Librarians
and
Labor
Relations

Recent Titles in Contributions in Librarianship and Information Science
Series Editor: Paul Wasserman

Public Knowledge, Private Ignorance: Toward a Library and Information
Policy
Patrick Wilson

Ideas and the University Library: Essays of an Unorthodox Academic
Librarian
Eli M. Oboler

Reform and Reaction: The Big City Public Library in American Life
Rosemary Ruhig Du Mont

Acquisitions: Where, What, and How
Ted Grieder

Information Sources in Children's Literature: A Practical Reference Guide
for Children's Librarians, Elementary School Teachers, and Students of
Children's Literature
Mary Meacham

The Vital Network: A Theory of Communication and Society
Patrick Williams and Joan Thornton Pearce

Cogent Communication: Overcoming Reading Overload
Charles L. Bernier and Neil A. Yerkey

The Librarian's Psychological Commitments: Human Relations
in Librarianship
Florence E. DeHart

Organization Development for Academic Libraries: An Evaluation
of the Management Review and Analysis Program
Edward R. Johnson and Stuart H. Mann

Social Science Reference Sources: A Practical Reference Guide
Tze-chung Li

Information for Academic Library Decision Making: The Case for
Organizational Information Management
Charles R. McClure

Defending Intellectual Freedom: The Library and the Censor
Eli M. Oboler

Management for Librarians: Fundamentals and Issues
John R. Rizzo

Corporate Authorship: Its Role in Library Cataloging
Michael Carpenter

Librarians
and
Labor
Relations EMPLOYMENT
UNDER UNION
CONTRACTS

Robert C. O'Reilly
and Marjorie I. O'Reilly

CONTRIBUTIONS IN LIBRARIANSHIP AND INFORMATION SCIENCE,
NUMBER 35

GREENWOOD PRESS
WESTPORT, CONNECTICUT • LONDON, ENGLAND

Library of Congress Cataloging in Publication Data

O'Reilly, Robert C   1928-
    Librarians and labor relations.

    (Contributions in librarianship and information
science ; no. 35 ISSN 0084-9243)
    Bibliography: p.
    Includes index.
    1. Librarians' unions—United States. 2. Collective
bargaining—Librarians—United States. I. O'Reilly,
Marjorie I., 1929-   joint author. II. Title.
III. Series.
Z682.2.U5074   331.89′04102   80-1049
ISBN 0-313-22485-4 (lib. bdg.)

Library of Congress Catalog Card Number: 80-1049
ISBN: 0-313-22485-4
ISSN: 0084-9243

First published in 1981

Greenwood Press
A division of Congressional Information Service, Inc.
88 Post Road West, Westport, Connecticut 06881

Printed in the United States of America

10 9 8 7 6 5 4 3 2 1

To
Dan, Debbie, Megan,
Tim, Diane, Sarah and Molly

CONTENTS

TABLES AND FIGURES

TABLES

FIGURES

PREFACE

This book is a combination of economics, politics, history, and the current scene of labor relations for librarians. That scene is changing rapidly as a consequence of new laws, new court pronouncements, new contracts, and changing manpower trends. This book is not a how-to-do-it book for either the librarians who choose union membership and representation or the library management and board of directors with whom they may negotiate. Rather, the book is intended to inform about specialized labor relations, to extend the understanding of collective bargaining and how it now bears upon American libraries.

At the outset, a special problem in terminology and word choice must be acknowledged. Is it appropriate to speak about manpower when addressing a field of employment in which females so heavily predominate? Good alternative words are hard to find; there is no uniform substitute. Such words as manpower and spokesman, as used in this text, have no gender connotation and are not intended to be chauvinistic or inflammatory. Clarity of word meaning has been the deciding factor in word choice.

To paraphrase Emerson, this is the best of times for librarians, if they but knew what to do. So it is with every professional group. That is, every time is a decision-making time, and when each professional group makes some particular decisions, those decisions will affect both the group and the clientele for many years to come.

For the past few decades a major question for librarians has been growing in intensity. Should librarians organize, follow a format for bargaining which has become rather well established for many occupational categories having parallelism to librarianship? Is there a viable employer-employee line that "rank-and-file" librarians can use advantageously? If organization and bargaining are suitable for librarians in some work settings, are they equally suitable in all work settings? Is there some minimum size of professional library staff that becomes a critical factor in effective bargaining? Upon close examination, it becomes obvious that the central question of unionization is the source of many subsidiary questions.

It has now been more than four decades since two librarians in the University of Washington presented papers devoted to the opposite sides of the question, that is, is unionization appropriate for librarians? At that time, those librarians were employed in the University of Washington Library, Seattle. Their papers were thoughtfully done. Each possessed its own strong logic lines. Neither was rancorous. Each position had its own share of supportive information and data. Present-day librarians are indebted to Ruth Hale and Barbara Falkoff for their brief but substantial expositions. They provided a reference point for comparisons, contrasts, and decisions; and, against that backdrop, present-day librarians can view current conditions of librarianship. One of their Washington colleagues, Bernard Berelson, became a librarian member of the university's local American Federation of Teachers (AFT) and quickly followed those pro and con essays with a lengthy description of the library-union condition. There was not the slightest intimation that membership in the AFT was parallel to membership in either the American Association of University Professors (AAUP) or the National Education Association (NEA)—and certainly, AFT membership was depicted as quite different from membership in the American Library Association (ALA).

It is possible to visualize the American labor scene as one divided by characteristics of the groups of laborers. Socioeconomic class designations can help to broadly categorize American workers. There are intellectual or professional workers, managers, clerks, service workers, craftsmen or skilled workers, and unskilled workers.

Here, intellectual and unskilled workers are conceived as being at opposite ends of the American labor continuum. It is an arbitary arrangement, without precise definitions; other categorical arrangements could be set forth. In this book, for example, reference will be made frequently to a two-category division: public and private employment. However, this loose, six-category arrangement that calls for identification by developmental level of workers emphasizes a characteristic that is timely for every group. There must be some attraction, some mutually magnetizing circumstance that molds the group's purpose and holds its membership.

A union of librarians must have that attraction. Lacking such central attraction, voluntarily formed social groups dissolve, if they are ever brought into being. In fact, to get a union "off the ground" is a more difficult operation than might, at first impression, be imagined. In Goldstein's colorfully described research of the 1960s, and from other sources, that difficulty becomes apparent, in reading of library unionization efforts that failed or noting the several library unions that formed and, after a few months, languished and disappeared.

For librarians, the question of association must be addressed. Should any library employees be excluded? Should membership be voluntary for all, or should membership and job eligibility be linked? Should the union be a local, or should it affiliate with some other regional or national group? If affiliation is desired, with what larger group should it occur? Should the local group request national sponsorship at the outset? Among intellectual workers—professionals—unionization, affiliation, and contact with the "laboring class" has always produced troublesome questions of protocol. Although less so than in an earlier time, it is still troublesome.

At the same time that librarians have had recourse to historical discussions about unionization, observed the labor scene, and raised many philosophical questions about librarians and union, they have also had to be practical. Librarians must address the changing work and mission of libraries in large cities today. In considering the working conditions for today's urban librarians, they must ask: What have been the effects of population growth, or decline? How about the racial composition and age distribution of the clientele? Will more than half the public library clientele be students? What about collaboration between public libraries, private libraries, and school and university libraries? Are facilities, inventories, and personnel shared? If libraries are not in an expansionist mode—if new branches are not being built with a view toward increased circulation—what does this hold for librarians? Questions are arising about the continued viability of cities. Libraries cannot stop riots; but libraries should surely be a major resource as cities try to get at the root causes of urban unrest. Libraries should provide service through which citizens can upgrade their social, spiritual, and economic positions. There is no evidence that unionization of librarians is antithetical to excellent service from libraries.

The reasons for unionization may be stated simply and candidly: higher wages, shorter hours, and better working conditions. All are relative reasons, susceptible of comparison. Each may change from time to time and by place. Reason #3 is a catchall, and within it could be built a long list of specific concerns. Few librarians would argue against any of the stated reasons, which embody the American preference for things that are integral to personal ease. It is pointless to decry the lack of concern for community welfare; candidly, that is just not a reason for unionization.

Arguments among librarian union members arise, when they do so, about selection of the means to the end. Many librarians who embrace the three goals would not advocate, or even accept, unionization as the appropriate means to goal achievement. This controversy is the foundation for the circumstance that, although best estimates indicate that there are in the U.S. nearly 120,000 workers who have been identified as librarians of one type or another, fewer than 25,000 of them have representation through collective bargaining units. Furthermore, the bulk of that represented segment is composed of librarians in elementary and secondary schools. When fewer than 20 percent of a group has been unionized, it is apparent that agitation for the extension of unionization will occur, if there is any job dissatisfaction.

For over a century librarians have been served by their own national organization, the American Library Association. In retrospect, it appears that, for the first half of the twentieth century, the ALA devoted enough of its resources to the economic welfare of librarians that unions of librarians did not emerge as a major professional question. Other factors, which may have included professional inhibitions against labor unions, have deterred library unionization; however, in some localities conditions were different enough that unionization appeared reasonable and attractive. For the most part, librarians found the protection they desired within the ALA. Now, that picture may be changing, for over 70,000 librarians—more than half of the total national group—are employed in schools or academic settings. Many of them have found their economic security as members of teacher unions that bargain collectively for all their professional members, including teachers, librarians, and other certificated employees (in secondary or elementary schools). Additionally, many of the remaining librarians, employed in both public and private settings, have sought unionization and have found no conflict between membership in a union and continued support of the ALA.

Restraint is not a union characteristic. Neither is compassion, given the union's focus upon self-interest. For professionals who are dedicated to service the moral conflict represented here must be resolved through some balance of opposing viewpoints. Increasingly, professionals are finding that position of balance.

Assistance for the development of this book has come from many places and from many people, and to them we are indebted. Special acknowledgments must be made to Mr. David Beasley of the New York Public Library and to Mr. Earl Baderschneider of the American Arbitration Association for their patient assistance in data gathering; to Professor Verne Haselwood, a friend and a colleague at the University of Nebraska at Omaha, who critically read parts of the manuscript; and to Miss Inga Ronke, who typed much of the manuscript from copy that was not always prepared in the best possible fashion. Other people in many job settings generously assisted, too, and for all their cordiality and willingess, we are grateful.

Robert C. O'Reilly
Marjorie I. O'Reilly

Librarians
and
Labor
Relations

A SURVEY OF LABOR UNIONS AND LIBRARIANS 1

SOME CURRENT ECONOMIC FACTORS

Collective bargaining among public employees was characterized by slow growth until about 1960. In 1960, Wisconsin enacted laws calling for school boards to meet and confer with teacher's associations (unions) and followed that act with more comprehensive collective bargaining laws; the Shanker-led strike of New York City teachers in 1962 was a vivid demonstration that some things could be achieved for professional workers through organizing; several presidential executive orders during the 1960s encouraged the organization of federal employees, an example not wasted on state and local governmental employees. Those and other events undeniably set a tone of political and social acceptance for the idea that public employees should organize, bargain, and work under contracts mutually developed with the employing governing boards. As over 75 percent of all librarians are employed in public agencies and institutions of one kind or another, heightened interest in labor relations by librarians was inevitable.

Other factors that contributed to the general growth of public employment collective bargaining included a new balance of workers in the labor force and the spread of state legislation authorizing public employees to bargain with the state. The new balance has come about because of an employment shift in the working force. When public and nonpublic employment are compared, the growth rate of public employment has been much faster. In 1953, state and local public employment stood at 8.6 percent (with all agricultural employment excluded). By 1970, the comparable figure was 14.0 percent. Projections from the Department of Labor indicated that 15.0 percent of the work force should be expected to be in state and local public employment by 1980. Of the increase, the preponderance was attributed to educational employment; another substantial portion of the increase was attributed to noneducational employment at both the state and local levels. The nonagricultural private sector of the nation's economy projected gains of 33 percent, an increase rate well below that for state and local public employment.[1]

One consequence of this altered balance of employment between the private and public sectors has been shrinking membership within the unions that have conventionally attracted private sector workers. In two years, from 1975 to 1977, the AFL-CIO shrank to 13.8 million total members, a loss of about 500,000 persons. That change in magnitude has cut in another way, too. One-third of all nonagricultural workers in America belonged to a union in 1957. Twenty years later, that same membership group ratio had shrunk to one in four.[2] Unions, but especially big unions, must be sensitive to their membership picture.

Coupled with the altered and altering employment-membership picture was the advent of increased activity in public employment organizing and bargaining. By 1980 over forty states had made statutory provisions for some kind of bargaining for some of their public employees.

Public employees may bargain in states lacking enabling legislation, if there is no specific prohibition against it. For example, teachers and librarians are among the public employees who bargain in Illinois and have done so for several decades in some localities in the state. Public employee bargaining in Illinois enjoyed a growth surge during the 1960s, and it is reasonable to think that that surge came on the heels of authorizations in many of the other states. During that same time, federal employees were told, through presidential executive orders, that they could organize. Even though Illinois' position still does not rest upon statutory obligations of public boards and trustees, that position can be seen as politically and sociologically in step with the times. At the same time, the lack of statutory direction may be a factor in the distance apparently maintained between the administration and the librarian's union in the Chicago Public Library (see Chapter 3 for details).

Court decisions have affected public bargaining. For example, the United States Supreme Court decided in the *National League of Cities* v. *Usery* (1976) that Congress could not extend the power of the National Labor Relations Board (NLRB) to cover public employees. The specific items in quesion had to do with controls over minimum wages, but the effects of the decision extend far beyond that narrow concern. That limitation on Congress makes it appear unlikely that any kind of federal legislation addressing public sector bargaining and designed to provide for uniformity between states will be enacted soon. That legislation has long been a goal of the National Education Association (NEA), which has vowed to pursue the goal even in the face of diminished chances for early accomplishment. For the 50,000 plus librarians employed in public school districts—many of whom are NEA members—this condition and effort has special significance. They are part of the effort and support it, if only as members of a large union. This persistence, after defeat of a long-sought legislative goal in the federal courts, along with other indicators, points toward continued growth among organized, unionized public employees. That growth is harmonious with present social moods, for much current legislation has been aimed at reducing paternalism and protecting individual rights. For example, the stereotype librarian of yesteryear has yielded to a more independent, audacious, and militant employee—one whose views on the work setting would have been shocking in an earlier decade.

Federal legislation may yet occur through existing state laws on public sector bargaining, as they will be made harmonious and uniform and some modest bargaining mandates be imposed upon those states now lacking such a law. Congress has not ignored labor relations. It has been conscious of its obligation to address questions of economic equity and to ensure industrial peace in the private sector. It may yet be persuaded to extend that concern to the public sector. In 1935, Congress enacted the National Labor Relations Act, also called the Wagner Act. That statute defined some of the rights and responsibilities of both employee and employer in the labor-management relationship. On balance, it provided more benefits to labor than to management and effectively encouraged the growth of unions, allowing for an expansion of the power of workers. This was not the first federal legislation related to labor, but it was, taken singly, a very important step for government to ensure some new rights and protections to employees. It was the harbinger of more such interest and legislation, a recognition that urbanization had created new problems deserving of government attention. All unions are voluntary associations of citizens, acting together in response to social and economic problems. As such, it was generally agreed that they deserved some protection by government.

LABOR RELATIONS DEFINED

Labor relations lacks a precise definition in that it may be defined broadly or narrowly. Either definition is localized, that is, what is understood to constitute labor relations in one setting may not be a valid definition or understanding of it in another setting. One characteristic seems central to all of labor relations, and that is tension, or conflict; beyond that, specifics differ.

When defined broadly, labor relations means anything and everything affecting the employee from interview and selection to job leaving and exit interview. In this broad understanding, labor relations includes all the things that might be in a contract and more. To set forth some extensive categorical illustrations would not be to limit labor relations to such things as recruitment and hiring, placement and promotion, and layoff and dismissal and to such specifics as wages, salaries, overtime, and fringe benefits of all kinds.[3] Broadly construed, labor relations is all of the above, and more. Bargaining itself is a procedurally necessary part of this comprehensive definition, but neither bargaining nor the contract produced by it form a very large part of labor relations, as the contract only authenticates and legitimizes the ultimately comprehensive view of the job setting. This broad definition is a viable one for public school or public library settings. It is especially appropriate for those job settings given the propensity of public boards to develop and use policy that would implicitly become part of local labor relations.

A contrary view may sometimes be appropriate. This narrower view of labor relations holds that everything having to do with labor relations between an employee group and an employer was stated in the document that became the contract. Anything not in the contract is not a part of labor relations. In this specific definition, resting upon the rationale that the contract is a written agreement into which more or less may be entered as mutually agreed upon, the contract says it all. All else is excluded.[4] The content of the contract represents the limits of labor relations in each local setting accepting that definition. Of the two definitions, the narrower one is more rigid at point of contract administration.

If the traditions of a locale, developed in contract negotiation and administration, follow the narrower definition, then employees have to understand that only those items explicit in the contract are a part of labor relations. Neither definition is necessarily better than the other. It seems unlikely librarians would be substantially more advantaged under one than the other definition. However, it is essential that a definition be mutually agreed upon at the time of bargaining as the minimum effort necessary to prevent unpleasant surprises to librarians or administrators after a contract is in force.

Several years ago, this necessity for a clear definition of labor relations was addressed in an agreement between the United Auto Workers and the General Motors Corporation. That contract clause exemplifies the wording necessary to define the comprehensive approach to labor relations. It has been used as a pattern for narrow interpretation in many labor agreements.

The parties acknowledge that during the negotiations which resulted in this agreement, each had the unlimited right and opportunity to make demands and proposals with respect to any subject or matter not removed by law from the areas of collective bargaining, and that the understanding and agreements arrived at by the parties after the exercise of that right and opportunity are set forth in this agreement. Therefore, the Corporation and the Union, for the life of this Agreement, each voluntarily and unqualifiedly waives the right and agrees that the other shall not be obligated to bargain collectively with respect to any matter referred to, or covered in this Agreement, or with respect to any subject or matter not specifically referred to or covered in this Agreement, even though such subject or matter may not have been within the knowledge or contemplation of either or both of the parties at the time they negotiated or signed this Agreement.[5]

Without any intent to diminish the values of a narrow definition of labor relations, the more comprehensive definition forces both parties to recognize how extensive labor relations may be. Librarians should choose the definition that they consider more usable through collective bargaining in shaping and improving their careers. Even if rejected in the contract, the following points demonstrate the suitablity of the comprehensive definition in any extended understanding of labor relations:

1. The politico-economic matrix that surrounds employer-employee relations; the industrial structure of the country; the characteristics of the labor force; the looseness or tightness of the labor market; management's personnel policies; and the balance of power in the political system.
2. The characteristics of the trade unions; whether workers are organized by plant, by craft, or by industry; whether power resides mainly in the local or national unions; the degree of membership attachment; the strength of union finances and leadership.
3. Trade union tactics; whether the labor relations program concentrates mainly on controlling the employer through collective bargaining or on influencing government through political action.
4. The structure of collective bargaining; the size of the bargaining units, the subjects regulated by agreement; the duration of agreements; the methods of resolving disputes over the application of the agreement; the use of strikes; and other forms of economic pressure.
5. The framework of public control, which determines about what the parties may bargain and what tactics they may use.[6]

EARLY LABOR RELATIONS

Momentarily disregarding the cause and effect relationship between union membership and worker prosperity, it is easy to show that American workers fare well in terms of what they can buy for the wages earned and the hours worked. American workers are envied by other workers all over the world—their production, their income, and their consumption are, relatively, high. Unions have provided a leverage for Americans through which they have been able to claim from that high production a higher equity for themselves. Labor relations encompasses that struggle, that fierce drive of American workers toward higher wages and improved working conditions. The change in political power accomplished by disciplined organizations of workers has forced change in the attitude of government, and a transition from intolerance of unions to acceptance of them, to endorsement and support, can be seen. Organizations usurp some power from individual members, reducing autonomy and freedom; however, unions, as organizations, have also provided political power, forcing elected officials to consider new ideas proposed from within unions.

As early technological breakthroughs in the eighteenth and ninteenth centuries ushered in the industrial revolution, work forces were assembled to run the plants. Workers, recruited from rural areas, endured work conditions that were, from today's perspective, terrible. Yet, such conditions have, historically, motivated people to strive for something better. The adage that misery loves company also means that misery can form a base from which people may collectivize, organize, and move against that misery. Every occupational group seeks prestige and advantage and escape from misery. Some of those early workers saw power in numbers, and over several decades, they established a pattern by organizing for what they saw as benefits for the worker group.

During this phase of development, capital was sacred. Owners and investors demanded—and got—consideration and protection from governments headed by people who were, themselves, often among the owners and investors. If workers wanted more, and that demand put strain upon capital and its regeneration, how could owners be protected? That question remains as a point of tension between workers and owners in the post-industrial world. It is a tension that is equally present in government-owned and government-operated enterprises. It applies to libraries, for each community wants extensive, prompt, accurate library service at low tax rates, while librarians want ever larger salaries in return for their expert services.

Early unions were formed by craftsmen. Their goals were narrow, concerned with wages and conditions of employment. Working within such narrow confines, they sought to secure immediate improvement for their members. They had no acquaintance with the complex labor contract so familiar to today's employment scene. Their concerns, narrow compared to the broad concerns of today's workers, epitomized the accretionary expectation within labor relations. Considering a current contract with a long list of nonsalary benefits, it can be seen that those early organized craftsmen laid a foundation for improvement that has been maintained. The rights of workers have expanded as improvements and additions secured over many decades have been continued in successive contracts.

With limited communications and with a high risk of job loss through mass firings, those early craft unions focused their efforts locally. Because each union acted as a contractor for its skilled craftsmen, it demanded a monopoly over the services of its members. This aspect of disciplining members created a scarcity of the skill, which must be maintained even today, or a union may collapse. Exclusivity of a desired service is a basic necessity to bargaining. Membership in those early guilds or unions was controlled in at least three ways: (1) joining fees, (2) apprenticeship rules, and (3) demonstration of skills in performance.[7] Today's librarians, like other occupationally organized groups, are aware of that heritage.

Another aspect of union development was coincident with the increasing populism of American-style democracy. The extension of suffrage provided for the masses another kind of leverage, i.e., the possibility of political control over elected government officials. Workers in all settings have never lost sight of the goal of improving their condition. Workers in some occupations found that, at some times and in some localities, advancement came under the shelter of their local union. Other workers found that by joining political activity and by gaining influence over elected officials, they could enact laws that were harmonious with union goals. Such gains did not have to be made at the bargaining table. In politics, power is numbers of voters, and unions have numbers. Unions have altered their points of emphasis, sometimes focusing energies upon the local work scene as the place from which to generate improvements and at other times into the political arena as money and manpower are expended, supporting political candidates sympathetic to union causes.

Job security has greatly increased in the last three or four decades. That security has been another enabling influence in the entry of unions into the political arena, and political action is now commonly accepted as one of the very few basic missions of a union. For those librarians who, as employees in the public schools, are also members of the NEA or American Federation of Teachers (AFT), political action has become a major mission, frequently addressed and calling for substantial money support.

Union membership fluctuates as the felt need for mutual protection under common bonds changes. Membership, or more specifically the work represented by it, has sometimes been evidenced in other ways. In the history of the nineteenth century, a correlation has been observed between union membership and times of economic growth. Conversely, in times of economic recession, unions faltered and political parties prospered, indicating that workers judged for themselves the organizations from which they could get the greatest help at the smallest risk, i.e., labor union or political party.[8]

Union specialty is not a new or surely American concept, but the well-established concept of like workers who centuries ago organized into guilds and found strength and satisfaction in those organizations. The American Federation of Labor (AFL) used the concept as many unions, each specialized by the occupational characteristics of the members, joined in a federation to secure the greater political strength of a large group. Moreover, the AFL had narrowed concerns, such as the improvement of working conditions and higher compensation for the membership of each of the separate unions. Initially, the members were blue-collar workers in trades and crafts and the industrial unskilled workers, too. Professional workers did not form a substantial part of the labor movement in the late nineteenth and early twentieth centuries in America. Employees of government agencies, generally, were also outside union membership.

With the arrival of industrial technology, job skills were frequently replaced by machines; unskilled workers, knowing no craft, could operate the machines. A cheap labor source for industrial production, fueled by also cheap sources of energy, made it possible for American workers to boost production and make new claims for higher wages. In 1938, the Congress of Industrial Organizations (CIO) was formed as a union to represent workers of low skills who provided labor labeled unskilled. The AFL and the CIO became rivals for members.[9] Every central union treasury is sensitive to the need to increase membership and increase dues receipts, too. Rivalry ceased with the amalgamation of the unions. The AFL-CIO was formed. Entering the 1980s, George Meany, the octogenarian president of the AFL, dominates American labor. As a reference point from which to judge the success of the federation concept stands one segment of the AFL, the American Federation of State, County, and Municipal Employees (AFSCME). In that single union of the federation are over 1,000,000 members, partially by way of union mergers in the latter 1970s. The AFSCME has become a very popular national affiliate for local library unions, accepting as members professional librarians of all classes, as well as supportive staff from secretaries to stationary engineers.

THE ATTITUDES OF GOVERNMENT TOWARD LABOR

Governments are concerned with stability. Each government, if intelligently operated, acts in its own interest to assure its continuation. It must be sensitive to crimes of violence and to loss of property. Such an attitude is a natural advocacy for conservatism, for the status quo. Coupled with the fact that people in government such as senators, judges, and governors have always been more available to people with money than to those lacking it, there was in the nineteenth century an environment in which government worked to preserve industrially created capital, which was closely held, and to discourage new systems for the distribution of wealth. In the labor-management concept and in the labor-capital concept, governments, right into the twentieth century, were antagonistic in their attitudes toward labor. The majority decision by the Massachusetts Supreme Court, In *Vegelahn* v. *Guntner* (1898) enjoined peaceful picketing and was so unsympathetic toward the plight of the worker that Justice Oliver Wendell Holmes penned a critical minority opinion:

One of the eternal conflicts out of which life is made up is that between the effort of every man to get the most he can for his services, and that of society . . . to get his services for the least possible return. . . . I can remember when many people thought that, apart from violence or breach of contract, strikes were wicked, as organized refusals to work. I suppose that intelligent economists and legislators have given up that notion today. I feel pretty confident that they equally will abandon the idea that an organized refusal by workmen of social intercourse with a man who shall enter their antagonist's employ is unlawful.

It is this view of Justice Holmes that has come to prevail. In the battle for equity between labor and capital, the strike is an acknowledgedly suitable weapon for private sector employees. It is not agreed, however, that public employees should strike, and many states with laws allowing public employees to bargain also have laws denying public employees the right to strike.

In just a little over half a century, the balance of power between labor and management has shifted, and in favor of labor. Federal laws have been instrumental in the shift, providing some protection for workers from huge, impersonal corporations. The Railway Labor Act, passed in 1926, required collective bargaining of those employers and protected workers who acted to form unions.[10]

In 1932 the Norris-LaGuardia Act was passed. It limited the liability of unions for unlawful acts by their officers and members, and it outlawed "yellow dog" contracts. Those contracts were agreements in which workers signed a side pledge that they would not join a union and by which, if it became known that they were involved in any union activity, they would face immediate job loss.[11]

In 1935 Congress passed the Wagner Act or more specifically, the National Labor Relations Act. This legislation included only those workers in the private sector of the economy but, by precedent and implication, affected public employment, eventually. The act reinforced the Constitutional freedom of association, giving workers the right, specifically, to form and to join a union and to elect their own representatives as spokesmen to management. The act delimited those procedures necessary for elections and identification of the representative union; it forbade management to interfere with employees as they explored the questions of organizing.[12]

In 1938 the Wage-Hour Act, or the Fair Labor Standards Act, was passed by Congress. The goal was new government control over such items as child labor, minimum wages, and overtime pay. Included were employment settings that carried on interstate commerce and the manufacture of goods for interstate commerce. Intrastate commerce and public employment were outside the purview of the act. Initially, the minimum wage was set at $0.25 per hour.[13] As mentioned earlier, through the decision in *NLC* v. *Usery*, minimum wage mandates from Congress do not apply to local political subdivisions; i.e., public libraries are exempt, although they may voluntarily comply.

With such a favorable attitude from government, unions expanded and, with the newly found muscle of large organizations, tipped the balance of power away from management, toward labor. A reactionary consequence was the series of amendments to the Wagner Act, which became known as the Taft-Hartley Act (1947). The intent of that act was to interrupt the growth of union power and to establish a new balance between labor and management in labor relations. It defined unfair labor practices and provided a new executive control by stipulating that strikes that endangered the health and safety of the nation could be halted after eighty days, if the president, for certain causes, sought an injunction ordering the union back to work.[14]

In 1959 the Landrum-Griffin Act, also called the Labor-Management Reporting and Disclosure Act, was passed by Congress. This was a labor reform act, providing assurances to members that they could not be persecuted by their own unions for holding views unpopular with some, or most, members. Its intent was to open union politics. The act demanded that union financial records be made public, and it extended controls over certain union administrative procedures. Assurances were given to members that they could freely participate in meetings.[15] The values of such legislation to library employment are obvious, for intimidation of workers was addressed from another direction.

Abuse of power, a characteristic of almost all large organizations, had become evident in many powerful unions. Members needed protection from their own association; Landrum-Griffin provided it. It also described a national policy toward collective bargaining:

Employees shall have the right to self-organization, to form, join, or assist labor organizations, to bargain collectively through representatives of their own choosing and to engage in other concerted activities for the purpose of collective bargaining or other mutual aid or protection, and shall have the right to refrain from any or all such activities except to the extent that such right may be affected by an agreement requiring membership in a labor organization. . . . (Sec. 7)

Surveying the private employment sector, the history of unions is rife with failures, animosities, and hostilities; yet unions have prevailed. Despite all the complexities wrapped up in labor relations, workers have been attracted to and have supported organizations. In a sense, there is more social reform encompassed in the development of public sector bargaining than in that of the private sector. The later entry of public employment upon the scene has made it only slightly less complex than the private arena. States have enacted individualized statutes, treating the public employees in their boundaries differently from other states. Restrictions and opportunities differ. Occupational categories and negotiable items differ, too. Across all of the states, it can be said that, as minima, wages, hours, and other conditions of employment may be negotiated.

PUBLIC EMPLOYMENT LABOR RELATIONS

If librarians are to improve their lot in their work setting, they must understand not only the jobs they perform but also the environments in which they work. Those environments surely include an understanding of what is allowed in labor relations. Traditional thinking about labor relations has led to the exclusion of professionals from the labor field; somehow it was difficult to bridge the semantic gap from professional employee to worker. Yet, in many ways, they are the same, and there is nothing to indicate that a conscious awareness among librarians that they perform work for money will make them less productive, less humane, less professional. By philosophical and political viewpoints, it is quite reasonable to focus upon commonalities between workers who are professional and workers who are not.

Studies at the University of Hawaii covered seventy-five state statutes, municipal ordinances, and professional regulations. All bore upon public employment. The study revealed the greater simplicity of public sector labor relations documents, partially controlled by statutes. Only one-third of the items provided for grievance procedures in written agreements. Simple, uncluttered contracts were encouraged. Impasse procedures were addressed in one-fifth of those laws. Several of the laws mandated that agreements should be for a term coincident with the budget of the state.[16] For example, the Teachers Professional Negotiations Act was passed in Nebraska in 1967, and it included school librarians. At that time, the state legislature met every two years and contracts could also be written for two-year terms.

Within that group of seventy-five items of the statutes bearing upon public labor relations, union security was a concern in fewer than one-third of the cases. At the same time, some strength was added to the union cause as a majority of the statutes spoke to the suitability of employer deduction of union dues.[17] Again, taking the whole group of seventy-five laws, nearly 90 percent addressed the manner in which governing boards could determine what local unit would be recognized for purposes of bargaining. Common among the statutes was a clause calling for the establishment of some administrative agency having general oversight of all aspects of bargaining.[18] The agencies have typically emerged as public employment relations boards or commissions, with broad powers. Nebraska has been atypical, with a unique Court of Industrial Relations playing a very restricted role as arbitrator of public employment disputes. In 1979, the Nebraska legislature changed the name of the Court to the Commission of

Industrial Relations. Some of its functions were changed, too, but it is still primarily a court, inferior to the state's Supreme Court.

As reported earlier, it was decided in the *NLC* v. *Usery* that Congress had overstepped its bounds when it tried to impose upon state and local governments the same kind of minimum wage provision which it had mandated upon private employers. Then Secretary of Labor W. S. Usery, Jr., was prevented by this decision from imposing this new regulation on governmental units, for the court held that it applied exclusively to the private sector through the National Labor Relations Board. Most librarians are publicly employed; however, for that smaller number in work settings under the jurisdiction of the NLRB, the new wage and hour minima apply and give to those library employees a worker protection by way of political activity.

A SURVEY OF LIBRARIANS AND UNIONS

Although the bookbinders in the United States were among the first workers to unionize in the early 1800s, the first movement toward unionization in libraries didn't appear until just before 1920. Unions were formed in five large eastern libraries—in the New York Public (May 1917), in the Library of Congress (September 1917), in the Boston Public (May 1918), and in the Washington, D.C., Public Library (June 1919). All were affiliated with the AFL.

The question of unionization created much comment, with two main arguments against library unionization at that time. The first argument was that always it had been the rule among professional men and women that an organization that sought to advance wages was unprofessional and undignified. Second, unionization would mean intrusion into the administration of the library—the territorial domain of the chief librarian. Of the four public libraries that formed unions, the one at Washington, D.C., was the most successful. It formed a branch of the National Federation of Federal Employees. Employees affiliated through the branches of their own departments and through the Library of Congress union. The other three public library unions maintained lower profiles, although records indicate some activity of varying levels in all three organizations.

The year 1934 marked the next movement toward library unionization with labor affiliation; but in the intervening fifteen years, protective activities were being carried out by some staff associations. One such group was the Boston Library Club, which (like some of its predecessors), when organized by the employees of the Boston Public Library, was to deal specifically with the problems of low salary and other working conditions. It proved successful in some of its goals, seeing in 1937 and 1938 the first general pay raises since 1925. A pay rate of a $20.00 weekly minimum was established: "Tactful, but unyielding opposition of library authorities stymied most further proposals of the group, and a decision was made to disband in 1942."[19]

The Great Depression convinced professional workers in many fields that the forces that gave impetus to the organization of manual labor were operative on them and that they, too, might find their solution in a professional union. The question did not arise as a purely academic matter; certain basic economic drives—emphasized and sharpened during the Depression—led many librarians to a consideration of the solution that unionization offered to some of their problems; and it was the point of interest in much emotionally charged discussion in professional groups.[20]

The first widespread library movement was that of mechanics' and apprentices' libraries; later, there were mercantile libraries, which were partly for clerks, that is, they were libraries for members of unions and worker's guilds. Libraries for working men's organizations, such as libraries in industrial plants and libraries for railroad workers, provide clear indications that nineteenth-century American libraries had an egalitarian aspect. Interestingly, the existence of these libraries was used by supporters of the library movement in their argument that the public library would "woo" the worker away from the union's library, where he was thought to be subjected only to union propaganda. There is also some indication that the more class-conscious of the workers suspected that the library, as a public institution, might be used against them by their more capitalist-oriented opposition.

Sidney Ditzion, in an unpublished master's thesis at City College of New York in 1938, concluded that the needs of the wage earner were implicated in all of the theories of the library movement as an important if not a paramount factor. The facts prove beyond a doubt that democratic forces were more influential in shaping and directing the course of free library service than was philanthropy. "In a later article Ditzion cites four factors involved in the social backgrounds of the library movement, one of which is the (favorable) attitude of organized labor toward mass education through the medium of books and reading."[21]

Closely synchronized, then, were the labor movement and its shorter working hours with the rapid multiplication of libraries between 1850 and 1890. The library movement also appears to be closely associated with the establishment of the public education system, also championed by the labor movement. Reasonably, the laboring man desiring free public schools for children also sought public educational resources in library systems that were staffed by nonunion professionals.

Although public libraries historically have failed miserably to communicate their problems to labor unions, existing library unions are reported to have received generous support, when they have asked for it, from older, well-established labor unions. In 1926, the following editorial appeared in the *American Federalist*, the AFL publication; presumably, it was written by the president of the federation:

A public library is a necessary part of the educational equipment of every city. Surely such an allowance (the A.L.A. minimum of one dollar per capita) for a service that extends to such groups and varied needs is a most constructive expenditure. Labor organizations and especially local committees on education throughout the jurisdiction of the A.F. of L. are urged to do their utmost to promote generous appropriations for library purposes. Make it your duty to find out the amount appropriated for library purposes in your community and compare this with the minimum maintenance standard recommended by the American Library Association. If your local appropriation falls short you are urged to do whatever may be necessary to secure larger appropriations.[22]

Library union membership in 1938 was estimated to be around seven hundred. Some librarians were members of staff associations as previously mentioned; some in schools and colleges were members of the American Federation of Teachers, which came into existence in 1916. Advocates of unionization based their argument on three main points:

1. unionization will improve the economic status of both the library and the library employees;
2. it will extend the democratization of library administration;
3. it will provide affiliation with a broad constructive movement for concrete expression of social attitudes and desires.

Unions in 1938 were concerned with the wide diversity in library salaries and its implications. Table 1.1 uses data adapted from ALA sources used by Berelson and treats numbers of librarians and high school educators in cities of over 200,000 population and librarians in the federal service. It illustrates the disparity in the salaries offered by public libraries in 1938. The factor that causes the difference to appear so sharply is the relatively low salary of the professional assistant. With the revelation of these facts, there is little wonder why in many staff associations chief librarians were excluded from membership.[23]

Table 1.1 **Comparisons of Salaries of Public Librarians, Librarians in Federal Service, and High School Educators in 1938**

	High Schools		Federal Library Service		Public Library	
					Prof.	*Chief*
	Teacher	*Principal*	**Grade P1*	*Grades P5–8*	*Asst.*	*Libr.*
Salary	$2,125	$4,233	$2,250	$6,600	$1,535	$6,000
Index no.	100	199	100	292	100	391

*Designations of the U.S. Personnel Classification Board in 1938.

Even though the need for better salaries, higher budgets, improved physical facilities, and the like were seen by librarians, organizers often ran up against a stone wall of prejudice and unreason. Librarians by the very nature of their work were led to have an unshakeable belief in their own impartiality. To serve their clientiele without bias did not indicate a transfer of this same impartiality in the formation of personal opinions. Strong feelings of fear of damage to professionalism by unionization handicapped even the most persuasive organizer.[24]

The Library Unions Round Table (LURT) was formed at the American Library Association Conference in Kansas City in 1938. One of its purposes was to coordinate the work of the existing CIO and AFL unions of library workers. Devoting much energy to publicity, a second aim was to promote improvement of library services and to act as liaison between the library movement and organized labor. The advancement of the professional status of library workers and promotion of democratic library personnel policies held high priority for the LURT. The promotion of projects beneficial to labor and to libraries and the representation of organized labor on library boards were items written into the aims of the LURT.

With the advent of the 1940s and the gathering crisis abroad, the urgency of domestic issues such as librarians' salaries and working conditions lessened and all but disappeared while the country built up the momentum to win a war. One of the more controversial issues at hand in the library world was the appointment by President Franklin Roosevelt of the poet Archibald MacLeish to head the Library of Congress, a position he reportedly filled with distinction from 1939 to 1944.[25] The LC did not flourish during Mr. MacLeish's administration.

In 1950, library unions were located in such cities as New York, Cleveland, Chicago, Newark, Milwaukee, Minneapolis, and Detroit. In all of these cities, unions were an accepted part of the social pattern. Surprisingly, in certain other strong union cities—namely San Francisco, Seattle, and Buffalo—there were no library unions.[26]

Gathering the threads of library union activity from the past and coming closer to the present state of labor relations situations in libraries, it can be said that the unionization, the collectivization, of librarians began around the first decade of the century. Few locals were established, and their influence was, on the whole, minimal, as most librarians allied themselves with the professional organizations. Activity suddenly burst forth in the mid-1960s; from 1967 to 1969, librarians and unions were the subject of more than twenty articles in major library periodicals—about twenty times greater than what had appeared in the preceding two years! Amid other social turmoil in the country came the birth on May 5, 1965, of the Library Chapter of the University AFT, Local 1474 of the AFT, AFL-CIO on the Berkeley Campus, University of California. On October 28, 1966, employees of the Brooklyn Public Library voted to join the AFL-CIO affiliate, the American Federation of State, County, and Municipal Employees (AFSCME).

MANAGEMENT PERSPECTIVES ON LIBRARY UNIONS

In the latter part of the 1930s, Mr. Justice Felix Frankfurter was solicited by his friend, Franklin Roosevelt, upon the question of who should be the next Librarian of Congress, as Herbert Putnam was retiring. Frankfurter responded by stipulating certain characteristics that should be present. "What is wanted in the directing head of a great library," Frankfurter wrote, "is a man who knows books, loves books, and makes books. If he has these three qualities, the craftmanship of the library calling is an easily acquired quality."[27] Amid widespread opposition and with a notable lack of professional endorsements, the president proceeded in the selection of a successor and appointed Archibald MacLeish, as mentioned earlier. The opposition gracefully faded, the ALA promised cooperation, and the new Librarian of Congress—a poet, editor, lawyer, and writer—moved into the position.

MacLeish himself recognized that in entering the position he was following the long and successful administrative career of Herbert Putnam. He set out to enhance the quality of the Library of Congress and to become known as a friend of libraries. In a retrospective commentary upon his five-year tenure, MacLeish stated that, "My predecessor, Herbert Putnam, had been a great librarian, but he had run the library like a feudal fief, and feudal fiefs had a way of hardening and solidifying in the mold."[28]

The library administrations that were represented in the persons of Putnam and MacLeish were worlds apart—in concept, attitude, and operation. Both were substantially different from the more professionally uniform administrators presently found in libraries across the nation. Neither particularly encouraged unionization in the Library of Congress, which, more often than not, was faltering; and there is evidence that their trustees were in harmony with that stance on the part of each director. On the time line of the twentieth century, they were well in advance of the changing cultural and social values that, in retrospect, seem to have advanced in strength since World War II and include a strong feeling of egalitarianism and the notion that all authority structures are open to question. This is a rather natural reaction of workers who see their won best interests served by their own group; who see themselves in a struggle with administrators, directors, or trustees (of whatever inclinations they may be); and who perceive the administrative hierarchy, generally, as task oriented, not people oriented.

Library administrations are aware that library employees of all types, when they form unions and affiliate, tend to choose the American Federation of State, County, and Municipal Employees as their national affiliate. [On the West Coast, employees have looked to the Service Employees International Union (SEIU) for their affiliation.] Library administrations are interested in the uninterrupted continuous service of their agency. Administrators recognize that, with the arrival of unions within the library, a second authority structure has been created and the likelihood of conflicts heightened. Jerry Wurf, AFSCME president, has commented on the necessity of developing workable mechanisms through which reasonable settlements are more likely and confrontations are less likely. He has also stated that public employees who are engaged in non-emergency services "should enjoy the right of withdrawing . . . services when the employer refuses to offer fair and equitable compensation for services rendered." In additional comments on unsettled disputes, Wurf stated the AFSCME position:

> We reject the politics of confrontation for confrontation's sake. We seek to avoid the strike option whenever it can reasonably be avoided. But we insist that public workers do not relinquish their basic rights to fair compensation and decent conditions of employment when they sign on for service to the public. The rights of most workers to strike and the right of all to choose to have their disputes arbitrated by truly impartial third parties are basic to all public workers and to the American ideal of a free and equitable society.[29]

This attitude can hardly diminish the hard lines that tend to build between library administration and employees, for administrators must see such statements as threats.

When compared to some other occupations, it is difficult to speak very specifically to the welfare problems of librarians. For such public employment occupational groups as police and firefighters, the Bureau of Labor Statistics periodically gathers data relevant to salaries and working conditions. In part, due to their relatively smaller size, librarians receive no such treatment, and, lack of an informational base from which to approach the problems of librarians is a real drawback for the group.

Moreover, library administrations are beleaguered with a host of problems. What about the changing clientele, which, for so many libraries means fewer whites and more blacks? What will be the result upon revenue of the tax revolt, which came to the forefront so explosively with California's Proposition 13? How are new cost obligations to be met as library buildings are remodeled in an attempt to make libraries more accommodating to the handicapped? Representative of the sweep and scope from which administrators must view libraries, such global problems include personnel problems and problems of labor relations—and form only one part of the library director's world.

TRUSTEES, MANAGEMENT, AND COOPERATION

A brief glimpse into some of the real aspects of smaller public library operations should provide additional insights about the suitability of organizing library employees, i.e., whether a union will likely confer benefit or distress. Money for operation is generated after a budget has been approved. The budget building process in the public library is a mutual venture between the library director and the library board of trustees, working with the city council (or some other tax-levying group). The trustees are the policy makers and the director the administrator of that policy; initially, the goals and objectives of each library must be established as the base from which the administration may address operational problems. Ideally, each public library board should have diversity of interest and occupation, as well as understanding of the community, its needs, and its resources, so that the board speaks to myriad community interests through the budget. The budget becomes the instrument through which the goals and objectives may be attained.

The director, being primarily responsible for the statistical reports of the library, sets up the basic items for budget consideration. Different organizational patterns will be used to fit a variety of situations, but basic budget categories might include the following:

1. personnel services, including salaries and benefits of personnel
2. library materials, including books, nonprint materials, binding, and those non-expendable items needed to build and maintain a collection
3. operating expenses
4. expendable supplies
5. repair and maintenance
6. utilities and fixed costs

Within categories, individual items must have consideration. For example, insurance is not an item to be overlooked, and it should be adjusted as the collection increases or diminishes in value and with cost of living data in mind.

Ideally, the trustees bring the needs of the community to the attention of the director. Together, they establish goals and objectives, and the librarian prepares a budget under the advisement of the board. In an organized library, collective bargaining is an activity stream that, in many ways, runs parallel to the budget-building process. The board takes responsibility for presenting the budget to its tax-levying agency and exerts every effort to insure that the necessary funds will be generated.

Many states have a maximum mill levy for the operational budget of public libraries. (Typically, such a local levy maximum might be three or four mills.) Upon presentation of the budget, a down-to-earth line-item analysis is conducted by the fiscal officer for the tax-levying agency, such as a city council or a county board. In the period of analysis, a board of trustees must be able to clearly articulate the goals and objectives of the library program, not only to defend the budget but also, in any instance of mandated cuts, to state priorities of programs to those not familiar with the operations of the library. In smaller cities, where informal relationships may prevail, city council members who can quote, at the drop of a hat, the cost of a load of cement may not fully appreciate the function of the card catalog. Without detracting from the talents of all persons involved in the budget development processes, the necessity for honest and open communication between the major groups involved cannot be overemphasized. In this time of intense scrutiny into the business of public boards, such openness must surely include the employee group, without regard to whether they are organized or not, if good personnel administration procedures are being followed.

Personnel salaries and benefits tend to be established by comparisons with prevailing rates in similar settings. If that seems a simple, clear basis for decision making, a sample of questions in only one category of personnel employment can point out its sensitive, emotion-laden complexity. For example, how much should part-time workers, employed at an hourly rate, be paid? Should part-time employees be excluded from bargaining units?

In a non-union setting, questions of pay equity are likely to increase in the near future. A municipality may determine that all part-time employees in every department—including the public library, as one fiscal department—must be paid at uniform rates, established on the basis of experience, preparation, responsibility, and so on. On the other hand, the library is a nice place to work for twelve or fifteen hours per week. Frequently, there is a labor pool of university-trained, uniquely qualified housewives who are willing to work for a lower salary and fewer benefits than the independent, self-supporting library assistant, who calls for higher wages and all the benefits the municipality offers. In many small-town libraries, the director's salary may be the only one at the generally understood place for lower-level professionals, which is the level at which librarians seem to find themselves. There are, then, several variables and complicating factors in establishing pay equity.

A sudden increase in budget caused by higher salaries and benefits—a first priority goal of all unions—can cause a real uproar in a usually calm and methodical city council or county board as a new budget proposal is scrutinized. Library directors who are in initial bargaining settings must stay very close to their trustees as negotiations progress and salary information develops. Personnel cost trends and comparisons must be studied and understood. In all program and cost considerations, a director cannot treat the trustees as fixtures around a table who must be endured once a month. Especially in times of new salary cost trends, library trustees and the library director must be in as much mutual agreement as can be developed through the period of negotiation.

For unionization to work, an attitude of mutual respect, grounded in the ethics of fair labor practices, must prevail. If unionization means increased costs, it is then to the advantage of all—librarians, trustees, and clientele—to deliver better services, that is, to increase production. Some libraries have found that this can be done through cooperative networks. For example, in the Omaha, Nebraska, area there is a regional network, one of several in the state; it is comprised of five counties and includes the state's two largest cities. Within the Metropolitan Network, one library has been designated as the regional library and receives funding from the State Library Commission, which has been used to maintain additional staff. This has been accomplished through an annual contract that actually places discretion for funds use in the hands of the director of the designated library. Any library in the network looks to the regional library for services to extend the performance of the local library. If a book, film, or in some instances, records, are are not part of a local collection, the regional library communicates with other libraries in the state to pursue what is requested. In sharing collections, cost of services are cut and quality of service is enhanced.

Special collections, such as large-print book collections, are housed in the regional library but are circulated throughout the network. A toybrary, a lending source for toys which are circulated much as are books, is handled in similar fashion. Patrons use the service free of charge with the local library paying a postage fee only.

Cooperatives have been formed at various places across the nation. Public libraries and university libraries have moved aggressively in such endeavors. Under such structures as are stipulated in the federal regulations that go hand-in-glove with their funding, the reports of their effectiveness in the extension of services have generally been quite favorable.

Without addressing such administrative complexities as split payrolls and new interagency relationships, the primary advantage of cooperatives merits specific mention. The cooperative, with rapid communication links, provides an extended collection. Collection building in the cooperative is more than selection and purchase; it is coordinated and aggregated to provide a broadened function, an extended tool. Selection, carried out judiciously within a cooperative, is an even more demanding demonstration of librarianship than is customarily the case, because it allows for the extension of the book and material portion of each participating library's budget. In traditional understandings of labor relations, the "library product" might be described as the provision of informational services, a residue of ideas and knowledge, organized in such a way as to be available to support the community's interests. To increase that product through some such technique as the cooperative, at the same time that substantial salary increases are sought in any of the local sponsoring libraries, is an idea that has obvious political merit and is worth the consideration of any beginning union.

SUMMARY

Although there have been locally exciting events, very little in the study of collective bargaining in libraries could be called intellectually dazzling. All of labor relations is after all, methodical, analytical, and reality oriented. Set within an array of complex problems, it is not receptive to sophisticated but rigid mathematical models. They lack the elasticity and flexibility necessary to accommodate the complexity of the librarian at work in a broad spectrum of settings. For librarians, and indeed for all support employees in libraries as well, when consideration of the possibility of organizing for bargaining arises, it is apparent that an extended appreciation of the library's costs and services should strengthen the underpinnings of the entire bargaining process.

NOTES

1. Ronald B. Ehrenberg, *The Demand for State and Local Government Employees* (Lexington, Mass.: Lexington Books, 1972), p. 1.

2. The *Washington Star*, 21 Dec. 1977; quoted in "National Right to Work Newsletter," 24 (January 1978): 8.

3. Harold S. Roberts, *Roberts' Dictionary of Industrial Relations* (Washington, D.C.: Bureau of National Affairs, 1966), p. 157.

4. Michigan International Labor Studies, *Labor Relations and the Law in the United Kingdom and the United States* (Ann Arbor, Mich.: University of Michigan, 1968), pp. 99–100.

5. Bureau of National Affairs, Inc., *Collective Bargaining, Negotiations, and Contracts* (Washington, D.C.: The Bureau of National Affairs, 1964), pp. 20: 346–47.

6. Lloyd G. Reynolds, *Labor Economics and Labor Relations* (Englewood Cliffs, N.J.: Prentice-Hall, Inc., 1970), p. 292.

7. Mark van de Vall, *Labor Organizations* (London: Cambridge University Press, 1970), pp. 1–3.

8. The University of the State of New York and the State Education Department, *Industrial and Labor Relations: A Core of Related Instructions for Apprentices* (USOE, ERIC Document ED 116 033, 1975), p. 23.

9. Ibid., p. 24.

10. Roberts, p. 270.

11. The University of the State of New York, p. 25.

12. Roberts, p. 274.

13. Ibid., p. 106.

14. Ibid., p. 274.

15. The University of the State of New York, p. 26.

16. Joyce M. Najita, *Guide to Statutory Provisions in Public Sector Collective Bargaining: Scope of Negotiations* (Honolulu: University of Hawaii, March 1973), pp. 1–2.

17. Joyce M. Najita and Dennis T. Ogawa, *Guide to Statutory Provisions in*

Public Sector Collective Bargaining: Union Security (Honolulu: University of Hawaii, May 1973), p. 1.

18. Dennis T. Ogawa and Joyce M. Najita, *Guide to Statutory Provisions in Public Sector Collective Bargaining: Unit Determination* (Honolulu: University of Hawaii, June 1973), p. 1.

19. John J. Clopine, "A History of Library Unions in the United States" (Master's thesis, Catholic University, Washington, D.C., 1951), p. 8.

20. Bernard Berelson, "Library Unionization," *Library Quarterly* 9 (October 1939): 477–86.

21. Ibid., p. 480.

22. Ibid., pp. 482–83.

23. Ibid., pp. 497–505.

24. Barbara Falkoff, "Should Librarians Unionize: Part II. The Librarian and the Closed Shop," *Library Journal* 62 (August 1937): 592.

25. Archibald MacLeish, *Champion of a Cause* (Chicago: American Library Association, 1971), pp. 2–6.

26. Clopine, p. 146.

27. Eva M. Goldschmidt, "Introduction," in Archibald MacLeish, *Champion of a Cause* (Chicago: American Library Association, 1971), pp. 2–3.

28. MacLeish, p. x.

29. Jerry Wurf, "Right to Strike Important," *LMRS Newsletter* 8 (October 1977): 3–4.

LIBRARY SERVICES, REVENUE, AND POLITICS 2

MUNICIPALITIES AND PUBLIC SERVICES

For the purposes of further studying municipal services, including public libraries, it is fruitful to look at the English commercial communities of five or six centuries ago to develop certain points about cities of today.

Jon Teaford provides a clear picture of the development of such municipalities as Liverpool, Berwick, and Nottingham. The fundamentals of political existence and governance embraced by fifteenth- and sixteenth-century freemen as they pursued manufacture and trade became deeply embedded in society. Municipal charters were sought and obtained from the kings; their grants of power were exercised within the discretion of a governing corporation whose officials were elected. Although the major reason for the municipality's existence was commerce, the records of those early municipalities show that the aldermen and councillors had extended interests, even then. Many communities encouraged and authorized the construction of streets and water conduits, and also dealt with such fundamental questions as the protection of health and safety.Some boroughs even managed to establish tuition-free grammar schools which promising young urban scholars such as Will Shakespeare might attend.[1]

The general picture of those early cities is clear. That concept has carried over the centuries. In both politics and revenue, first attention was given to economic health, and second attention was given to services that enhanced the quality of life in the city. Table 2.1 shows the categorical concerns of those early cities.

From the table, two or three pertinent generalizations can be made. First, the primacy of concern for the economic welfare of the city becomes ob-

Table 2.1 **Governance Concerns of Early Municipalities**

Ordinances Relating to	Cities	
	York (a)	Beverly (b)
1. trades and markets	114	16
2. relief for the poor	53	2
3. public works	19	1
4. health and safety	8	6
5. regulating crafts and vocations	—	16

SOURCE: Jon C. Teaford, *The Municipal Revolution in America* (Chicago: University of Chicago Press, 1975), pp. 6-10.

(a) York Book of Common Minutes, 1570-1588
(b) Great Order Book of Beverly, 1516-1670

vious through the attention to trades, markets, crafts, and vocations. Second, the lesser, but still apparent concern for public services is clear. Third, although each city stands as an illustration of the municipality signifying a social break with the agricultural antecedents of the preceding centuries, it is clear that each of the cities, through its locally elected governing commission, perceived different areas of concern, at different levels of magnitude, and at different points in time.

Analysis of similar, comparable concerns of major American cities at the beginning of the nineteenth century showed that such cities as New York, Philadelphia, and New London maintained that strong interest in trade and commerce, but they also had begun to devote large efforts to public service, public safety, and public works.[2] Strong municipal support for public libraries—and such other agencies as public museums and zoos—did not come until the last half of the nineteenth century.

If this circumstance could be called a trend, it cannot be described as one without variations and interruptions. For example, Philadelphia was studied extensively as a part of its own bicentennial observation. With the rise of crime and similar problems, which have beset other cities, tax monies were shifted from service agencies, which came to be viewed as luxuries. From 1968 to 1973 that city reduced the personnel in the free public library by 29.2 percent. That datum demonstrates that attractive services can be curtailed.[3] One sociologist has declared that there are five social functions which are essential for every community:

1. producing and distributing goods and services
2. transmitting values
3. enforcing norms
4. facilitating participation in community life
5. assuring mutual support[4]

Libraries were invented and developed to carry out some part of at least four of those five functions. Experience attests to the suitability of the functions and of that part of the functions accomplished by libraries. Those parts are basic operational values in the institutional design of libraries and should not be forsaken. To curtail those functions does not speak well for communities—nor, candidly, for librarianship as an occupational category.

There are reasons for such reactionary positions by cities. Almost all such positions relate to the scarcity of money. Unionization has been widespread among public employees of local political subdivisions. Embracing both collective bargaining and a new leverage in the traditional forms of political pressure, unionization has emerged as an influential element in city budget-building. The organizational strength, spread across the spectrum of public employment, has contributed to increased budgets. Evidence of that strength and its debilitating aftermath became evident in the budget crises that became epidemic for cities in the early 1970s. The political strength of the unions became a major force in deciding when, how, and for whom the tax funds of the cities should be spent. Indeed, the question was raised by some observers as to whether union power had preempted the power of elected public officials, with regard to budget.[5]

Compensation claims have come from firefighters, police, sanitation workers, clerks, and other employees, unionized to bargain for "their share" of the municipal budget. The claims have included salary, fringes, pensions, and some special perquisites. As American cities have responded, a cycle has become discernible within only a few years. Fringe benefits, for example, represent a category of employee interest in which there has been a continued drive for improvement. That drive for improvement is, doubtless, parallel to a similar drive in the private employment sector. Private-public employment comparisons could be made which would show that public employees are at some substandard level. Yet, that political influence aspect of public employee unions, which sometimes is coupled with an aspect of critical services, looms as a distinct factor in influencing budget-building and money distribution.

There certainly has developed in cities a trend toward increased services to citizens. Librarians deliver some of that service. They comprise an occupational category that is both an inside and an outside group. They are an inside group in the sense that they are public employees who may unionize. They are an outside group in the sense that they are small in number and have marginal political clout. Given such political facts of life, the money shift noted in Philadelphia, used here as an example, becomes a rational activity for the city as its various services are reviewed and funded—more or less.

OPPORTUNITIES AND HUMAN CAPITAL

In a broad sense, politics is any condition where opposing ideas come into tension and confrontation. Libraries are services. Services do not produce raw products, finished products, or reserve capital. Yet, that observation is not altogether true, for studies of the economic growth of post-World War II societies led to the discovery that some nations, with their raw products held in a statistical constant, grew much more rapidly than did others. To account for this difference, the notion of human capital was advanced.

Human capital is generated as citizens seize opportunities for personal development and advancement. Those opportunities have been housed, largely, in service agencies. The foremost among the American service agencies is, of course, the systematic, compulsory education provided in the school districts of every state. The free public libraries have also made their contribution to this human capital in America, as citizens have patronized the libraries. The library impact is much more difficult to measure, in part because it lacks the regularized, compelled attendance aspect of public schools. Nonetheless, it is fair to assume that because this growth of human capital is harmonious with the historical mission(s) of American libraries, they have had an impact, even if not handily quantifiable and measurable.

Such global observations about library mission and operation tend to gloss over the hostilities and tensions—the politics—under which library services are offered. An understanding of library politics can be strengthened by looking in two directions, inward toward the staff and outward toward the community.

Historically, communities have extended their strongest support to the commercial interests of the city, and that fact of city political life was well illustrated by the early English cities. Even present-day America, with a strong commitment toward maximizing opportunities through which individuals may develop, still hearkens back to those old, old attitudes of city expenditures and gives but little acknowledgment of human capital. There is only grudgingly a recognition that money must be spent and services made available if American communities are to be maintained and flourish. The condition may be decried by many who see the necessity for services clearly. Some may see it as a competition against an almost feudalistic attitude, but it is the reality of late twentieth-century American politics, the realm in which public libraries must compete for the funds that support their services. In this competitive setting, it is not possible for libraries to set forward a precise, persuasive description of their effect upon citizen growth and development as public schools have done for many years. However, it is possible for libraries to claim an important place. On the straight line that shows the one-way relationship between investment in education and availability of opportunities, libraries have a significant place. The question is how does this justifiable claim to position influence the flow of revenue?

The difficulty of the question is well illustrated in Figure 2.1, a tax effort model. Tax revenues constitute a category of scarce commodities. Competi-

Figure 2.1 Attitudes Toward Tax Support for Services

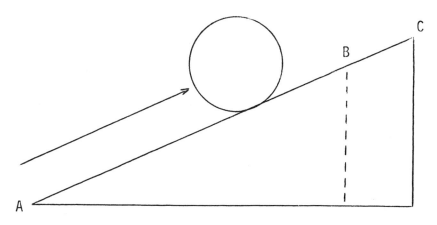

(ADAPTED FROM THE BLOOMBERG-SUNSHINE TAX EFFORT MODEL)

SOURCE: William E. Sparkman, "Tax Effort in Education," in Kern Alexander and K. Forbis Jordan, eds., *Educational Need in the Public Economy* (Gainesville, Fla.: University of Florida Press, 1976), p. 323.

tion for them is high. The tax effort a constituency will develop and maintain or increase is related to many factors, some of which are beyond the ability of an agency to influence. For example, variations in both general and particular support may include such factors as population density, urbanization, debt position of the local government, and industrialization. This discouraging array does not decrease the need for persuasive presentation of the services of the library. (These comments have focused, narrowly, upon the library as educative agency in order to reference that service against any other agency in an educative posture; however, a total services consideration must be the position from which each library advocates its own case for tax revenue support.)

Figure 2.1 carries three primary implications:

1. To move from the starting point A, and to achieve and position on the inclining line of tax revenues, demands effort
2. To maintain that position on the sloping revenue line requires effort
3. The effort to move to point B, with the volume of resources such a move would enclose, if that is considered the minimally desirable support level, is substantial. Yet, the effort to move to point C, a higher resources point, if that is considered the most desirable support level, is truly outstanding

Like every area in which money is spent, citizens want to get the most for
their money. Taxes (and especially local taxes), more than any other costs
that citizens bear, arouse antagonistic attitudes when there is talk of increase.

To some extent, opportunity for the development of human capital—as
one of the major reasons for library services—can be assessed by studying
the tax performance of the states and securing a measure of tax effort. That
is, services depend upon tax revenues that support the free public libraries.

Table 2.2 is, in effect, a survey index of tax effort. Although only selected
states have been listed, the survey provides a complete picture of the range
of tax effort. The differences in total tax collections between the highest and
the lowest of the states is of the order of magnitude of 2.6. The political environments in which libraries seek money for their services have characteristic
maxima that will influence the extent of the services. Those historically
characteristic maxima also carry a message to librarians who are interested
in their own professional economic welfare as they address questions of collective bargaining in their work setting, that is, "be aware of money sources."

Looking outward into the politics of the library's community, many problems become apparent. Other problems have been laid to rest. For example,
civil service reform, now almost forgotten because accomplished so long
ago, protects government employees from exploitation by politicians who
could, before that reform, seek campaign funds and campaign services from
employees. Progress toward better working conditions and relief from
political chicanery—politics at its worst—may be slow, but progress can be
seen when the whole work setting is considered over time.

MANAGEMENT, GOVERNANCE, AND THE SOVEREIGNTY DOCTRINE

The word "politics" is not used to connote intrigue or deceit; it is a
broader and more honorable term. Politics is tension within a social system.
Movements within organizations to secure relocations of the locus of power
have been more or less characteristic of all organizations through time.
Organizational politics may include artfulness and wariness, but when
politics includes deceit, its moral justificaion and attractiveness are jeopar-
dized. Libraries are political organizations existing within larger political
organizations, and in many areas employees have accepted collective
bargaining as a device to generate new authority and seek more control
over their unit of employment.

Public libraries have been a major interest area of the lower classes, those
people having found in the public library one avenue to their own personal
improvement and advancement. There is a connection between this historic
interest in American libraries, the way libraries are governed, and their

Table 2.2 **Tax Performance as a Measure of Tax Effort**

	Per Capita Local Tax Collections 1969-70		Per Capita State Tax Revenue FY 1970		Per Capita Total of Tax Collections, State and Local Governments 1969-70	
	highest	*lowest*	*highest*	*lowest*	*highest*	*lowest*
State	NY	SC	HI	NH	NY	AR
Amount	$317	$64	$422	$128	$652	$251
Rank	1	50	1	50	1	50

SOURCE: Adapted from William E. Sparkman, "Tax Effort in Education," in Kern Alexander and K. Forbis Jordan, eds., *Educational Need in the Public Economy* (Gainesville, Florida: The University Press, 1976), pp. 308–9.

Table 2.3 **Library Support in the Most Populous States (FY 1975)**

State	Population	Grants-in-Aid Total Federal	State Aid/Appropriation	Total Public Library Income
CA	20,800,000	$3,924,000	$ 1,000,000	$160,887,000
IL	11,113,000	3,565,000	11,138,000	70,281,000
NY	18,243,000	1,123,000	25,000,000	170,223,000
PA	11,800,000	2,417,000	8,220,000	44,894,000
TX	10,525,000	5,832,000	500,000	37,967,000

SOURCE: *American Library Director*, 30th edition.

general level of support. Table 2.3 reveals that support for library services varies regionally; more emphatically, the data reveal the heavy dependence of libraries upon local tax sources. Typically, it appears that local taxes supply about 80 percent of the dollars needed to operate libraries.

Revenue, both in amount and by source, must be of more than passing interest to all library employees. The philosophical orientation of American public libraries has been toward free access. The development, processing, storage, and retrieval of information have costs. In a time of constant or rising costs, and strong resistance to increased local taxes, what is the financial future of libraries, as American have come to know them? In a thoughtful address, Russell Shank, the incoming president of the American Library Association, made several pertinent comments. He called attention to some user services of relatively high cost that are, increasingly, being paid for by fees. "Word is going around that the free library, that is the public library, freely accessible at no cost to the user, is doomed." Shank pinpointed this circumstance as a change in the American culture, if it happens. He also acknowledged that the trend away from tax-supported services through which information is supplied and toward fee charging to users for services is symptomatic of a philosophical shift within many branches of American governments. He concluded with a position statement, declaring, "Whatever we do we must not let the powerful new technology in the information service field slip behind the greenback curtain, there to be an exotic tool for the exclusive use of the well-heeled."[6] His resistance to this trend can be supported by the observation that the measurable ability and knowledge of its individuals comprises the ability, knowledge, and effectiveness of the citizenry.

In some related events centering upon revenue and costs, libraries have experienced recently both feast and famine. Fort Lauderdale, announcing a need for stricter accountability, attempted to raise the building rent charged the county library from one dollar to $190,000 annually. In New York's Nassau County, tax support was cut off for a reference center established to serve all types of libraries in the area. On the other hand, the Detroit Public got a $3.1 million boost, coming from both state and local sources, upon its recognition as the state resource center. In Bismarck, North Dakota, citizens turned out in record numbers to support a referendum calling for a new level of tax support to the public library.[7] It is clear that revenue, in amount and constancy, is a mixed bag; its strong, voluntary continuation cannot be assumed.

In the cities, service employment has become the principal source of jobs, surpassing manufacturing and commerce. This major change in the economic life of cities has had an effect upon, and contributed to, the "urban crises" in several ways. Every metropolitan area has a large number of political subdivisions, and Chicago can stand as a good example. It is a municipality. In fact, it is many municipalities. It is also many townships, special districts, and several counties. By one system of counting, Chicago consisted of 599 political subdivisions.[8] The competition among these subdivisions for tax dollars from citizens must necessarily be intense; likewise, that tax dollar pursuit must be irritating to those upon whom the taxes are levied. (Some citizens must experience what they perceive as double taxation.) That irritation can only be accentuated when the proportion of tax-supported jobs is rising and the proportion of industrial jobs is declining.

When such factors are coupled with the long-standing doctrine of managerial sovereignty in public employment—which precludes the necessary give and take of collective bargaining—divisiveness in the manpower of the library may result. If management, in the form of the trustees or chief executive, stands firm in defining public sector management as the implementation of employment conditions fixed by statute, then they must turn aside employee organizations that may attempt to bargain. Historically, managerial sovereignty was the public management posture. It is a fading position, with a pragmatic acknowledgment that it is no longer workable because employee attitudes changed and new statutes concerning employment support those organized workers.[9]

INSIDE THE LIBRARY

A comparison across time is helpful to understanding the climate in which library supervision occurs. In 1940, the Chicago library union demands included the "adjustment of employee grievances through the adoption of a modern, democratic personnel policy." That sentiment grew from the condition of the 1930s in which libraries operated under archaic personnel policies. Personnel management throughout the public service agencies was acknowledged as far below the standards accepted by progressive managers in the private employment sector. Library service stood below a median position with respect to attitudes toward library employees by supervisors.[10]

Theodore L. Guyton's comprehensive research into the working conditions of librarians provided information about attitudes of librarians toward their immediate supervisors, in the work setting climate. Table 2.4 reveals two job-related attitudes and indicates that the librarians of the 1970s had, in large part, favorable opinions of the "administrative aspects of their supervisor's job."[11]

One research project of the late 1960s revealed some pertinent facts as well as uncertainties about collective bargaining and management attitudes

Table 2.4 **Survey Respondents' Attitudes Toward the Library and Its Administration**

Attitude	Pro-union (%)	Anti-union (%)	Total Sample (N)
Toward job satisfaction:			
Favorable	53	47	89
Unfavorable	53	47	11
Toward immediate supervision:			
Favorable	51	49	82
Unfavorable	57	43	18

SOURCE: Guyton, *Unionization: The Viewpoint of Librarians.*

in eighty large American libraries. Seventy administrator respondents replied to a question about the encouragement of collective bargaining. Three percent said they would encourage library unionization; 20 percent stated they would discourage it; 68 percent said they would be neutral; 9 percent declined to respond. While responding to another question, the administrators established a mildly contradictory finding when 63 percent of them said that they felt that both professional and nonprofessional library employees should have access to collective bargaining and 11 percent stated that library employees should have the right to strike. Finally, this 1967 survey revealed that a preponderance of the librarian-administrators in the survey wanted more information. They stipulated the need to:

1. clarify tasks and responsibilities of professionals and nonprofessionals
2. provide information of the experience, of other, similar professions
3. guide the library, as an employing agency, in determing effective bargaining units at both the local and national levels[12]

Problems within the professional work force of libraries that have their origin in employee-supervisor conflict cannot be solved by hearkening back in time to simplistic models of administrative behavior. Managers must be able to assure themselves that their behavior reveals sensitivity to the needs of the work group. Employees have that human need for belonging to groups. For managers to set out to thwart groups, to prove that they dominate the employee group, to bureaucratically isolate the group, are all sure ways to create a climate of distrust, low morale, and low motivation. Through personal orientation, managers can establish a climate of self-direction, open communications, and shared decision making; then, productivity is likely to increase. Directionless management is no answer. But open management with defined goals actually encourages the employee group as each person moves to accomplish his own tasks within the organization's framework.

A balance of power must prevail if the library is to flourish. The relationship between employer and employee must be perceived as based upon managerial integrity. Job performance, job satisfaction, and productivity are not likely to prevail where mangement demands conformity, submissiveness, and dependence. Lapses in communication may be signs of distrust within the organization. In the face of so many strains, coming from without but influential within, it is essential that the library administration strive toward trust building through integrity in management. Such managers are:

1. honest and straightforward
2. aware of both strengths and limitations
3. consistent in demonstrating esteem for human dignity
4. flexible in managerial style
5. morally courageous[13]

Inside the library, another environment exists as each employee finds diverging, and sometimes contradictory, conditions calling for testaments of loyalty. Tensions exist internally which are part of the politics of the work setting. How can professional librarians, especially those who are newly hired, cope with influences that may be subtle, that may be, occasionally, at the verge of ethical behavior? How about the contradictory pressures of some work groups that have become, for some reason, points of polarization? Management methods, role perceptions, and work attitudes all are present, creating the internal politics of the library.

In reporting the study by Presthus, Plate stated that 53 percent of the 397 manager librarians in that survey agreed that "a librarian's loyalties should be with the organization hiring him rather than to his particular service." Taken in the context of specialization, that finding cast doubt upon the eventual full professionalization of librarianship. Further, Presthus' findings were substantiated in Plate's later research, which indicated that middle management librarians in large, prestigious libraries, exhibited a strong tendency to become locals in their job orientation.[14] Some might read that finding as an indicator of strong opposition toward unionization, and of strong support for conforming librarians by the librarian-manager types.

Figure 2.2 A Large Urban Library Organizational Model

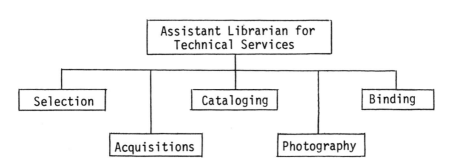

That finding for localism and high conformity may exacerbate already tense internal politics of libraries, in which unionization becomes all the more attractive to some, and all the more fearful to others. For example, Figure 2.2 portrays what might be a typical organization plan for a large urban library. The figure portrays five middle managers, each of whom heads a department employing several professional librarians. For management to insist that those varied professional librarians hold in higher esteem the interests of the library than their interest in the advancement of their own specialization is an effort to force a difficult choice. In a general observation about the personalities of organizations, it is fair to say that choices forced upon professionals by management are likely to cause rancor and dispute along with the choice.

LIBRARY ORGANIZATIONS

For over one hundred years, the American Library Association has been the primary organization devoted to the improvement and expansion of library services. With almost 35,000 members, the ALA is the oldest and strongest nongovernmental library organization in the world. It has been a forum from which spokesmen, from time to time, have addressed problems of information services. Consisting of thirteen special interest divisions in 1975-76, the ALA's membership included 27,600 personal and 4,400 organizational members. Organizationally split by special interests, the Association includes such units as the Association of College and Research Libraries, the Children's Service Division, and the Public Library Association. With interests in legislation, accreditation, and publishing, the ALA has been a potent force in American libraries.[15] However, the ALA has not emerged as the unit in which librarians have found advocacy for their professional financial welfare or for the improvement of their working conditions locally.

Although the focus of both service and support for libraries was originally local, each of the fifty states now has a state library agency located somewhere in its state government. For thirty-eight of the states, those agencies are either within the state department of education or in an independent library board or commission. There are nineteen agencies in each arrangement, and the remaining twelve states have various other organizational plans. For example, in Delaware the library agency is in the Department of Community Affairs; in Missouri, it is in the Department of Higher Education; while in North Dakota it is in the Department of Institutions. From those agencies has been formed a group called the Chief Officers of State Library Services (COSLA). Formed in 1973, COSLA has a membership of fifty, and its purpose is to extend interaction within the group, and between the group and the federal government. Network and systems development is a natural concern at the state level, but COSLA members are also concerned about the problems of local libraries within each state.[16] If funding of public libraries through the federal government is going to increase, COSLA will surely play a key role in securing that revenue for local libraries.

Like other members of the professional world of work, librarians have a wide array of associations which they may join. Some are comprehensive and open; some are limited and exclusive. Many could be listed, but the ALA and COSLA are both indicative and exemplary. Many professional association opportunities are open to librarians, but they are focused upon the special interests of the job setting and, clearly, are not associations through which librarians have gotten support for their own personal welfare as they perform their professional tasks. That statement in no way detracts from the influence wielded by such associations upon the work environment; it merely points out the fact that the influence is of a particular, and limited, nature.

FEDERAL LEGISLATION AND LIBRARIES

In recent years, libraries have benefited from several public laws, but especially from three: (1) the Library Services and Construction Act, (2) specific titles of the Higher Education Act, and (3) the Elementary and Secondary Education Act. Libraries have also been assisted by the Congress in such areas as postal and tax amendments, arts and humanities amendments, and telecommunications demonstrations. Much of this legislation, in both the original and renewed forms, has carried a demand for maintenance of effort from state or local financial resources. Such a demand precluded the substitution of federal for local funds. The maintenance of effort requirements were lessened in 1976. That is, they were kept in place, but the level or rigor was diminished, and in some localities federal funds were used to relieve the call upon local tax revenues.

A word must be said about the relationship between population and federal funds. Table 2.3 shows some data on the five most populous states. Estimates for 1977 by the Bureau of the Census showed these states are still the five largest but also showed that while New York and Pennsylvania had lost in population, Texas, California, and Illinois had gained in population. It now appears likely that the 1980 census will lead to a restructuring of the House of Representatives, which will affect thirteen states. Those gains and losses will take effect in the 1982 election. The gross redistribution of the population will affect type, amount, and distribution of federal appropriations.[17] Additionally, the 1980 census included questions designed to more accurately identify minority groups, with the aim of assisting the Congress in its efforts of special support to disadvantaged citizens.

In these brief comments about the federal government and library support, some clues usable in planning may be found in the viewpoints expressed toward President Jimmy Carter's urban policy. The U.S. Chamber of Commerce was initially warm toward the national urban policy, but as the legislation is being considered in the Congress, the Chamber has come forward as a critic. It has become especially critical of the large tax burden seen in federally financed local public works programs that have rigid specifications about who may be employed and locating new federal facilities in central cities. Another critical group, the National People's Action (NPA), has called for neighborhood impact analysis, rather than urban impact analysis, as the plan presently requires. NPA has also deplored the lack of any major neighborhood housing strategy.[18] Incomplete legislation such as this should be considered only as exemplary. It is a prime example, however, of the federal government's interest in special categories of citizens. It is exemplary of fund sources that have been, and will be, important to libraries for both operation and construction.

Funds available for programs in libraries and for the construction and organization themselves are shown in Table 2.5. The very largest sums have been made available to programs not shown in the table. For example, library programs and services were expanded substantially under the Elementary and Secondary Education Act, Title I, Educationally Deprived

Table 2.5 **Selected Federal Funding for Library Programs**

Library Programs	FY 1976 Appropriation	FY 1977 Appropriation
Library Services and Construction Act	$ 51,749,000	$ 60,237,000
Title I Library Services	49,155,000	56,900,000
Title II Public Library Construction	———	———
Title III Interlibrary Cooperation	2,594,000	3,337,000
Elementary and Secondary Education Act (ESEA)		
Title IV-B Libraries and Learning Resources	147,330,000*	154,330,000*
Higher Education Act (HEA) Title II	11,475,000	
Title II-A College Library Resources	9,975,000	Deferred
Title II-B Library Training	500,000	Deferred
Title II-B Library Research/Demonstrations	1,000,000	Deferred
Title II-C Research Libraries	———	Deferred
Title VI-A Undergraduate Education Equipment	7,500,000	Deferred
Library of Congress (LC)	119,125,400	137,895,200
LC National Program Acquisitions and Cataloging	10,173,391	10,767,497
National Library of Medicine (NLM)	22,632,000	27,234,000

SOURCE: Adapted from Eileen D. Cooke and Sara Case, "Legislation Affecting Librarianship in 1976," in *The Bowker Annual of Library and Book Trade Information*, 22nd ed. (New York: R.R. Bowker, 1977).

*Advance funded program

Children, for which $2,285 million was appropriated in FY 1977.[19] The table is not a comprehensive display of federal support to library programs.

SUMMARY

In the United States, there were 8,504 libraries listed in the *American Library Directory* for 1976-77. The same directory identified 5,477 branch libraries, 1,606 university and college libraries, 1,129 junior college libraries, and other special category libraries to total 29,345 libraries in the U.S. The professionals who staff them not only have an interest in the service that can be provided but in securing from each employing library the most advantageous working conditions. This may mean collective bargaining coming out of unionization. For that larger group of unionization service specialists—the librarians and media specialists certificated to work in the libraries of the 16,000 school districts of the nation—the number included under collective bargaining agreements is already increasing each year.

If the professional librarian attitude could be described as professional militancy, it is a condition that is continuing unabated. To some extent, the attitude has been nourished upon anxiety. Some present-day concerns of public and university librarians include new challenges to the legal validity of the M.L.S. degree as a job requirement; the task analysis approach to work role definition and increasing use of volunteers and nonprofessionals in both public school and public library settings; and the uncertainty of the impact upon jobs that are being created through computer technology and rapid information retrieval services. These concerns are compounded by questions of job title. For example, are workers certificated to man school libraries really media specialists—and professionally different from public library professionals—or are they, really, librarians, too?[20]

In every complex social setting, some factors must be seen as threats, producing tension and anxiety. To face the tough problems of revenue and politics, librarians of every persuasion obviously need to "get their act together."

NOTES

1. Jon C. Teaford, *The Municipal Revolution in America* Chicago: University of Chicago Press, 1975), pp. 6-10.

2. Ibid., p. 109.

3. Peter A. McGrath, "Bicentennial Philadelphia: a Quaking City," in Dennis Clark, ed., *Philadelphia: 1776-2076, A Three Hundred Year View* (Port Washington, N.Y.: The Kennikat Press, 1975), p. 90.

4. Hedley Donovan and others, eds., *The Community* (New York: Time-Life Books, 1976), p. 141.

5. Sterling D. Spero and John M. Capazzola, *The Urban Community and Its Unionized Bureaucracies* (New York: Denellen, 1973), p. 215.

6. John Berry, "Fighting Fees in California," *Library Journal* 103 (January 15, 1978): 119.

7. Noel Savage, "News Report 1977," *Library Journal* 103 (January 15, 1978): 133.

8. Bennett Harrison, "Public Service Jobs for Urban Ghetto Residents," in Harold L. Sheppard and others, eds., *The Political Economy of Public Service Employment* (Lexington, Mass.: Lexington Books, 1972), p. 237.

9. Paul Prasow and Edward Peters, *Arbitration and Collective Bargaining* (New York: McGraw-Hill, 1970), pp. 235-36.

10. Theodore L. Guyton, *Unionization: The Viewpoint of Librarians* (Chicago: American Library Association, 1975), p. 126.

11. Ibid., p. 132.

12. George L. Gardiner, "Collective Bargaining: Some Questions Asked," *ALA Bulletin* 62 (September 1968): 975.

13. E. G. Bogue and Robert L. Sanders, *The Educational Manager* (Worthington, Ohio: Charles A. Jones, 1976), pp. 101-102.

14. Kenneth Plate, *Management Personnel in Libraries* (Rockaway, N.J.: American Faculty Press, 1978), p. 32.

15. Clara S. Jones, "American Library Association," in *The Bowker Annual of*

Library and Book Trade Information, 22nd ed. (New York: R. R. Bowker, 1977), pp. 51–53.

16. Joseph Shubert, "Chief Officers of State Library Agencies," in *The Bowker Annual of Library and Book Trade Information,* 22nd ed. (New York: R. R. Bowker, 1977), pp. 71–75.

17. "More Political Heft for the Southwest," *U.S. News and World Report* 84 (February 6, 1978): 45.

18. *ALH: Administrative and Legislative Highlights* 78 (April 13, 1978): 3.

19. Eileen D. Cooke and Sara Case, "Legislation Affecting Librarianship in 1976," in *The Bowker Annual of Library and Book Trade Information,* 22nd ed. (New York: R. R. Bowker, 1977), p. 100.

20. Savage, pp. 138–39.

PUBLIC LIBRARIANS 3

INTRODUCTION

A comprehensive study of libraries and unions was done by Goldstein. In the late 1960s, he sought through correspondence to secure information about the attitudes and history within which library unions were formed across the nation. Along with the information flow generated by his research emerged a strange reticence to talk about labor relations in public libraries, especially from the "side" of management. That is, many library directors did not want to talk about unions of public librarians, and some did not even want to admit that a local union professional librarians existed. The situation cut both ways, too, in that some local union officers revealed information grudgingly or not at all. The environment for labor relations in public libraries during the 1960s was permeated all too frequently by an attitude of distrust and secrecy, if this national survey can be taken as an indicator.

For example, Goldstein reported that inquiries to the library administration of the Chicago Public Library elicited brief, noncommittal, noninformative replies, acknowledging only that there was a union of professional employees in the Chicago Public Library. The literature documented the existence of a union, whose strength had waxed and waned over a few decades, but which was strong enough to threaten a strike in 1967. (That was averted through the personal intervention of Mayor Daley.) Yet, in 1968, neither the librarian nor the director of the local council of the American Federation of State, County, and Municipal Employees were willing to join in a candid correspondence with Goldstein describing the conditions of labor relations in the Chicago Public Library.[1]

The emergence of AFSCME as a leading national affiliate for librarians was clearly documented by Goldstein's listing of such public libraries as

Cleveland, St. Paul, Minneapolis, and Baltimore as places where librarians and some library support personnel negotiated through their own AFSCME local. His research, too, revealed independent units, other affiliations, and exceptionalities based upon statutory limitations. With each state developing its own public employee bargaining statutes, the public employees of each state must be in conformity with the statutes of the state. For the professional librarians of the Boston Public Library, the Massachusetts law contained a controlling qualifier to membership. That law stipulated that professionals and nonprofessionals in a single public employment setting could not form a single collective bargaining unit, except upon the agreement of a majority of the professionals to do so. That is, an AFSCME local for nonprofessional library employees could not also represent the professional group, except by a majority vote of the latter group to affiliate.[2]

By initially focusing upon the Chicago Public Library as an early example, it is possible to better understand labor relations in libraries. The AFSCME has been the librarian's union since about the mid-1930s. Illinois was—and is—one of the few states with no bargaining law for public employees. Public administrators and boards of trustees not wishing to bargain cannot be forced to do so, lacking a statutory mandate. Those public administrations that do bargain in Illinois do so voluntarily. For an understanding of the current drive for bargaining among librarians, and for contrast with the older Chicago unit, the New York Public Library has been chosen here as an extended example. However, before examining two specific settings, a glimpse into the manpower situation should be helpful.

One additional note should be borne in mind. Any discussion of labor relations in libraries implicitly includes personnel management and the interpersonal relations characteristic of organizations. The appraisal of librarians in the performance of specific tasks for which they have responsibility is important to the employees themselves, as well as to the library administrators and trustees. For example, it is hardly a controversial notion that job performance appraisal should be specific to the assigned tasks, but that notion should be explicitly stated in a negotiated contract if it is not a part of policy. Further, the manner in which assigned tasks are described and distributed should be clear to all. Although this general comment about some characteristics of organizations is aimed at public library work settings, it applies equally in school-university libraries, except that the distance from the trustees to the library would be greater in the latter settings.

MANPOWER AND JOBS

Librarianship has long been seen as an occupation of gentility. It has many of the distinctive features of a profession. Librarians have less autonomy in their work settings than do persons in some other professionlike occupations. Librarians work in a bureaucracy. There is a tendency for bureaucracies to follow the subordinate-superordinate organization scheme that predominates in the military and in business organizations. That work setting decreases autonomy, the self-control which librarians can exercise as they apply the general knowledge in which they are expert. Nonetheless, the service orientation of professionalism prevails, and librarianship as an occupation is sufficiently attractive and prestigious that the current manpower pool is more than adequate.

Table 3.1 reveals a generally upward trend in the beginning manpower pool, the new library science graduates, and reveals a progressively upward trend in salaries, too. The table, augmented, also accounts for the inflationary instability of the dollar; and with a beginning salary index of 100—when the Cost of Living (COL) was 100—the accumulative data reveal that the compensation levels to beginning fifth-year library school graduates have been slipping. While the beginning salary index rose from 100 to 145, the COL rose from 100 to 162. There may be several reasons for that real money loss, but one of the reasons must be the supply of manpower. When the manpower supply in any occupational category reaches a point that allows employers to pick and choose from among many applicants, compensation for both beginners and experienced persons tends to sink. Obviously, that is a too simplistic explanation of the relationships; other factors influence compensation, too, but unemployed, available professionals have a strongly depressing effect.

Table 3.1 **Beginning Salaries of Fifth-Year Library School Graduates**

Year	Number of Graduates	Average Beginning Salary	Beginning Salary Index	Cost of Living Index
1967	4,030	$ 7,305	100	100
1969	4,970	8,161	112	—
1971	5,670	8,846	121	—
1973	6,336	9,423	128	—
1975	6,010	10,594	145	162

SOURCE: Carol L. Learmont and Richard L. Darling, "Placements and Salaries, 1975: A Difficult Year," in Nada Beth Glick and Sarah L. Prakken, eds., *The Bowker Annual of Library and Book Trade Information*, 22nd ed. (New York: R.R. Bowker Company, 1977), p. 355.

THE EARLY CHICAGO UNION

From the mid-1950s to the mid-1960s, the Chicago library administration restricted the activity of the union merely by refusing to deal with it. In

1967, the union forced the matter with a strike threat. The mayor interven-
ed, the strike was called off, and the library administration agreed to meet
with the union representatives to discuss union demands, grievances, and
other personnel procedures.[3]

Earlier, in the mid-1930s, the Chicago librarians formed the Chicago
Public Library Employees Union, Local 88 of the State, County and
Municipal Workers of America, affiliated with the Committee for Industrial
Organization. That group published a newsletter, the *C.P.L. Union News*,
for about ten years. The first issue bore a December 1937 date. That
publication, which in its first few years must be called a distinguished and
enlightening newsletter, was the primary reason that the Chicago library
affords a unique opportunity to understand labor relations and librarians. It
was an outstanding record of those events, revealing many of the major
problems that still plague labor relations.

In the order of things, unions are not called upon to discipline themselves.
That pressure comes from the outside. Self-regulatory functions are not part
of unionism. Regulatory functions and the long-range viewpoint are part of
administration. That attitudinal conflict constitutes a part of the tension in
the employee-employer relationship. It is a puzzle which calls for analysis,
for the sane approach, for the application of good sense—in short, for
adherence to fair labor practices by both sides. That puzzle was well
reported in the Chicago newsletter.

Amidst a strong and persistent drive for members, the Chicago Public
Library Employees Union (CPLEU) secured the services of consultants to
analyze problems of organization finance, and to recommend action lines.
The program of the union, stated in Figure 3.1, was set forward clearly and
concisely. The CPLEU affiliated both regionally and nationally and stated
its program generally, to be for the good of the library and for the good of
the employees as well. Those concerns were specific to the 1930s, but it
would take very little imagination to revise them in such a way that forty
years later they would be applicable in many localities. From the newly
employed beginning librarian to the director of libraries, that ten-point program had—and has—real meaning.

The organizational procedure and format for CPLEU were explained in
an early editorial.

The Union was organized by representatives of the State, County and Municipal
Workers of America, affiliated with the Committee for Industrial Organization.
There is nothing unusual about this. The aim of the C.I.O. is to organize the
unorganized and no one can deny that the Chicago Public Library employees were
unorganized.

The Union has elected officers, an executive committee, a board of branch and
department stewards, and several functioning committees. In addition to membership meetings, two successful organizational meetings have been held in order that

Figure 3.1 Ten-Point Program of the (CPLE) Union

1. Strict enforcement of civil service for all library employees.
2. An adequate staff at all times.
3. Definite classification of duties within each grade.
4. Re-classification of grades upward to bring compensation in line with that in other city departments.
5. A minimum wage of $1,200 a year for all full time employees, with part time paid on a proportional basis and time and a half for overtime.
6. Promotional examinations and appointments from qualified lists at regular intervals.
7. Automatic increases within grades.
8. Four weeks vacation with pay, and a thirty-five hour week (30 hour week in long range program).
9. Proper working conditions and the safeguarding of employees' health by the provision of adequate heat, light, ventilation, and rest-room facilities.
10. Adequate facilities as to space, equipment and supplies, for carrying on the duties of all employees.

SOURCE: *CPL Union News 1* (December 1937): 1.

all members of the staff might have the opportunity to learn more about the activities of the union.[4]

Statistical comparisons have long been a primary basis from which judgments can be made. Are librarians adequately paid? Is revenue appropriately distributed in the operation of the library? These were questions which the CPLEU faced, and it developed sets of comparative data from a list of forty-five cities having more than 200,000 population. Some of the statistics have been summarized in Tables 3.2 and 3.3 from data gathered in the latter 1930s.

Those tables represent a kind of comparative information that librarians, at any time or place, must know. The "must know" obligation applies to librarians as employees or as directors, for both sides in a negotiations setting must have complete, accurate information as a prelude to desirable contracts.

By late 1938, the CPLEU was deep into a program of many facets. The Union hosted a first anniversary dinner with invitations sent to administrators and directors, trustees, other union officials, and city dignitaries. The Union sponsored a free fall lecture series under the auspices

Table 3.2 **Library Revenue**

City	Per Capita	Library Staff Salaries	Nonsalary Appropriations
Chicago	$0.51	60%	40%
Detroit	0.67	66	34
Los Angeles	0.81	66	34
New York	0.48	75	25

SOURCE: *CPL Union News* 1 (December 1937): 4.

Table 3.3 **Librarian Work Times**

City	Hours Per Week	Days of Vacation	Special Holidays
Chicago	41	18	8
Detroit	37	20	6
Los Angeles	40	12	7
New York	40	26	11

SOURCE: *CPL Union News* 1 (December 1937): 4.

of its own Education Committee. The five lecture titles indicated the span of the Union's interest:

1. "Youth and the Public Library"
2. "The Clivedon Set and Fascism"
3. "Professional Standards—Union Standards"
4. "Adult Education"
5. "The Library as a Social Force."

The Union also unveiled its own program for the improvement of library appropriations from the state legislature, with a news story to its members.

The first shot in a spirited campaign to muster more support for the library and to increase its revenue has sounded. The Executive Committee of the C.P.L. Employees Union at its last meeting October 19 adopted a memorandum on proposed library legislation to be presented at the next session of the State Legislature. The Union goes on record favoring the amending of the Library law to increase the pegged levy for maintenance and operation of the Public Library from $2,000,000 to $3,000,000, the additional sum to be used partly for increasing the staff and for more adequate salaries, and partly for needed additions to the book stock; and increase in the tax-levy for building purposes from one-tenth to two-tenths of a mill on each dollar of assessed property valuation. The memorandum was presented to candidates at the Legislative Rally sponsored by the While Collar Council at the Midland Hotel.[5]

The extraordinary interest span of the Chicago union, turning its attention to a variety of endeavors both peripheral to and supportive of better wages and better working conditions was evidenced by these endeavors and by the high quality of the newsletter itself. The CPLEU spectrum of concerns included public relations and political action. The resolution from its Executive Committee, presented at the first national convention of the Committee for Industrial Organization in November 1938, revealed its strong commitment to political action.

RESOLVED, that we members of the Chicago Public Library Employees Union, Local 88, State, County and Municipal Workers of America (C.I.O.) assembled at a membership meeting, on Sunday, November 6, 1938, at 155 N. Clark Street, of the Committee for Industrial Organization convened in Pittsburgh on November 14, 1938, to go on record supporting a National Program of Library Development, and favoring Federal Aid for Libraries, and be it further

RESOLVED, that the C.I.O. Convention urge all its constituent International, National and local industrial unions to support local library legislation, and be it finally

RESOLVED, that copies of this resolution be forwarded to the Hon. Harold Ickes, Secretary of the Interior, to the American Library Association, to the State, County, and Municipal Workers of America, the Bulletin of the A.L.A., the Library Journal, the Wilson Bulletin, the press, and other interested organizations and individuals.[6]

Despite its initial vitality, the good wishes it received from many public administrators in Chicago and elsewhere, and the letters of admiration for its newsletter from all over the nation, the CPLEU showed signs of faltering in the early 1940s. It has been both strong and weak since, but mostly weak. Perhaps it came at the wrong time, just before World War II. Perhaps its program was too broad. Some earlier, private sector unions suffered and disappeared from the scene as a consequence of operating too broad a front. When a present-day researcher turns back to that time and takes note of the union's concerns, and expectation of leadership among library unions is built. That expectation was, at best, only partially fulfilled.

THE NEW YORK UNION

The NYPL Organizing Committee issued its first newsletter in March 1967, announcing its intentions and existence. At the April meeting, the agenda encouraged discussion from the floor and was devoted to five primary concerns:

1. Current status of librarianship as a profession
2. Importance of a democratic grievance committee
3. Wage increases for the clerical staff
4. The welfare fund
5. The negotiations committee[7]

That paradoxical problem the "wait and see syndrome" plagued the union organizers. People wanted to wait, to see what the group could accomplish before committing themselves or their money to the group. The paradox, of course, is that no group can prove itself without members, workers, and money.[8]

Two things need to be said about the New York Public Library and the initial records of the unionization of librarians. First, the name of the New York Public Library is misleading. The New York Public Library, Astor, Lennox, and Tilden Foundations is really a private library open to the public that has some support from public funds. It has its own self-perpetuating board of trustees. The Main Branch is the Central Building and houses the research libraries. The NYPL is administratively separate from the other borough libraries in New York City. Some employees are paid from private endowments, and some are paid from public funds. Predominant in the latter group are those who staff the branch libraries. Administratively a hybrid, the NYPL has some unusual problems and opportunities, as bargaining and contract management have come upon the scene.

Second, this description of unionization has focused upon current efforts. There were earlier attempts at unionization in the NYPL. At least one of the attempts, in the 1930s, was an apparent response to the national economic fluctuation from inflation to depression. The Depression, with its uncertainties, brought a fear to citizens in this technological society that, to some extent, they tried to alleviate through unionization. James Henderson spoke to that point directly, when he said,

> I know there were at least two such attempts (at earlier unionization)—in the forties and also at an earlier time, probably during the period of the Depression. The Depression group published a periodical called *The Classmark*.[9]

In November 1969, Local # 1930, NYPL Guild of the AFSCME, made its first publication to members, "The 1930 Local Line." The first issue was devoted to explaining the procedures for election of officers, the use by the local of library bulletin boards, a salary increment for a second M.S. degree, and other items. It was apparent from the publication that the method of election was based upon an open democratic format.[10]

Newly elected President David Beasley, at the helm of # 1930, demanded that the "staff (of 1930) does not want a simulation of an association. We

Table 3.4 **Mean Salary Comparisons for Selected Librarians**

Employing Agency	July 1970	Jan. 1971	Oct. 1970	Oct. 1971	Oct. 1970	Oct. 1971
			Time			
New York Public Librarians	$8,000	8,600				
New York City School Librarians			$9,950	10,900		
City University New York Librarians					$11,960	12,700

SOURCE: *1930 Local Line Newsletter*, no. 13 (August 13, 1970): 1–2.

want a strong, aggressive trade union."[11] Salaries, pensions, and working conditions received attention early.

A comparison was developed among librarians in different employment settings in New York. (Research librarians were excluded upon the basis that they were paid at a substantially higher rate, and from private funds.) Table 3.4 revealed that the NYPL employees did not fare well in the comparison. From the table it became clear that not only were the present salaries in NYPL #1930 low, but when anticipated gains were compared with the extended contracts of the two other groups, the picture remained bleak. Parity with school librarians and an extended-year contract became high priority items.

Much of what occurs in any job setting is a response to perceptions of conditions which may differ between management employees. The "1930 Local Lines" issues of 1971 revealed that management threatened to close the performing arts library and the bindery. Local #1930 demanded an agency shop and took the position that if other city employees struck about pension plan issues, the librarians would join them. Like 1930, these other unions were affiliated with AFSCME. Management continued to speak of a financial crisis, and at the end of 1971, jobs were being abolished and staff terminated—events that had not happened previously in the library's seventy-five year history.

In 1973 and 1974, the union achieved certain gains:

1. two successive nine percent raises
2. compensated maternity leave
3. restoration of compensatory time for specified employees
4. permanence of tenure, even after job transfer

Yet, all was not well for the employees. At the end of 1974, the administration announced the closing of several branch libraries, and in only a few months over sixty professionals from the Research Libraries were also terminated. The administration also initiated firing, job downgrading, and rehiring during this period. Amid such uncertainty and frenzied activity, local members had a need for news, promptly distributed. To meet this need, the union president wrote and frequently issued a new organ, "The Local Bulletin." The intent was to keep members abreast of developments immediately after they occurred.[12]

A basic point of contention in all bargaining between Local #1930 and the administration was the temperature-humidity index (THI). Simply described, the THI is a measurable point at which the work area becomes annoyingly cloying in a high temperature and humidity combination. If the index goes beyond that point, employees are relieved of duty, but are compensated. This compensated absence is based upon the notion that it is the responsibility of the administration to provide a safe, desirable work place. After the experience of paying for hours and hours of time away from work, the administration became terribly annoyed itself with the THI. The NYPL Main Branch is a grand but old building. Located on an island, where high humidity is the rule, THI has become a very big item, occasionally blocking negotiations and settlement on other items. Although peculiar to a single bargaining setting, the THI is symptomatic of similar blockage that may arise in other libraries elsewhere. Such items must be reassessed according to their true importance as part of the sane analysis, alluded to earlier.

Whenever local unions affiliate, they get some advantages from the larger unit—and some disadvantages, as well. The Chicago union was affiliated regionally and nationally. The New York union affiliated with District Council #37, American Federation of State, County and Municipal Employees, AFL-CIO. Many of those advantages and disadvantages can be seen in the liaison between the NYPL Guild, Local #1930, and the AFSCME District Council #37.

DISTRICT COUNCIL #37, NEW YORK CITY

Size is clout. In DC #37, there are over 100,000 members. Other AFSCME members in the state of New York (some by way of a recent public employee union merger) bring the statewide total to 400,000 members. AFSCME's national membership has passed the one million mark, making it the single largest union in the AFL-CIO. Union leaders pointed out that this newly achieved size would allow them to ". . . concentrate their efforts more effectively in taking on management, and anti-labor politicians, at both the national and local level." This statement presumes a political cohesiveness among the workers and a power base developed from the solidarity of the group.[13]

Service to members is clout. In a series of related stories carried in several Spring 1978 issues of DC #37, *Public Employees Press* (PEP), the Council's services were extolled. Safety at work was the central concern of an investigation of a truck crash in which three members of Laborer's Local #376 were accident victims. DC #37 sent its own safety director to the wreckage, inspected it, and then loosed a barrage of criticism against the Highways Department for sending out workers in trucks known to be mechanically faulty. The Leadership Conference of Local #272, Schools Division, was warmly reported in PEP. That story related that over 600 delegates had attended the conference, which was devoted to such topics as problems in government funding, collective bargaining, and political lobbying. Service for all was detailed in a PEP story about the new District Council Dental Service. Every kind of preventive and primary dental care is available at no fee to members and dependents, who are covered for full dental benefits.

The attitude of members toward their union was revealed in a 1978 survey of DC #37. The results of the survey were portrayed through the eyes of a mythical average member. If there were such, the "average" member would be a clerical worker

. . . in her 50's, earning about $10,000 per year and living in a rented apartment in Brooklyn. She's proud of her job and her work, but feels she should be paid more. She's distrustful of public officials, but thinks her union had done a good job of protecting its members during New York's extended and extending fiscal crisis. She's a regular voter, an optimist, and a faithful reader of this newpaper.[14]

For such advantages as these to members, is there a cost? The answer is yes, and it can be described as being of two dimensions. First, there is a money cost, that is, a charge is levied for affiliation. Second, there is an autonomy cost; the locals must negotiate their specific needs within the enlarged membership and interests of the council. This two-dimensional cost can be understood by using Local #1930, the NYPL Guild with a membership of about 1800, as an exemplary unit in the over 100,000-member District Council #37, AFSCME.

Table 3.5 was excerpted from the local treasurer's report. The membership dues in Local #1930 rose from initial monthly charges of less than five

Table 3.5 **Treasurer's Report, 1976, NYPL Local #1930**

Income from dues collected			$160,411.25
less allocations:	District Council 37	$ 97,017.00	
	AFSCME International	40,557.45	
	checkoff charges	917.55	
total allocations:		$138,492.00	
Net amount available to Local #1930			$ 21,919.25

(Note: Expenses of #1930 were $32,524.52, causing the union to draw on previously accumulated balances.)

dollars in 1969 until, in 1977, dues for full-time employees were $9.70 per month and for part-time employees, $5.85 per month. Those dues generated the gross annual income of over $160,000, which was distributed as shown in the table. The table speaks to the cost of affiliation and reveals that the local union claimed only about 15 percent of the collected dues for its own operations.

The occupational category spread in AFSCME is extensive. DC #37 is no exception to the national rule. Librarians are near the top of that membership in preparation for the job and in compensation. Local #1930 itself includes beginning clerks and principal librarians. In terms of any preparation or professional measurement scale, the span of DC #37 would be much more extensive. When the great bulk of an organization is composed of members whose median annual salary hovers near $10,000, interest conflicts and divisions arise, and the group is likely to deliver only marginal support to the compensation-benefit drives of the professionals who constitute a small subgroup already well above the median.[15]

Large numbers give strength, but diversified interests can become a debilitating weakness. The union officers must be alert to communication responsibilities lest their membership desert them. Merely reading the treasurer's report, it would be easy for members of Local #1930 to become cynical of the value of unionization and to see affiliation as an undesirable burden. Such conflicts in perception are not new. One arose in the 1960s in the United Steel Workers of America when David McDonald was the national president. He introduced or accepted innovations aimed at reducing strikes. Primarily, this innovation was a very small group of union and management representatives who met and identified and discussed potential problems with the aim of avoiding a head-on, highly visible clash. It was a secret group, unknown to union members. When its existence became known, the workers thought they had been "sold out," and the union president was ousted.[16] The point is that every local must be in close, two-way communication with its affiliate groups, for there are always visible reasons from which to doubt the desirability of affiliation. Librarians, more than most occupational categories, use questioning as a regularized approach to problem solving, thereby increasing the need for communication. Mediocrity of mind or obscurity of purpose is a handicap that will defeat any system of affiliation. Affiliations must justify their existence to members through persuasive evidence.

THE PRESENT UNION PICTURE

In the latter 1960s, when library unionization was on the rise, the trustees of the Queens Borough Library sent a sternly worded message to a union seeking to represent that library staff. The trustees pointed out that they were ". . . exempt from the provisions of the (New York) city's Executive Order 49" under which city employees could bargain collectively.[17] Later on, however, following the lead of the Brooklyn Library Union, the Queens union was established.

In Youngstown, Ohio, the staff of ". . . the Youngstown and Mahoning County Library System" voted to accept as their sole bargaining agent the Federation of Library Employees. No written contract had yet been developed by the summer of 1968.[18]

A variety of *Library Journal* articles described unionization of libraries in 1968-1969. In the Los Angeles Public Library, the Librarians Guild, Local #1634 of AFSCME, was formed. Shortly after, that local decided to organize on a statewide basis and added the San Francisco and Santa Monica public libraries to an affiliated list. Meanwhile, in a sharp departure from the near strikes or neo-strikes in Chicago and Brooklyn, the Contra Costa library unit of Local #1648 AFSCME went on strike in Contra Costa, California. Picket line service was a new experience and a new concept for the librarians who walked the line.

Personnel in a variety of occupational categories must work together in a library, if it is to function satisfactorily. This, alone, makes of the library a complex organization. The introduction of collective bargaining has not decreased the organizational tension or the complexity of the unit. However, it is reasonable to expect that, with the establishment of collective bargaining over the years, controversy and tension will decrease as management routines will become stabilized in accumulative contracts.

The costs of membership and benefits received merit a brief glance. Cost benefit analysis, a technical accounting term, is much too grand to apply to what might be identified and analyzed in contemporary union membership for librarians. Excluding those librarians who are employed in public schools and in colleges or universities, dues of seven, eight, or nine dollars per month are characteristic. Some, levied as a percent of salary, may cost over twelve dollars per month.[19] What benefit comes to the employee for the cost? Is the library's service enhanced in any way as a consequence of a fee-supported union? What proportion of the fee should stay local, and what part should be sent to support the regional or national union?

There is a lack of clear, uncontroverted evidence that libraries, as a consequence of unionization, have produced higher wages or fringe benefits for the librarian employees. Generally, library administrators view unionization as the onset of a decreased autonomy for themselves, which may or may not be true. They may suffer a loss of power. The lack of clarity and uniformity in unionized settings makes it impossible to generalize about preferred conditions. That is, do employees truly enjoy some gains, and does management truly lose? The answer is not known. Some guarded generalizations are helpful, however.

Whether higher wages are produced with a union present or are perceived to be the result of union activity are questions to be judged in a particular library setting. The evaluation of the impact of higher wages would also have to be assessed in terms of library service and the administrative decision-making process. There is no inherent contradiction in stating that higher wages for librarians and other library employees may have a beneficial effect on the institution as a whole. Careful analysis is required to ascertain the impact of higher wages or of a number of other factors, such as decreased workload on the character of library service.[20]

There is a terrible tension between the long-range and the short-range views of the benefits that should come from union membership. It has to do with the old story of the goose that laid the golden eggs. How can you get the biggest eggs, regularly, and still keep the goose in good health for future years? Unfortunately, in the clamor for short-range improvements—which, admittedly, may be badly overdue—there is a tendency to overlook the long-range view. Such an approach lacks rationality and coherence and carries within it the seeds of its own destruction. This conflict of viewpoints is generally exemplified in the structure in which managements take the long view (protecting the organization), and the employees take the short view (protecting the workers). Ironically, in that structure, if management is weak, both management and labor will lose eventually, because the service will have priced itself out of business. That eventuality can be seen in many American localities without a cost benefit analysis!

In that dilemma there are overtones of moral responsiblities. That is, should the union share or accept responsibility for the continuation of the agency from which it is attempting to bargain an increase in wages? Should the union consider the welfare of the clients served by the agency and the social consequences of any kind of disruption to the agency's services? Slogans are not enough to ensure the continuation of any organization. Given the singularity of purposes to which unions can subscribe, it is imperative that management accept the responsibility for extension of the organization and represent that interest strongly in negotiations.

Surveys conducted during the 1960s made it clear that library administrators —who must, in the nature of things, be administrators first and librarians second—were overwhelmingly opposed to unionization. Other surveys made it equally clear that librarians favored the labor and librarianship duo. Unions were formed in such places as Philadelphia, Detroit, Boston, Milwaukee, and Brooklyn and in many smaller cities as well. They were devoted to such common causes as

1. delineation of professional from nonprofessional roles
2. securing information on private sector employment
3. developing guidelines for action at both the local and national levels[21]

The recent negotiations of Local #1930 reveal the concerns of a union in a city with financial troubles. Their big concerns in 1977 were

1. cost of living adjustments (COLA)
2. productivity give-ups to the administration
3. clarification of seniority, lay-offs, and recalls
4. new fringe benefits[22]

At the same time, that library management sought

1. an extended work week
2. union assistance in fund development
3. reduction of leave time
4. reduction of THI compensated time off[23]

The tension between the board and the administrators and the librarians exemplified by these contradictory positions could be found in Baltimore, in Los Angeles, or elsewhere. Such tension is not an indication of indifference to personnel problems on the part of library trustees, necessarily. Their funding problems are part of the picture, and although it is an exciting notion that every American should become rich, it is unlikely that any union can accomplish this. The history of librarianship seems not to indicate that professional preparation is the route to riches. The financial crisis of New York must impinge upon bargaining there and, to a lesser extent, in other municipal settings. If it is not a rosy picture, it is a reflection of the changing proportion of payrolls in cities described in Chapter 2. Industrial and commercial payrolls have declined while public service payrolls have increased, and this fact impinges upon the amount that can be paid to any single public employee, or to any single category of employees.

With such stark facts of life staring unblinkingly back at each library local, librarians must bear in mind two important points. First, the librarians must court the support and assistance of their community, including other segments of organized labor. Such broad support is necessary if lobbying is to yield the legislative appropriations that appear to be necessary. Second, librarians must recognize that their colleagues are not administrator-librarians; their colleagues are among other union people in the sense of support to finance their services. To develop or maintain an elitist barrier between themselves as the professional group and their nonlibrarian fellow employees could hardly enhance the stature of the library as a service institution or as an employer. As an occupational category, librarians compose a small group and must respond with the professional's disciplined intelligence to a realistic appraisal of the situation.

SUMMARY

The availability of qualified persons to fill positions in libraries has fluctuated over the years. When persons in that manpower pool enlarge it beyond the needs of employing libraries, as was the case in the late 1970s, that condition has an economically depressing effect upon librarians. Not only are salaries depressed, but because of this financial condition, other job performance characteristics tend to suffer, too. Many librarians who are among the better workers, sensitive to the job limitations and sensitive to attractive opportunities in other work settings, forsake their library work. Consequently, teamwork is disrupted and valuable services, as performed by outstanding professionals, are lost. The manpower pool has a salutary effect upon the quality of service the library clientele receives and must be realistically considered in union organizing, goal setting, and negotiating.

From the first organizing efforts until the present day, unionized librarians have devoted themselves to the accomplishment of such goals as adequate compensation, grade classifications within job titles, systematic evaluation and promotion, and working conditions with adequate ventilation, heat, and light. In fifty years of union library history, the main goals for library employees have remained remarkably consistent—which is certainly not to say that no improvement has occurred. Through most of those years, librarians serving as spokesmen for colleagues have acknowledged the need to stay abreast of the facts of financial support for libraries.

As unorganized librarians contemplate organizing into local guilds or unions, the intercommunications among eligible employees must be considered. Timing, recipients, authors, and content are a few of the items which must be resolved as newsletters and periodic reports are developed and distributed. Organization is seldom an easy task, and a communications system that is late or inaccurate can undermine the best efforts. After organization, too, unions have an obligation to keep members informed, lest they wonder what their dues are being spent for. Communications has a central position in both creation and maintenance, and it must be two-way communication. For that matter, in the management-labor model, communications between trustees and director is no less important as bargaining leads to contract and on to library operation through contract administration.

Compensation for librarians has never been more than minimal. Librarians do not get rich. Among professional librarians, those employed in public libraries tend to receive smaller salaries than their colleagues employed in public schools and universities. Even in situations where unions bargain aggressively and successfully for higher salaries, the outcome may not be good for all employees. That is, when higher individual salaries, pressing upward against budget ceilings, sometimes force administrative decisions to curtail hours of operation or termination of positions, the employee position is not altogether well served. Within the world of work and especially within such institutions as libraries, workers seek what they see as their just share from the resources for the work roles they fulfill. Administrators tend to conserve resources for any of many reasons they deem important. The tension and adversarial conditions of collective bargaining follow naturally.

As locals are formed, they face the decision of affiliation. Some locals do affiliate with huge national unions, and some do not. Those that do accept such advantages as the availability of expertise and experience in bargaining and the political leverage generated through large membership. Disadvantages include increased dues and decreased local autonomy. That is, the larger union brings diversity of interests and must necessarily also bring an increased member discipline, lest it lose its solidarity.

In the decade of the 1970s, and shortly before, viable library unions emerged across the nation. Library employees organized in Boston, Brooklyn, Queens, New York Public, Baltimore, Chicago, Santa Clara, and Los Angeles. It is not possible to list all of the gains—and losses—that employees accomplished through their union activity. Library administrators have generally opposed unionization. Yet, as with the employees, it is not entirely clear what administrators may have lost, if anything. It should be noted, guardedly, that some short-term gains for "one side" can now be seen as long-term gains for the "other side." concern for cost effectiveness, budget ceilings, and reductions in financing have contributed to the insecurity epitomized in labor relations.

NOTES

1. Melvin S. Goldstein, *Collective Bargaining in the Field of Librarianship* (Brooklyn, N.Y.: Pratt Institute, 1969), pp. 78–84.
2. Ibid., pp. 88–89.
3. "Strike Threat Cancelled at Chicago Public Library," *Library Journal* 92 (April 1, 1967): 1398–99.
4. *CPL Union News* 1 (December 1937): 2.
5. *CPL Union News* 1 (April 15, 1937): 1.
6. Ibid., p. 3.
7. *NYPLOC Newsletter* 1 (April 15, 1967): 1.
8. *NYPLOC Newsletter* 1 (June 1, 1967): 2.
9. Personal correspondence with James W. Henderson, former director of the NYPL Research Libraries, April 4, 1978.
10. *1930 Local Line Newsletter*, no. 1 (November 13, 1969): 1.
11. *1930 Local Line Newsletter*, no. 4 (January 11, 1970): 1.
12. Statement by David Beasley, former president of Local #1930, in a personal interview, New York City, May 23, 1978.

13. "We're the Biggest in the State and Nation," *Public Employee Press* 19 (May 5, 1978): p. 24.

14. Bill Schleicher, "How Members Rate Their Jobs and Their Union," *Public Employee Press* 19 (May 5, 1978): p. 8.

15. Statement by David Beasley, former president of Local #1930, in a personal interview, New York City, May 23, 1978.

16. Gerald I. Nierenberg, *The Art of Negotiating* (New York: The Cornerstone Library, 1968; 1977 ed.), p. 18.

17. "Queens Borough Trustees Refuse Union Negotiations," *Library Journal* 92 (February 15, 1967): 722.

18. "Youngstown Library Staff Gets Union Representation," *Library Journal* 93 (March 15, 1968): p. 1090.

19. Marilyn A. Oberg and others, "Unionization: Costs and Benefits to the Individual and the Library," *Library Trends* 25 (October 1976): p. 441.

20. Ibid., p. 446.

21. "Union Study Figures Released by ALA," *Library Journal* 93 (September 15, 1968): p. 3068.

22. *1930 Local Line Newsletter* 2 (October 1977): pp. 2-4.

23. Ibid., p. 1.

LIBRARIANS IN SCHOOLS AND UNIVERSITIES 4

OCCUPATIONAL IDENTITY

Taken as a group, librarians have a problem in occupational identity. Partially, that problem can be attributed to the fact that librarians are not a single group, in many senses of the word. As a group in search of status and attempting to accommodate specializations, librarians have been forced to recognize that among them are at least four major subgroups identified according to employment settings. Some are employed in public (or private) libraries; some are in occupationally specialized or professioanl support libraries; some are in the college-university setting. By far the largest subgroup, however, is the school librarian group. Are these people in these various settings really librarians, or are they functionally in some other occupational category, people who received professional librarian's training for application in some other field?

There was a time when librarians devoted substantial time and effort to discuss whether librarianship was a profession or an occupation. There is an attractive aura about the word professional. It stands at the apex away from charlatanism and deception. It connotes power, prestige, self-governance, and upward mobility. Occupational categories strive for the label and sometimes confer it upon themselves, even when the claim to the label is clearly pretentious. Some groups have sought the label because they have seen that professional workers receive higher incomes than most workers and, in a conspicuously naive rationale, have deduced that to have the label would yield the income. Such reasoning, with its terribly frail cause and effect base, cannot stand for long; to test the notion is to disprove it. In terms of library services, and in terms of the personal welfare of librarians, continued pursuit of the question of most appropriate label does not seem to be a promising line of activity.[1]

Librarians join a variety of societies and associations related to their work settings. For example, in the 1930s Bernard Berelson was a member of the American Federation of Teachers while employed at the University of Washington as a university librarian. Much of his writing of that period was devoted to questions about librarians and unions. He was not involved in a search for status; he was involved in a search for improved employment benefits through a federation of teachers. Despite the uncertainties that designation as a professional would actually yield some tangible benefits for people who are employed in public institutions, today persons who are employed in elementary and secondary schools to man those libraries can be seen in a strong drive toward professionalism, as that is conceived by, largely, public school teachers.

From a certain vantage point, the problem of identity for librarians is, really, of two major dimensions:

1. Are librarians professionals? Should they be, if they could be?
2. Are those persons who are trained as librarians, but who find employment in school or college settings, really librarians—or are they more accurately labeled faculty members?

There is at least one more aspect about librarian identity that merits attention. As librarians are educated, graduate, and locate jobs, they also find that, inevitably, they are in some employee category. These categories are made in the nomenclature and definitions of each locality, and they are far from any national standards. Initially, these newly hired librarians are not officers of the board of trustees which has governmental, policy, and fiscal responsibility for the library. Customarily, at least in all public libraries, only one librarian will have been designated as the principal librarian. Actual titles vary, but this person—the librarian, or the Director of Libraries, or some similar title—is a functionary who (1) has direct liaison with the board of trustees and (2) is at the peak of the organization's salary. Further, this administrator comes to the position from a position as a librarian and with the passage of time.

Similarly, such an administrator-librarian will be found in many of the school libraries and nearly all of the college and university libraries. Organizational size is a prime factor influencing how this person functions. Is the university librarian a librarian or an administrator? Even though a Director of Libraries might not meet with the university's board of regents, the position would be viewed as managerial by those same regents. Even though that person might not be at or even near a negotiating table, that person would still be perceived as part of the management team, in an adversarial position to the librarians, who would be perceived as employees. In the contemporary labor relations milieu, the librarian who aspires to and becomes a director of libraries forsakes an earlier identity in the assumption of a new identity as manager of librarians.

ELEMENTARY AND SECONDARY SCHOOL LIBRARIANS

By law, certain minimum standards have been set for the public elementary and secondary schools in each of the states. Those standards are applied, about equally, to the private schools conducting elementary and secondary education because, although private in their organizational format, they are functionally performing a public service. For this discussion, then, the term public school means all of the elementary and secondary education under the supervision of the state department of education. Actually, in most states, about 90 percent of that education is conducted by public agencies and about 10 percent is conducted by private agencies performing public functions. The certificated personnel in both employment settings are very likely to share a common membership in the same association or union, the National Education Association (NEA) or the American Federation of Teachers (AFT). For example, the teaching faculty of Boys Town, Nebraska, a private educational agency, are members of the NEA; including the certificated librarians.

PUBLIC SCHOOL FACULTY AND PROFESSIONALISM

With about two million members, the NEA is the largest public school faculty union. (Although the NEA has a division devoted to higher education, it is primarily the union for elementary and secondary school teachers.) Over 50,000 persons trained as librarians are employed in the public schools. They are credentialed as librarians or, under its certification euphemism, as media specialists. They, along with such other groups as elementary teachers and secondary teachers, make up that NEA membership.

Do librarians maintain a spearate and visible identity with the NEA? The copies of the annual *Proceedings of the Representative Assembly of the National Education Association* for the years 1971 to 1976 were examined. The reports, speeches, and business session transcripts were scrutinized. Librarians could not, in any year, be distinguished from any other members. That dues-paying membership, which represented a wide variety of certification, was consistently molded into a single, unified group under such generic terms as educators, staff, faculty, or teachers. Although the NEA reports included attention to such goals as professional excellence and professional security for educators, it was clear that professionalism within the NEA was closely attached to certification. Counselors, elementary teachers, secondary teachers, and librarians, for example, were perceived as sharing in a common concern for professional identity and were not seen as differentiated subgroups.

In 1977, the Educational Research Service conducted a survey into the types of orientation conducted in public schools for new employees. The survey included both very small and quite large school districts. Data were presented from 349 respondent schools, and about two-thirds had orientation programs of some sort. It is reasonable to assume that in several of those districts some of the new employees were certificated as librarians or as media specialists, as the case might be. Yet, in hardly any of the workshops, programs, or handbooks were librarians recognized as a singular employee group needing some special orientation apart from other new employees. Overwhelmingly, the orientations called for the joint participation of all new employees, without regard to the position for which they might carry certification.[2] Taken together these two surveys—one of NEA convention reports and the other of on-the-job indoctrination—emphasize the identity submersion of librarians into the generic terms such as faculty or staff. The differentiation of labor characteristics were deemphasized; the commonality of labor was emphasized.

Public school faculty have a concept of professionalism that merits mention because the school librarians are in that group. It is a concept of professionalism that has philosophically evolved; recently the concept has come to harmoniously incorporate collective bargaining as a part. The term, professional, encompasses an understanding of the occupation as (1) based upon certain academic minima; (2) trust by the public to perform job tasks independently and accurately; and, (3) abilities to handle a wide variety of job centered problems. It is a reasonable way in which to think about school librarians, and indeed, all librarians.

Some occupational categories, but only a few, have been able to develop an academic routine in which entering students must have first completed a four-year university program. Those occupations have, in part, legitimized their claim to status as professionals on the basis of a complex and extended period of preparation. To complete the prescribed academic requirements prior to entry into those professions, the aspiring student may face an obligation of from one to four or five additional years of university training and specific additional degree programs.

For public schools, the bachelor's degree is the professional, that is, the vocationally qualifying, degree. Additional degrees, advanced certification, and new compensation levels are achieved after initial employment and along with job performance. Public school faculty income is not such, at least for beginning teachers, that the NEA or any other whole membership group can insist that higer degrees be a minimum for job entry.[3] Society cannot demand a too-extended academic preparation from people who will enter high-tension jobs at comparatively modest pay. The entire faculty, as it aspires toward professionalism, then, does so through a general and technical education that can be coupled to both the common and particular problems shared by all other employees in elementary and secondary schools.

It seems likely that librarianship is not enhanced by the variety of preparation programs, which in some instances may be undergraduate and in others graduate degree programs. Neither does it appear that it is enhanced by employment settings of such wide variety or by frequent isolation from colleagues of similar training and service inclination. This last is, of course, the typical work setting for the school librarian. Yet, these are job characteristics with which the occupational groups must reckon as they contemplate their own welfare in their job setting.

A cursory survey of the professional library journals revealed that there is a paucity of literature on the well-being of the profession. This may mean that the profession lacks cohesiveness simply because it lacks a mutuality of concern for the welfare of the occupational group, as members of the group are frequently faculty first and librarians last.

SCHOOL LIBRARIANS AND CERTIFICATION

There is comparatively little published data on school librarians. Even though state education departments may gather some data on the school libraries in their state, annually, those data customarily are not published and, because of interstate difference, are not susceptible of aggregation to form some picture of the national scene. The USOE's National Center for Educational Statistics publishes very little information on school libraries, perhaps because there are so many units, with one per school building. The USOE survey of school libraries, done in 1962, remains the best "recently published source of detailed information on school libraries."[4] Now nearly twenty years old, its date depreciates its value, somewhat.

School libraries, as places in which librarians may find employment, are shown within Table 4.1. That table not only allows a glimpse into the history of the profession but also provides some guidance for anticipation of the future. Like every projection, this one, originally done by Anne Kahl, carries forward certain assumptions on funding and demand for services. The central message of the table was that, among four categories of libraries in which growth was anticipated, school libraries are the category in which both rate and magnitude of growth will be greatest.

People who become school librarians do so through a certification process. With the certificate in hand, they become eligible for employment. In Table 4.2, certification requirements for the five largest states have been

Table 4.1 **Past and Projected Employment for Librarians by Type
of Library**

Type of Library	1970	1980	1985
All libraries	115,000	141,000	162,000
school	52,000	64,500	79,500
public	26,500	30,000	33,000
academic	19,500	26,500	27,000
special	17,000	20,000	22,500

SOURCE: Edward G. Holley, "Librarians, 1876–1976," *Library Trends* 25 (July 1976): 182.

briefly stated. Varying in the name under which the certificate is issued, the states characteristically call for some graduate work, but for less than a completed master's degree in a school accreditated by the American Library Association.

A parenthetical comparison, as a reference point for clarification, seems appropriate at this point. Scanning current issues of the *Chronicle of Higher Education* for its "positions available" section, some differences in training between elementary-secondary librarians and college-university librarians become apparent. For the librarian in a university, the academic librarian, no certification is required; however, the initial academic credential required was, typically, higher than that for the school librarian. The academic librarian positions customarily specified a Master's Degree in Library Science, with other complementing and supporting work to go along with it. For example, a position might call for the M.L.S. plus a second master's degree in art, science, or some other area. It might specify the M.L.S. plus training or experience in some pertinent background area.

SCHOOL LIBRARIANS AND SALARIES

Salaries have been, nearly always, at the top of the bargaining list for elementary and secondary school locals. By the 1975/76 school year, several public schools offered starting salaries of $11,000 or more to certificated employees. That minimum salary has been pushed upward with each successive round of bargaining. Experience indicates that for the school year of 1979/80, a $14,000 minimum base salary will not be an entirely uncommon starting point for certificated public school employees.

Table 4.2 Certification Standards for Professional School Librarians

State and Date	Certificate Name	Hours of Coursework	Institution Accredited or Approved
California (2/77)	Librarian	Master's in L.S. or 30 graduate hours in school librarianship	Approved
New York (1/73)	School Media Specialist (provisional thru permanent)	From 12 hours (provisional) to Master's or 36 graduate hours in approved program	Approved and/or regionally accredited
Illinois (9/77)	Media Professional	18 graduate hours	Recognized institution
	Media Specialist	32 graduate hours	same
Pennsylvania (1/70)	L.S. K-12 Instructional Certificate	Standards set, but credit hours not prescribed	Approved program and institutional recommendation
	Instructional Media Specialist		
Texas (5/76)	Learning Resources Endorsement	21 specified hours, of which at least 12 must be graduate	Accredited institution and approved program
	Learning Resources Specialist	36 post-bachelor's hours, of which 27 must be graduate and 21 must be L.S./media	

SOURCE: Adapted from Ann Y. Franklin, "School Library Certification Requirements: 1978 Update," *School Library Journal* 24 (April 1978): 44–50.

Table 4.3 **Salaries of Librarians in 1,060 School Systems, by Size, 1976-77**

Categories	Enrollment Groupings				Total, all reporting schools
	25,000 or more	to 24,000	to 9,999	2,400	
Respondents (N)	139	248	306	117	810
Mean	$17,847	$18,040	$17,492	$15,338	$17,410
Median	17,984	18,300	17,414	15,178	17,411
Range: low	12,374	11,076	9,970	8,550	8,550
high	25,708	24,966	27,946	27,054	17,946

SOURCE: "Scheduled Salaries for Professional Personnel in Public Schools, 1976-77" (Arlington, Va.: Educational Research Service, Inc., 1977), p. 24.

Table 4.3 shows salary conditions for school librarians in 1976-77, by arithmetic mean, median, and range. The data, further structured by school district size, reveals that the average school librarian in the sample of 810 reporting schools earned $17,410 for that school year. The display also makes quite plain the likelihood of higher salaries in larger school districts.

Yet, school librarians have interests beyond salary, too. When the first library acquisitions funds were made available under the Elementary and Secondary Education Act (ESEA), the appropriations were distributed by a formula of need. However, librarians were not initially included in either the planning or acquisition under ESEA in the New York City schools. Newly acquired books stayed in cartons, unpacked for months because of a lack of resources to process them and, in many cases, a lack of shelves upon which to place them. Librarians heatedly pointed out that administrators had bypassed them and generated needless work problems for librarians, and the librarians successfully demanded, through the United Federation of Teachers (UFT) representatives, a voice in planning for future acquisitions. Librarian interest may exceed the narrow focus upon salary concerns and extend into a broader realm of professional concerns.[5] Those concerns may be carried forward into the organization by the union representatives. However, it should be understood that such interests have never comprised the primary group of concerns in strong unions, in either public or private employment.

Whereas Table 4.3 was developed to show salary conditions by size of school district, Table 4.4 was developed to provide some indication of salary by region. Once again, the table includes the five largest states, augmented by another (Kansas) to represent the smaller states. The school districts were selected from the alphabetical list of the comprehensive Educational Reserarch Service (ERS) salary report, in which counselors, teachers, and librarians were paid at identical rates. (The exception was

Table 4.4 **Wages and Salaries for Professional School Librarians, 1977-78**

	Selected School Districts	Scheduled Min.	Scheduled Max.	Salaries Paid Min.	Paid Avg.	Max.
CA	Atascadero	$ 9,788	$18,117	$ ——	$17,388	$ ——
	Barstow	9,626	18,289	12,961	15,963	18,964
	Cajon Valley	9,875	19,954	12,641	17,044	19,954
NY	Ardsley	11,802	27,302	18,173	20,902	24,213
	Bay Shore	11,886	25,555	17,472	21,104	24,961
	Brentwood	11,171	25,382	14,580	21,108	24,806
IL	Alton	10,000	19,000	12,200	15,600	19,000
	Arlington Heights	10,300	21,700	15,245	16,074	17,489
	Decatur	9,000	19,600	9,000	14,835	20,670
PA	Albert Gallatin	7,000	16,300	8,450	12,567	16,350
	Bristol	10,100	21,917	———	13,332	22,013
	Central Cambria	9,600	16,100	12,200	14,150	16,100
TX	Alvin	10,260	17,122	10,900	13,744	15,490
	Austin	9,500	16,558	9,500	14,400	15,558
	Birdville	9,810	15,925	10,510	14,770	15,925
KS	Geary County	8,500	15,750	9,600	11,575	13,350
	Haysville	8,700	15,660	12,534	14,730	16,775*
	Iola	8,750	14,787	11,375	———	14,975*

SOURCE: Adapted from "National Survey of Salaries and Wages Paid in Public Schools, Parts 1 and 2" (Arlington, Va.: Educational Research Service, Inc., 1978).

*The maximum salaries exceeded the scheduled maximums, presumably for such duty as an extended school year.

Texas, where counselors are obligated to a longer work year, for differentiated pay.) Given the rather closely standardized certification regulations set forward in Table 4.2, the salary range between states is especilly noticeable. If the service of a certificated librarian is comparable from state to state, it would appear that some states have agreed to pay more for that service than have other states, for reasons unrelated to certification.

COLLEGE AND UNIVERSITY LIBRARIANS

Writing in the *American Library Journal* in 1876, Melvil Dewey stated his belief about the librarian's role. He contended that

It is not now enough that the books are cared for properly, are well arranged, are never lost. It is not enough if the librarian can readily produce any book asked for. It is not enough that he can, when asked, give advice as to the best books in his collection on any given subject.

Speaking of librarians broadly, Dewey contended that, additionally, librarians had a teaching obligation to guide library users in the study of their own wants and needs. After a hundred years, the concept still has appeal and an obvious rationale and would appear to be a firm basis from which academic librarians could approach the question of faculty designation, in their drive for faculty status.

The American Library Association, through the Association of College and Research Libraries (ACRL), has been a vocal proponent of faculty status for university librarians. Professional duties have been analyzed and, in some instances, reconstructed; criteria have been developed through which qualitative development could be discerned as prelude to tenure and advancement in rank.[6] In addition, the ACRL took a position on collecive bargaining in higher education in 1975:

The policy of the Association of College and Research Libraries is that academic librarians be included with their faculty colleagues in units for collective bargaining and that such units should be guided by the *Standards for Faculty Status for College and University Librarians* and the *Joint Statement on Faculty Status of College and University Librarians.*[7]

With a strong orienting statement by a "founding father" of American librarianship; with encouragement from the national level for librarians to secure for themselves the traditional academic roles and titles in higher education; and, with an official position statement favoring contractual inclusion, an observer of librarianship might easily conclude, in error, that academic librarians have accomplished these goals.

Analysis of role, title inclusiveness, and negotiated contracts reveal a startling lack of uniformity among academic librarians. Some have achieved faculty status, while others have remained within the staff designation. It seems fair to observe that there is a generally held view that librarians are not, in many ways, on parity with faculty, who possess specialized knowledge through which they identify with some academic area or department. Such a view complicates the role and identity conflicts on nearly every campus.

In fact, settlement of role is quite different by campus, as the following examples demonstrate. At the Indiana University Libraries, persons are appointed to positions as professional librarians. In that single job title, such persons may work through a probationary period and receive tenure in a designation parallel to faculty tenure. At the University of Nebraska at Lincoln, librarians of professional standing move through the familiar job titles of instructor, assistant, and associate professor to professor—upon accomplishing specified performance within the library at each rank. The ranks have no academic specialty designation. Tenure is awarded in a fashion parallel to the academic departments of the campus. At Duke University, a four-step progression occurs under the titles of Assistant Librarian, Senior Assistant Librarian, Associate Librarian, and Librarian. Continuing appoinment (tenure) is possible at Duke under rules established for librarians only, and apart from the rules that apply to the faculty generally.[8] Clearly, there is no single way for academic librarians to enhance their status through assuming facultylike titles and roles.

ACADEMIC LIBRARIAN SALARIES AND CONTRACTS

In the early 1970s surveys were conducted under the auspices of the Council on Library Resources to determine the compensation levels of librarians in institutions of higher education. Table 4.5 reveals that compensation for the library directors was a little above that for professors, but the salaries were calculated on different work years. It is also apparent that, among librarians, a very small percentage is at the top salary levels, in sharp contrast to the professors, comprising one major group of the faculty. The intervening years since this research was conducted have changed the particulars, certainly, but they have done little to change the validity of the interoccupational setting within the academic setting.

Table 4.5 **Annual Compensation Patterns for Two Personnel Categories in Universities, by Types of Controls**

Position title	Percent of staff, all universities	Average Compensation		
		all combined	*public*	*private*
LIBRARIANS				
library director	2%	$25,930	$26,710	$27,700
assoc. & asst. director	5	18,779	18,610	20,080
curator-specialist	12	13,070	13,000	13,630
dept.-branch head	27	13,380	13,720	13,290
other professional				
5 yrs. + service	17	11,680	12,010	11,340
less than 5 yrs.	37	10,290	10,290	10,460
FACULTY				
professors	31%	$21,680	$21,000	$24,390
assoc. prof.	20	16,060	15,980	16,740
asst. prof.	32	13,160	13,160	13,470
instructor	18	10,120	10,080	10,620

Notes: (1) Compensation includes salary and fringe benefits.
　　　(2) Faculty year is 9 months; librarian year is 11 months.

SOURCE: Donald F. Cameron and Peggy Heim, *How Well Are They Paid?* (Washington, D.C.: Council on Library Resources, Inc., 1972), p. 6.

In that salary comparison with faculty, academic librarianship did not emerge favorably. It is just such comparisons that have stimulated librarians to seek faculty status, in the belief that money flows to title. In reality, that is a mixed bag, for as often as not there is great variation in pay at each rank. Even after accomplishing rank designation and even within a negotiated contract, librarians are, realistically, likely to find themselves at the bottom of the range for each academic rank.

It seems clear that if librarians are to be a part of the negotiated contract, they must be included with faculty. That is, academic librarians simply lack the clout and the community of interest to secure the recognition for themselves as a unique group which must precede bargaining. This is not an unsuitable arrangement, for the most commonly bargained issues are of interest to professional librarians and faculty alike. They are, in rank order of frequency:

1. salary and fringe benefits
2. grievance procedures and a dispute resolution mechanism
3. rights and privileges for the union
4. employment conditions, such as load, credit-hour requirements, and faculty office space[9]

Unfortunately, if librarians are included with faculty in bargaining units, they are likely to find themselves outside the library's community of interest, in the strict sense of the term. For example, within the New York Public Library, workers from a wide variety of occupational titles were organized into a single guild. All guild members employed in the same library by the same board of trustees shared a community of interest. The characteristic separation of people who have academic status in university settings from those who do not, then, calls for a parallel separation of personnel within the library, if the librarians stand with the faculty in the bargaining unit. The library, itself, is a too narrow base from which realistically to approach collective bargaining. Ordinarily, personnel could draw upon the shared community of interest as a source of strength, but that is not a viable factor in organizations of university employees.[10]

Current contracts at twenty institutions of higher education were analyzed to determine the status of librarians at those institutions. The data are displayed in Tables 4.6 and 4.7. The displays make clear that variety is a predominating feature of contracts between employees in higher education and their employing boards of regents. Table 4.6 includes only those institutions where the employee's representative was an agency other than the American Association of University Professors (AAUP). Table 4.7, on the other hand, includes only those institutions in which the AAUP was the

Table 4.6 **Librarians as Employees in Contracts from Selected Public Institutions (N=10)**

Institution	State	Contract Dates	Affili-ation	Librarians		
				Full time	*Part time*	*Workload stated*
Central Michigan	MI	1974–77	Indep.	yes	no	no
Fitchburg State	MA	1964–	NEA	yes[1]	no	no
Florida State University System	FL	1976–78	Indep.	yes	no	no
Massachusetts College of Art	MA	1973–75	AFT	no	no	no
Nebraska State Colleges	NE	1976–	NEA	no[2]	no	no
New Jersey State Colleges	NJ	1977–79	AFT	yes	no	yes
Northern Iowa	IA	1977–79	AAUP/NEA	——[3]	——	no
Pennsylvania State Colleges & Universities	PA	1974–	———[3]	yes[4]	no	yes
Saginaw State	MI	1976–78	Indep.	no	no	no
Youngstown State	OH	1977–81	NEA	——[3]	——	no

1. Librarians with academic rank only; included evaluation of libraries by teaching faculty.
2. Librarians on one campus were mentioned; the contract itself was in litigation in 1978.
3. Undeterminable from contract analysis.
4. Librarians with faculty status only.

Table 4.7 **Librarians as Employees in AAUP, Contracts from Selected Universities (N=10)**

Institution	State	Contract Dates	Private or Public	Librarians Included		
				Full time	*Part time*	*Workload stated*
Adelphi	NY	1973–76	PR	yes	yes	yes
Cincinnati	OH	1975–77	PU	——[1]	——	no
Fairleigh Dickinson	NJ	1976–77	PR	no	no	no
Hofstra	NY	1976–79	PR	yes	yes	no
Oakland	MI	1976–79	PU	yes	no	yes
Rutgers	NJ	1975–77	PU	yes	no	yes[2]
Temple	PA	1976–80	PR/PU	yes[3]	no	yes
St. John's	NY	1974–77	PR	yes	no	yes
Wayne State	MI	1976–78	PU	yes	yes	yes
Western Michigan	MI	1976–77	PU	yes	yes[4]	yes

1. Undeterminable from contract analysis.
2. Stipulations were general and nonprescriptive.
3. Some full-time librarians excluded.
4. Part-time people with faculty rank only.

representative. Each table is designed to reveal the place of librarians in the academic collective bargaining environment and in one aspect of contractual specificity. The chance sample reveals a distinction between the two bargaining groups. Some specific librarian concerns were generally treated and included as contract items within the settings where the AAUP was the representative. The contrary was the rule for those units not represented by the AAUP. Regarding the inclusion of librarians for separate and distinct treatment in the contracts bargained for by the AAUP, there was no apparent difference between the private and public institutions.

Under a proposed format for distinguishing types of issues raised by professional librarians, the Level I goals included wages, hours, and working conditions. Within that labeling system and in the chance sample of twenty institutions, it appears that the goals of librarians are better served when they are members of units represented by the AAUP.

During the past ten to twenty years, in public schools where there was not a strong tradition of faculty self-governance, those faculties—including librarians—have taken new portions of self-governance unto themselves through collective bargaining processes. Those public employees recognized that power could be developed through statutorily controlled adversarial settings devoted to questions of employment.

For many decades, American universities have had a strong tradition of self-governance. University senates and extensive committee systems were developed to maintain and extend the collegial, self-governing work setting. It is true, of course, that generalization is susceptible of overstatement, and to some extent these two generalizations about work settings are overstated. The truth of the generalizations merits special consideration, however, for some conditions seem to be changing. John Ryor spoke to this phenomenon recently when he asked some hard questions about university governance, such as, Did collegiality exist at present levels because administrators found it satisfactory to allow it? Has self-governance been stifled "under the weight of a sprawling upper management superstructure that is neither responsive nor responsible to faculties"?[12] There appears to be occurring some reversal of the roles of faculties in public schools and higher education, at least as regards their potency for self-governance. Librarians in both settings are affected by that power shift.

New kinds of problems are arising for both school and academic librarians. One in which both groups share involves budget and service reduction. Yale University, with a library budget of over ten million dollars for fiscal year 1977, has responded to a stringent budget by cancelling several hundred journal subscriptions, by passing on some acquisitions costs to the colleges serviced, and by reducing the number of professional and assisting professional librarian positions.[13] Such reductions point out the need for librarians to speak to the positive benefits received from libraries, lest those reductions become, increasingly, real obligations for libraries in schools and for public libraries as well.

Candidly, the fiscal future portends budget cuts that may reach into personnel categories. Although the librarians employed in schools and universities are more distant than are the public librarians from policy-making boards, all share a mutual concern for salaries as the first priority in personnel welfare. Although the school librarians are typically in work settings with much more unionized strength than those of the academic librarians, the "signs of the times" indicate the appropriateness, for those academic librarians who are seeking to enhance their conditions of employment, to continue their drive toward faculty status, which might include coverage in a negotiated contract.

SUMMARY

Librarianship is seen differently from the vantage point of different occupational settings. There are media specialists, reference specialists, cataloguers, circulation librarians, research librarians, and so on. The titles represent a variety of employment settings, too. Although all might share some commonality in professional training, the actual training and certainly the professional missions differ. Some even see a pecking order among librarians, further adding to the disunity of the group, further confusing any surge toward a common occupational identity. Given the additional split that comes when the director, the administrator-librarian, aligns with the trustees in the adversarial setting of collective bargaining, it is little wonder that librarians have an identity problem, despite the fact that they are a relatively small occupational group.

Among all the persons trained in library science, the largest subgroup finds employment in public elementary or secondary schools. Probably they also find a union firmly in place—the NEA or the AFT—for which their membership will be sought. Among themselves, school librarians share the commonality of a certificate issued by their state department of education as testimony of certain competencies in librarianship or media use. Their professional colleagues all have certificates, too, attesting to some special abilities through which their competence may be demonstrated. It is a different set of linkages at the work setting than prevail for other librarians. Moreover, it is far removed from the administrative seat of power that controls collective bargaining for the employing board of education. Salary surveys in over 800 schools for 1976/77 revealed that the school-year salary average for this group was $17,410.

Librarians who find employment in higher education settings tend to find themselves in the salary ranges that prevail at the levels of assistant professor in the academic departments. Rank for librarians is not the rule, making it difficult for librarians to advance monetarily. Once hired into the university library, there is little opportunity for promotion; denied rank status, librarians quickly drop behind their colleagues in the professoriate. Many university librarians see as the solution to their dilemma membership in the professoriate, with rank and promotions as a possibility. Only a few institutions offered such opportunities to university librarians in the latter 1970s. Partially, this situation is a reflection of an aspect of the larger American society where power tends to become stratified as some groups get and some do not.

NOTES

1. William J. Goode, "The Librarian: From Occupation to Profession?" in Phillip H. Ennis and Howard W. Winger, eds., *Seven Questions about the Profession of Librarianship* (Chicago: University of Chicago Press, 1962), pp. 23–27.

2. Joan P. S. Kowalski, *Orientation Programs for New Teachers* (Fort Meyer, VA: Educational Research Service, Inc., 1977), pp. 4–10.

3. Everett C. Hughes, "Education for a Profession," in Ennis and Winger, eds., *Seven Questions*, pp. 40–44.

4. Mary Edna Anders, "Statistical Information as a Basis for Cooperative Planning," *Library Trends* 24 (October 1975): 234–35.

5. Karl Nygren, "Libraries and Labor Unions," *Library Journal* 92 (June 1, 1967): 2115.

6. Lewis C. Branscomb, ed., *The Case for Faculty Status for Academic Librarians* (Chicago: American Library Association, 1970), pp. 22–26.

7. Association of College and Research Libraries. "Statement on Collective Bargaining" (Chicago: American Library Association, 1975), p. 1.

8. "Tenure Guidelines [of the] All University Librarians Promotion and Tenure Committee, Indiana University Librarians" (Bloomington, Ind., 1973, unpublished; augmented at the University of Nebraska at Omaha 1976).

9. Kenneth P. Mortimer, "A Survey of Experience in Academic Collective Bargaining," in Millicent D. Abell, ed., *Collective Bargaining in Higher Education: Its Implications for Governance and Faculty Status for Librarians* (Chicago: American Library Association, 1976), pp. 30–31.

10. Donald H. Wollett, "The Nature of Collective Bargaining," in Abell, *Collective Bargaining*, p. 13.

11. Margaret Chaplan and Charles Maxey, "The Scope of Faculty Bargaining: Implications for Academic Librarians," *Library Quarterly* 46 (July 1976): 235.

12. John Ryor, "Straight Talk about Collective Bargaining and Academic Governance," *Chronicle of Higher Education* 16 (April 17, 1978): 14.

13. "Yale Reports Rising Cost, Staff Cuts, More Security," *Library Journal* 103 (April 15, 1978): 802–04.

ORGANIZING, ELECTIONS, AND PROPOSALS 5

INTRODUCTION

Certain preliminaries must be accomplished before any union activity can occur. For example, it must be clear to the members of the group anticipating unionization that their personal-professioanl risk is low, that is, they now may form a union without reprisals. Historically, the development of organized labor in the United States is really a chronicle of increased freedoms for workers. McConnell recognized three stages of organized labor on the American scenes:

1. Repression (1790–1930)
2. Encouragement (1930–1947)
3. Intervention (1947–to the present time)[1]

From its beginnings, organized labor has had a difficult time overcoming the stands taken by management and government, especially as carried out by the courts, since disputes went into the courts for decisions. From the time that the nation was being settled until the early 1900s, it was difficult for employees to choose a bargaining unit because, typically, courts did not allow bargaining units and issued injunctions against them. The doctrine of criminal conspiracy explains much of the legal attitude of those times:

The hostility of the courts was first given vent in the criminal conspiracy doctrine. This doctrine, "imported" by the American courts from English common law at the turn of the 19th century, was unbelievably narrow by modern standards. The doctrine flatly concluded that combinations of workmen to raise wages were criminal conspiracies and hence, illegal. . . . The shadow of the conspiracy doctrine hung heavily over organized labor throughout most of the 1800s.[2]

Injunctions against most of the leverage actions invented or adapted by unions were easily secured. Only with the passage of the Norris-LaGuardia Act (1932) and its successor legislation did workers begin to escape from such reprisal techniques as were embodied in the "yellow dog contracts," a promise (contract) made by a worker to the employer not to join a union and acknowledgement that any intention by the worker to join a union would be sufficient grounds for dismissal. Although professionals, librarians are in no less need of protection from reprisals than other workers.

From Bureau of the Census data, it was possible to document an aspect of the comparative costs of local civilian public employment. Table 5.1 reveals several public employee groups that are, to some extent, involved in union activity. In the sense that the functions represent personal services, the number of employees is a key to relative costs. In this comparative setting, libraries are low-cost community services.

When considering unionization, employees must become involved in the establishment of goals felt to be suitable for the organizing group that also have some realistic likelihood of accomplishment. With but a very slight adaptation, most of the goal statements of the AFT could be accepted by public librarians:

1. salaries—to secure compensation consistent with expertise and experience
2. fringe benefits—to establish sick leave, medical and dental insurance, and other group benefits
3. job security—to secure the passage of permanent employment statutes, after probation, and to protect from discharge except upon just cause revealed through impartial due process procedures
4. academic freedom—to protect the right to exercise professional judgment in both substance and style as job responsibilities are carried out
5. retirement—to make possible a retirement funded at such a level that life can be maintained in comfort and dignity
6. equal rights—to eliminate differentials in pay and assignments based upon sex discrimination
7. political action—to engage the membership in a more active aspect of the democratic political process[3]

Other goals could be developed; some might be local in orientation. The point is that library employees lack neither opportunity nor reason when the question of organization of employees arises.

The AFSCME publications that speak to professional dignity through union membership point out that unionism offers advantages of moving toward better wages and working conditions than can be expected from the various professional societies for librarians. The goals that have been stipulated by AFSCME include:

Table 5.1 Employees of State and Local Government by Selected Function

	All employees (Full-time & Part-time) (in 1000s)			Full-time employees (in 1000s)			Full-time Equivalent Employees (in 1000s)		
	total	state	local	total	state	local	total	state	local
Education	6272	1400	4872	4471	805	3666	4952	952	4000
Hospitals	1002	506	496	894	465	429	944	485	459
Police	609	69	540	529	68	461	545	69	476
Fire	291	—	291	209	—	209	214	—	214
Libraries	90	—	90	55	—	55	64	—	64
All others	—	—	—	—	—	—	—	—	—
Total	12097	3268	8823	9410	2538	6872	10111	2742	7369

SOURCE: Bureau of National Affairs, Governmental Employee Relations Report (1976), pp. 71–2113.

1. professional standards
2. individual dignity
3. better wages
4. improved working conditions
5. effective representation
6. improved public services
7. strength through unity.

The increasing cost of living is a stimulus for the consideration of unionism. In planning for the future, librarians and other workers have come to grips with inflation and the way in which it evaporates the purchasing power of the dollar. Prices climbed 6.8 percent in 1977, as measured by the Consumer Price Index (CPI). At that point in the latter 1970s, observers of the economic scene predicted an annual inflation rate of about 8 percent into the 1980s. That proved to be a substantial underestimate. The CPI for January 1980 reported 13.9 and 14.0 percent as the one year increases for the U.S. city average.

How does inflation of this magnitude affect buying power? Table 5.2 reveals how a specific amount—$1,000—will shrink in real value over the next ten years. Such factors influence the thinking of workers as they consider how to protect their personal welfare. In examining the history of labor relations, many workers see in unionism a possible solution to problems of personal welfare.

ORGANIZING LOCAL UNIONS

Organizing can be a peaceful, low-cost, smoothly developing activity. On the other hand, it can be a brutal, shocking, expensive, and extended series of activities in the work setting, in which antagonisms develop out of

Table 5.2 **Purchasing Power of $1,000—after Inflation**

On January 1	At 5% Yearly Inflation	At 7% Yearly Inflation	At 8% Yearly Inflation	At 10% Yearly Inflation
1978	$1,000	$1,000	$1,000	$1,000
1979	$ 952	$ 935	$ 926	$ 909
1980	$ 907	$ 873	$ 857	$ 826
1981	$ 864	$ 816	$ 794	$ 751
1982	$ 823	$ 763	$ 735	$ 683
1983	$ 784	$ 713	$ 681	$ 621
1984	$ 746	$ 666	$ 630	$ 564
1985	$ 711	$ 623	$ 584	$ 513
1986	$ 677	$ 582	$ 540	$ 467
1987	$ 646	$ 544	$ 500	$ 424
1988	$ 614	$ 508	$ 463	$ 386

SOURCE: *U.S. News and World Report* 85 (September 25, 1978): 73.

disruptions. It seems appropriate to first consider some characteristics of the more simple, peaceful union organizing activities.

Most public libraries have independently elected or nonpartisan appointed governing boards. Most public libraries are not fiscally independent, as most of those boards are fiscally dependent for all or part of their funds to some political subdivision with taxing powers (e.g., a city council or a county board). Most public libraries are small. The *American Library Directory* (30th edition) has counted 8,504 public libraries. A scanning of four pages of that directory, selected by chance, found forty-seven public libraries listed. Of that number, fifteen registered at least 25,000 book titles, while 32 showed fewer than 25,000 titles—giving some indication of the preponderance of small libraries. Most union organizing activity occurs where there are larger libraries and more employees.

If a library exists in a state that statutorily provides for bargaining among all public employees, such as Iowa, then the librarians may consider organizing. Likewise, librarians may organize in states that allow public sector bargaining as a matter of practice, such as Illinois. For purposes of illustration, presume a library of forty to fifty professional or assistant professional employees and a budget of $750,000 to $800,000, a reasonable size for such an organization. If all or some of those librarians can be convened by someone in the group who is interested in unionization, a start toward organizing has been accomplished. It is unreasonable, it is overly optimistic, to think that a majority of librarians will upon first meeting decide to organize; but experience indicates clearly that it is reasonable to anticipate additional meetings, at which the topic will be further discussed. Meetings convened for the purpose of exploring whether workers should organize must be in harmony with local laws. For example, the Florida Public Employee Collective Bargaining Law (1971) stipulated that:

Employees shall have the right to self-organization, to form, join or assist labor unions or labor organizations or to refrain from such activity to bargain collectively through representatives of their own choosing, and to engage in concerted activities, for the purpose of collective bargaining or other mutual aid or protection (Florida Statutes, 447.03, 1).

Similarly, Section 1 of the Iowa Public Employment Relations Act (1974) states that:

The general assembly declares that it is the public policy of the state to promote harmonious and cooperative relationships between government and its employees by permitting public employees to organize and bargain collectively; . . .and to protect the rights of public employees to join or refuse to join, to participate or refuse to participate in, employee organizations.

These statutes are fairly typical of what might be expected in other states that have general public employee relations laws. With statutory assurances and authorizations, it is safe to assume that in discussions of the question of organizing, some librarians will be persuaded, some dissuaded.

Returning to the example of the library with forty to fifty professional employees and presuming that a majority agrees to organize and form a union, the next step is to approach the board of trustees in anticipation of bargaining. Although boards occasionally procrastinate and engage in delaying tactics because they do not want to bargain, boards will generally recognize the petitioning local. For exclusive bargaining rights with the trustees, an open election and/or valid membership list may be demanded. Boards do not want to, and typically will not, bargain with locals having less than a majority of the employees within their validated membership.

If the organizing has occurred in as simple a manner as portrayed, the group (now a local guild of librarians in fledgling form) may wish to consider affiliation. That is, should the emerging local seek affiliation with an existing national group or some state or regional group, or should it develop as an independent local? It is reasonable to assume that it will follow the direction of greatest presumed benefit, measuring additional costs (dues) against probable gains. The gains would include expertise from the national on all aspects of labor relations and political leverage. The additional costs would include money for dues and reduction in local autonomy as well as extension of responsibility and accountability. That is, problems of other affiliated unions would become the problems of newly affiliating unions, to some degree.

Using another example, presume a library that, with its several branches, employs 400 to 450 professional and assisting librarians, with many specializations represented. Speaking candidly, it must be pointed out that such a library staff, simply as a function of its size, may be attractive as a potential local for some regional or national union. For example, AFSCME, as the foremost union with which library locals have affiliated, might initiate organizing activity rather than passively wait for the possibility of organization from within. As in the smaller library, a first move toward organizing could also begin within the library staff itself, statutes permitting. With increased size and a commensurate increased potential for dues, larger libraries become more attractive as potential sites for new unions when assessed from the national or regional viewpoint. Large central unions must address this question: should they attempt to organize a new local, that is, spend money to attract the librarians into their own union on the basis of benefits that might be secured to those librarians through negotiations and from whose dues they could add to the wealth of the central union itself?

In such situations, organizing activity by "outsiders" may occur. In fact, organizing activity may involve more than one union, each vying for new members and the establishment of a new local. For obvious reasons, no single local employee group can organize into more than one union and still expect recognition from the employing library board of trustees. There will be one, and only one, recognized organization, finally.

In situations of organizational competition, a work force chooses through elections the union or association that it wishes to have as its exclusive representative in the collective bargaining that will eventually follow. It is in the competitive setting where workers are involved in more than one organizational thrust that individuals may find themselves in the middle of a tugging and pulling—and sometimes an abrupt pushing—contest. It is in such settings that organizational activities may turn ugly and brutal. Such an occurrrence is enough of a disruptive factor in library administration to influence the thinking of many library directors and trustees away from unionism. Seeing its undesirable employment characteristics, they are disenchanted by it. Happily, such incidents in libraries are few in number.

In 1968, the ALA conducted an informal inquiry into this question: why should there be collective bargaining in libraries? The respondents were directors in libraries that had negotiated contracts with employees. Some selected answers are included here for two specific questions in the inquiry. The first question was: why do professional librarians organize?

   Administrators:
1. Encouraged by recently enacted state laws authorizing public employees to organize and bargain collectively;
2. Spectacular success of teachers' organizations in achieving salary raises;
3. Impetus and support of the international overall unions;
4. Philosophy of the labor movement appeals to many librarians.
   Professional librarians, as in the case of other professional groups, and indeed as in the case of employees in general, organize into unions to permit them to have a voice in the decision-making process regarding conditions of employment. Such matters as job security, salary, and promotion policies and procedures are of immediate and intense concern for professional librarians.

Workers, librarians included, want a voice in the decision making that is a part of their work setting. As librarians view other professional occupations, many of them see great improvement in working conditions, which they attribute to organization. Especially among younger librarians, no professional stigma is attached to unionization.

The second question was: why do nonprofessional employees organize?

Administrators:

Usually the underlying reason for unionization is concern with employee welfare. Employees were unionized as part of a general organization drive of municipal employees.

Nonprofessional library employees organize essentially for the same reason that professional library employees organize, since their aspirations do not differ from professionals in kind but rather in degree. In addition, nonprofessional library employees frequently are drawn from the socio-economic strata of our society in which labor unions are not only accepted but often become a way of life.[4]

EARLY LIBRARY ORGANIZING

Organizations must have members' welfare as a central concern. Sometimes those concerns can be approached in a quasi-union fashion. Recalling the surge in library organizing of the 1960s, an incident from Mississippi is worthy of note. In 1968, an article in the *Mississippi Library News* revealed standards for minimum salaries for public librarians as recommended by a state committee. At that time, Mississippi librarians worked for less money than library technicians employed by the federal government received. It was recommended by a committee of librarians and trustees that salary levels for librarians be set on a comparative scale to public school teachers with equivalent education and that public librarians' salaries be supplemented by state appropriations. A bill was introduced into the legislature, and local support of it was urged.[5]

Without mentioning unionization, the Library Club of Cleveland put membership recruitment as its item of top priority in 1956. Obviously an already well-organized group, the Club was an "almost union."[6] In early 1957, the Club and the Cleveland Public Library Staff Association petitioned the city's budget commission on particular interests of their members, including leaves, vacations, and pensions. Shortly after, as reported in sequential issues of *News and Views*, extending through May 27, 1959, library representatives were invited to present their views on salaries to the library board. One outcome was the formation of a committee to evaluate and categorize personnel; finally, in 1959, the board established a graduated salary schedule, recognizing experience, levels of preparation, and performance.

The point is that workers organize for a cause. For librarians, that cause has sometimes led to a group, actually something less than a formal organization of workers into unions. Although there is a socialization aspect in labor unions, the primary orientation must be toward rewards for individual members. To the extent that those rewards are achieved prior to formal organization, the likelihood of a strong union's coming into being is diminished.

Establishment of the rights of public employees has paralleled that of private labor. Regarding union membership for teachers, as exemplary of professionals in unions, a Chicago court said in 1917 that ". . . it was inimical to proper discipline, prejudicial to the efficiency of the teaching force, and detrimental to the welfare of the public school systems."[7] Schools would not hire teachers who were union members, and teachers who were organizers were dismissed from their jobs. Inasmuch as organizing must precede election and recognition, such attitudes were effective deterrents.

Now, however, that issue has apparently been resolved with the ruling in *McLaughlin* v. *Tilendis* (1968), a circuit court decision. That court declared that First Amendment rights include the right to form and join a labor union, and that the Civil Rights Act of 1964 provides a remedy for employees dismissed because of their exercise of Constitutional rights. There is no reason to believe that any court would now rule differently in a similar suit coming from any category of public employment—public libraries included. Apparently, then, it is now an established condition that librarians who engage in union organizing activities are engaged in Constitutionally protected activities of free speech and association, and the criminal conspiracy doctrine at last has been laid to rest.

ELECTIONS

State statutes on elections vary. Obviously, elections must conform to prevailing statutes or be open to question, with the possibility that they may be overturned in court. Existing statutes from two states that address the topic of choosing an organization that will represent the employees of the unit reveal both similarities and differences. From Connecticut, the 1965 Act Concerning the Right of Teachers' Representative stated:

Any organization or organizations of certificated professional employees of a town or regional board of education may be selected in the manner provided herein for the purpose of representation in negotiations with such boards with respect to salaries and all other conditions of employment. A representative organization may be designated or elected for such purpose by a majority of all employees below the rank of superintendent in the entire group of such employees of a board of education or school district or by a majority of such employees in separate units. . . . [Section 10–152b]

Acting nearly a decade after Connecticut, and with substantial national experience to draw from, the Iowa legislature passed a comprehensive public employment relations act in 1974. Within the Iowa Public Employment Relations Act, the legislature addressed the topic of elections, in detail:

1. Upon the filing of a petition for certification of an employee organization, the board shall submit two questions to the public employees at an election in an appropriate bargaining unit. The first question on the ballot shall permit the public employees to determine whether or not such public employees desire exclusive bargaining representation. The second question on the ballot shall list any employee organization which has petitioned for certification or which has presented proof satisfactory to the board of support of ten percent or more of the public employees in the appropriate unit.
2. If a majority of the votes cast on the first question are in the negative, the public employees shall not be represented by an employee organization. If a majority of the votes cast on the first question is in the affirmative, then the employee organization receiving a majority of the votes cast on the second question shall represent the public employees in an appropriate bargaining unit.
3. If none of the choices on the ballot receive the vote of a majority of the public employees who could be represented by an employee organization, the board shall conduct a runoff election among the two choices receiving the greatest number of votes. [Section 15]

The Iowa legislature was determined to leave little to chance and mandated, in detail, much of the labor relations for public employees in various government agencies of the state. Typical of most statutes in that dependence upon the majority was the device chosen to assure local boards that they would not face two employee groups, each purporting to represent all, the statute also provided that under certain circumstances, boards could recognize newly formed locals with as few as 30 percent of the agency's employees.

Ohio, even though it has a strong industrial base and strong unions in the private sector, has not yet provided a collective bargaining law for public employees. When employees in the state's prison system attempted to organize unions, officials found that they faced multiple unions in single job settings, each laying claim to sole rights to represent all other employees. Guidelines for unionization were developed by Ohio's Department of Administrative Services. Negotiations in Ohio will continue to lead to contracts, thanks in no small part to the state's executive branch, which stepped in and filled a legislative void.[8] In collective bargaining, there is very little gift-giving; the tension of bargaining indicates the suitability and necessity of governmental oversight.

In order to ensure that elections for the identification of a representative union occur in fairness, neutral outsiders may be called upon. In some states, those persons who control and oversee the election are provided by the public employment commission. The American Arbitration Association (AAA) is an independent, nongovernmental agency with a growing interest in public labor relations. The AAA has panels of persons specializing in different aspects of labor relations within its membership and certainly has the resources to conduct representative elections. This is a service for a fee, proportional to the size of the job. Within AAA procedures, typical questions would be

1. Who will be eligible to vote? It may be helpful in answering this question to list those classifications of employees who will be ineligible to vote. Consideration must be given to long-term substitute employees, contract employees on official leave, etc.
2. When will the vote be held? On what day and during what hours will the polls be open? What will be the date of run-off election if one becomes necessary?
3. Where will the polling places be located? Junior and senior high schools are logical locations because they are strategically located throughout the district and usually have ample parking facilities. Where there are competing unions, one of the unions may argue for polling places on the basis of the location of its membership. The expense of establishing a polling place in each school is usually prohibitive. Polling places at locations other than the schools provide a satisfactory arrangement.
4. Who will be the election clerks at the polls? How many official observers from each organization on the ballot will be allowed at the polls?
5. What procedure will be used to list eligible voters, identify voters, challenge ballots and resolve the challenges?
6. What safeguards will exist to protect the secrecy of the ballot?
7. What shall be the wording of the question to be presented to the eligible voters on the election machine or paper ballot?
8. In what order will the choices be placed on the ballot? This can be determined by the flip of a coin. The ballot should provide for a choice of "no organization" as well as for the choice of the organizations, by exact title, seeking to represent the employees.[9]

When a board of trustees recognizes a library union, it is recognition for a term. Annual recognition is common. Proof of continued representativeness may be demanded by the board. Termination and renewal of recognition may be for a length of time set by statute; or, it may be part of the negotiated agreement. Control of the time span covered by the recognition is an interest which must be shared, for no board wants to get caught in a situation of contractual commitment to a union fading from power while a new union comes forward with clear proof of majority representativeness.

After elections, precise constituency may still be debated. For example, employees designated by such titles as supervisors, directors, and department heads may be in the management group and ineligible for membership. Yet, they might wish to join the union. Or on the contrary, such titles with localized connotations might identify people who would not be considered management but who might shun union membership, based upon a personal ambition for identification as managers, no matter how ephemeral.

THE DEMAND FOR BARGAINING

It is only realistic to take note of some of the current conditions prevailing in libraries. Library unions are changing the ways in which libraries can be managed. This is not a comment on the quality of library services; it is only an observation of what is happening. The union voice is influential because it is an expression of political power. Especially in cities, where alliances between many different public employee groups provide for a unified voice, politicos and boards must recognize that voice. In fact, some elected officials must view it as an appalling power, as they occasionally have faced unified threats from police, firefighters, trash haulers, hospital workers, teachers, and librarians. In assessing the extent to which those occupational groups provide a critical service, the position of librarians is glaringly apparent. Librarians need alliances.

In the sequence of initiating union activity, recognition follows election. Recognition leads to bargaining, the presentation of proposals and demands to the library administrator or the board of trustees. The written list of proposals and demands is a formal presentation, chaaracteristically done at the time required by the statute of each particular state or mutually agreed upon as desirable practice.

As librarians put forward demands and proposals, all are priced or costed against the organization's budget. Management bargainers discuss the financial capacity of their agency, and frequently at the bargaining table. They must know the tax base from which revenues will be generated and the operational cost expectations and be able to speak frankly about what money is available for what demands. They must not cry "Wolf!" and destroy trust, for that approach will only generate defiance and hostility. It is not a union goal to bankrupt the library, but neither is it acceptable to be duped by a bargainer for the board who pleads poverty when the facts, revealed later on, prove it not to have existed.

Good faith is an elusive term. It incorporates fairness and trust. Some specific conditions of bargaining developed by the National Labor Relations Board and from bargaining experience exemplify the conditions which must be present if bargaining is to occur in good faith:

1. there must be a serious attempt to adjust differences and to reach an acceptable common ground.
2. counter proposals must be offered when another party's proposal is rejected. This must involve the "give and take" or an auction system.
3. a position with regard to contract terms may not be constantly changed.
4. evasive behavior during negotiations is not permitted.
5. there must be a willingness to incorporate oral agreements into a written contract.[10]

Good faith is a relative term, one which eschews exaggeration. The establishment and maintenance of good faith is something of a paradox. For example, when the library union presents wage demands, how high an increase should be asked for? As the employee negotiating team discusses strategy and decides to demand a pay increase, how high can the demand go and still be defensible as good faith bargaining? And on the other side, when bargaining is focused upon salary, how conservative can management be in a salary counterproposal and still maintain the trust that is part of good faith? It is a worrisome condition with a balance having its own rationale. Proposals and counterproposals must incorporate the interests of the team making them but cannot be so outlandish as to violate good faith.

When a proposal is made by one team, there are four possible responses:

1. reject it
2. ignore it
3. modify it with a counterproposal
4. accept it

The bargaining table is a setting of action and reaction as the teams analyze demands and develop positions from which to address the proposals. Investigation, consideration, and consultation may be part of the analysis.

No proposal should involve illegal or proscribed areas. That is, if the library board, as a public board, has been legislatively forbidden from entering into certain agreements, it is pointless for a union to pursue such items, hoping to see them incorporated into contracts as restrictive clauses. Examples of such forbidden areas are included in the following list:

1. items not directly affecting the welfare of members of the negotiating unit
2. items with a primary function of determining educational policy (in schools)
3. items that may encroach directly upon an area inherent to management, such as the hiring of personnel[11]

Proposals are generally developed through a solicitation and filtering system. Through such a system, suggestions and gripes work their way up from individual members and work settings to refinement and preparation as proposals. Once identified and accepted by members as generally desirable, proposals are moved forward in the union's consideration. If not accepted immediately at the bargaining table, the union may decide to exercise patience and restraint, upon the judgment that chances of acceptance will be better at another time. Perseverance and insistence are routines through which unions accomplish many goals. When based upon the development of solicited suggestions from the membership at large, proposals will be perceived as supportive of the membership.[12]

Proposals should not be subterfuges. They should be sincere requests. In a prioritized arrangement of proposals, wage and salary proposals nearly always top the list. For librarians that would mean the maintenance and expansion of a salary schedule, with pay arranged by job classification and experience on the job. Salary schedules have a mutual value to both employees and trustees. They provide a reference point from which the union can approach questions of salary and form the first salary demand. For a library board, an existing schedule is a source of planning, as initial budget development proceeds prior to settlement of negotiation. Ultimately, negotiation decisions must be expressed in terms of earning more money, increasing the pleasantness of the work setting, or some similar satisfaction. Every specific demand must arise from one of those very few needs that will provide worker satisfaction when met.

BARGAINING AS AN EVENT

Although, for example, the Nebraska statute talks about professional negotiations for certificated employees in school, the word long used in the private sector is bargaining. In the past, the National Education Association sought to maintain a distinction: laborers bargained, but professionals negotiated. Time has proved the distinction meaningless, and the NEA has forsaken it. There are two sides at every bargaining table, labor and management. Each has something to give, and each wants something. Librarians have professional expertise they want to sell. Their preparation for work as librarians had to be premised on the expectation that there existed a place where that service would be valued and where a willingness to pay for the service existed. Bargaining is carried on in an adversarial mode, for neither side is able or willing to give as much as the other side would willingly take. One way to control the amount that might be granted for pay raises is to put constrictions upon local budget expansion. Some states did just that in 1979, by referendum.

How to bargain while keeping trust and respect at a level allowing for operation of the library at a high standard, as the bargainers move back and forth between the table and the workaday setting, is a problem. In large libraries where the bargainers are unlikely to meet in the work setting, it is a remote and unlikely problem. In smaller libraries, where the organizational distance from the director to the most junior librarian is but a few people, the problem can cause counterproductive reactions. Bargaining creates tension and hostility. Occasionally, professionalism is overwhelmed. The bargainers of both teams must work at keeping cool and developing restraint. Carry-over into work settings must be suppressed, for it is not beneficial to either group for the library to suffer an efficiency loss as a spin-off from bargaining.

The antagonisms of bargaining are real enough that trustees need to be satisfied that those antagonisms do not enter work settings. Cases reveal serious problems in which supervisors have harassed librarians involved in bargaining and also reveal that librarians have sometimes tried to sabotage the operation of the library, venting rage against library administrators. One way to decrease such unfortunate side effects is to have the board select as its representative at the bargaining table a person hired from the outside. Although qualified outside negotiators are in short supply, they can be hired. They relieve the local administration from hostilities that sometimes become personalized as bargainers' tempers flare.

Over the next few years, library boards probably will continue to use their own administrators on special short-term assignment as negotiators or hire nearby available professionals who appear reasonably well suited to the task. Obviously, any special directions, qualifications, and limitations must be made explicit by the employing board and accepted by the negotiator. The board must assure itself that job performance conflict is not being built into the work setting through the negotiation process and that it can speak to the problem through control of its own negotiator. Either arrangement, whether with an insider or an outsider, could be strongly supportive of the positive development of labor relations and the enhancement of the organization's work mission; the alternative that is chosen must bear intense scrutiny for its particular frailty.

Trustees have more flexibility in selecting someone as a bargainer than do library unions, simply because of the disparity in financial resources. Very few library locals have a membership of such size as to create from dues a financial reserve that will support hiring an outside agent. The local union's representative probably will be a person from the ranks, with brief training for the job. If affiliated, the local may get bargainer training and procedural guidelines. It may get the services of a central union bargainer if the local is large enough, which is rare among library locals. It is up to the elected or appointed local bargaining representatives to develop quickly the necessary skills for bargaining. That is not so ridiculous as it may appear initially, for librarians are professionals in the information system, accustomed to learning from books and media, and they have prime motivation for self-improvement. Nonetheless, it does appear that management, with its greater financial resources, has some advantages in deciding whether to hire an outside bargainer or use someone on the administrative staff. Demands that arise from discussion must have merit of their own, but whether they are accepted or discarded is also related to the skill with which they are handled at the bargaining table. As local library boards approach the question of the insider or the outsider to represent board interests, they must consider (1) organizational distance, (2) the goals to be accomplished through bargaining, (3) the availability of high-quality people, and (4) cost limitations on the bargaining effort.

As bargaining commences, selected strategies may reflect changing times. For example, employees characteristically drive for multiyear contracts during stable or near-stable economic times. Employers resist extended contracts at such times. When inflation is running at a double-digit figure, employers are receptive to long-term contracts and may even propose them, but employees are usually cautious at such times. Tactics and strategy must be determined prior to the start of bargaining, with built-in provisions for shifts and alternatives.

Some bargainers advocate long lists of initial demands. Boards have faced long lists of demands when the bargaining team has solicited the employee group, asking "What would you like to demand of the board this year?" Even after eliminating all duplications, such an open approach may yield seventy or eighty items, a list far in excess of what can be bargained within ordinary time constraints. This approach has several benefits. It is an avenue of expression through which the rank and file gain an active identification with the bargaining effort. It allows for many "give-aways," as the bargainer agrees to decrease the length of the list. It allows the administration to count gains, just by reducing the number of demands. It is not for all situations and times because within it are inherent weaknesses. For every demand there must be back-up information. The union bargainers must be prepared to support every demand with a knowledge of the cost and the likely impact.[13] To do less would be to expose the list as including inconsequential demands. Such a criticism could become a terrible mistake if seized upon by the administrative bargainer and used as a question to address other demands. Additionally, if some solicited demands are not included in the list because the bargainers view the issues as liabilities, the deletion can cause disharmony within the union. The initial list of demands should be controlled for length, according to what the union's guiding committee sees as most appropriate issues.

After the initial letter from the local union is received by the trustees, bargaining commences. Discussion is an essential element of free, civilized societies. Bargaining is structured, systematic, legalized discussion for the purpose of increasing the acceptability of the burden of work. Discussion implies persuasion, and persuasion should produce new viewpoints and altered positions. The board's first reaction to the union's initiative may be a noncommittal acknowledgment of the union's list and a statement of willingness to meet and confer. It may identify places, times, and people for the union as first meetings are considered. That message from the trustees could speak to the list of proposals, disavowing or accepting; it could include some new proposals or counterproposals. Generally, the message will be an acknowledgment of receipt of the list and a promise to meet and bargain on some items of employment at an appropriate time and place. Concessions are not made in a letter of acknowledgment.

During bargaining sessions the participants drive toward agreement. Proposing and compromising must occur. Sensitiveness to screened and cautious responses must be cultured because compromises are seldom accomplished with massive, all-at-once concessions. The heart of compromise is the counterproposal. Each side must be ready and inventive. For example, if the librarians propose a thirty-five-hour work week, it might be reasonable for the administration to counterpropose, tentatively agreeing to a reduction in the work week but at the same time linking it to a reduction in the number of paid holidays during the work year. Counterproposals should supply a line of defense for a bargainer while encouraging the continued discussion of the points at issue. The bargainers keep in their minds the need of their constituencies and the restrictions under which they are working at the table. They must not give up on an issue before exploring every possible solution they can develop, because impasse is not the goal.

Although agreement is the goal of bargaining, impasse may occur. The parties may acknowledge that, finally, on some issues(s) there is only an agreement to disagree and a stalemate has been reached. Examination of bargaining sessions to determine the role of good faith as a contributor to settlement has yielded ambiguous results. That is, bargaining that rested upon a plan containing some such bad-faith characteristics as subterfuge or deception has sometimes produced acceptable contracts. Contrarily, bargaining admitted by both parties to have been carried on in good faith has sometimes ended in impasse. Good faith is essential for honest bargaining, but its presence—though acknowledged by both bargainers—may not be enough to guarantee settlement. However, its absence or circumvention over extended periods of time cannot be tolerated if labor relations are to enhance the quality of work. Without good faith, without trust, bargaining must collapse, for it cannot continue when the parties lack respect for each other.

Hard bargainers press for their position on an issue with skill, resourcefulness, and tenacity. Hard bargaining is characterized by persistence in advocating preferred positions. Hard bargaining does not connote unreasonableness or lack of good faith. It is reasonable to select persons who have the capacity to hang tough, who have the ability to meet controversy head on. Practices that are advocated by unions are not likely to be those that are also advocated by the labor relations staff of any public employer. Yet, what is important to union members varies by location, occupation, and affiliation. During negotiations, each side may press its own points, and unless it uses such ploys as untruth or utter unreasonableness, it is not likely to be found guilty of lack of good faith in bargaining.[14]

Good faith is epitomized by trust and appreciation. It does not imply ready acceptance by a board of a set of demands, whether the list be long or short. Acceptance of union demands, or of counterproposals from the trustees, is only one among many indicators of good faith. As trustees act within their title, as guardians of some aspect of public welfare, they are obligated to a good faith approach to the expressed needs of their employee groups, meaning that they must accept demands with genuineness, sensitivity, and appreciation.

SPECIAL LIBRARIES

How to treat special libraries in a book devoted to librarians and labor relations has proven to be a difficult question. The near absence of special libraries and the professionals who staff them from this text is *not* an indication of their level of importance, but it does recognize that

1. Special libraries employ a relatively small proportion of the professional librarians.
2. Special libraries must carry out bargaining, if it occurs—and it rarely does—under rules laid down by the National Labor Relations Board or under court rulings. That is, statutes devoted to public employee bargaining do not apply.

Gale Research's *Directory of Special Libraries and Information centers* (5th edition) gives some indication of the magnitude of employment opportunities for librarians in "special" settings. The definition of special library is:

. . . substantively, special libraries are libraries built around a special collection limited by subject or form in accordance with the interests of its users; functionally, these libraries, which may at times have collections of a general nature, operate in support of their sponsoring organizations.[15]

The 14,000 such libraries in the United States do not form a comparatively significant employment grouping nor do they merit extensive treatment in a book devoted to the collectivization of librarians as a professional group. Scanning the listings of special libraries with attention to collection size, Gale's *Directory* revealed that many collections totaled fewer than 1,000 volumes. A few were much larger, and many had extensive holdings in periodicals or other special information sources. Nonetheless, it was not difficult to form the impression that the vast majority of special libraries are very small libraries. Individually, they employ few full-time professional librarians, and perhaps none. As library union action is taken by individual local units, special libraries generally lack the characteristics of libraries in which unions are likely to take root and prosper. Without a minimum number of employees, organization is impractical.

Another characteristic has diminished the importance of special libraries here. Many special libraries are parts of other, larger libraries. For example, the Antioch College Glen Helen Library (Gale entry #511) is described as holding 478 books devoted to environmental protection, resource management, forestry, and so on. At the same time, the Antioch College Library, found in Bowker's *American Library Directory: 1967-77*, is described as devoting part of its collection to eleven special subjects, including environmental studies and natural sciences. Both entries have the same address and telephone number. As a part of the larger library, and thereby part of a college faculty, the professional librarians of the institution might be organized and unionized.

A similar situation occurs with noticeable frequency as special libraries are identified in the Gale *Directory* as part of county or municipal, but local, public libraries. Special libraries hold some opportunity for professional employment, but for librarians who would prefer to work in a unionized setting they present a very restricted opportunity, except as they are parts of larger libraries that may become—or already are—unionized.

SUMMARY

When librarians consider organizing into a union to further their own welfare, the statutes or practices of their particular state must be incorporated into the planning. Affiliation with a national or regional group may be considered. Presumably, affiliation would provide expertise and assistance, but at some cost. Lest there occur damage in the areas of interpersonal relationships and personnel management, both professional employees and the library administration should know of intentions to organize at some fairly early date. Both employees and administration need to assess carefully who their respective negotiators will be and make selections according to both short- and long-range considerations. Care in preparation for unionization and bargaining in good faith will do much to reduce the hostilities that can arise from tension-laden events—which, after all, center on the questions of power and authority. There is no need for either side to fear the other, yet each side must be aware of the ambitions and limitations of the other side.

NOTES

1. Campbell R. McConnell, *Elementary Economics: Principles, Problems and Policies* (New York: McGraw-Hill, 1960), p. 627.

2. Ibid., p. 327.

3. "Goals of American Federation of Teachers" (Washington, D.C.: The Federation, AFL-CIO, 1977).

4. "Collective Bargaining: Questions and Answers," *ALA Bulletin* 62 (December 1968): pp. 1385-6.

5. M. B. Denny, "Section Reports of Convention," *Mississippi Library News* 32 (December 1968): p. 136.

6. Cleveland Public Libraray Staff Association, *News and Views* 21 (October 1956).

7. John Phillip Linn, "Collective Bargaining and the School Superintendent," in M. Chester Nolte, ed., *Law and the School Superintendent* (Cincinnati, Ohio: W. H. Anderson, 1971), p. 187.

8. Paul D. Standahar, "Prison Guard Labor Relations in Ohio," *Industrial Relations* 15 (May 1976): 177-90.

9. Linn, pp. 215-17.

10. Benjamin J. Taylor and Fred Whitney, *Labor Relations Law* (Englewood Cliffs, N. J.: Prentice-Hall, 1971), p. 332.

11. Donald Wollett and Robert H. Chanin, *The Law and the Practice of Teacher Negotiations* (Washington, D.C.: The Bureau of National Affairs, 1974), pp. 126-32.

12. E. D. Duryea and others, *Faculty Unions and Collective Bargaining* (San Francisco: Jossey-Bass, 1973), pp. 46-48.

13. Robert C. O'Reilly and Doug Nollette, "Negotiations, Impasse and Settlement," *Nebraska State School Boards Association Bulletin* (April 1976), pp. 9-10.

14. David Levin. "Collective Bargaining Impacts on Personnel Administration in the American Public Sector," *Labor Law Journal* (July 1976), pp. 426-36.

15. Margaret L. Young and Harold C. Young, eds. *Directory of Special Libraries and Information Centers*, 5th ed. (Detroit: Gale Research Company, 1979) p. viii.

CONTRACT
ITEM ANALYSIS 6

CONTRACT ITEMS, DATA AND RESEARCH

The Bureau of Labor Statistics periodically issues its selected file of state, county, and municipal collective bargaining agreements. Their file includes virtually all of the agreements with a minimum of 1,000 workers or more; they also maintain a sampling of agreements that cover fewer than 1,000 workers.

Examination of that file for the fall of 1975 revealed a very small number of contracts in which librarians were identified as the specific workers who were covered. There were two apparent reasons for such a small listing. First, many of the contracts were between cities or counties—as one of the parties—and listed worker groups as general municipal employees, public employees, and all municipal employees, as the other parties to the contract. Doubtless, many of those generic, inclusive groups of workers included librarians in an arrangement parallel to the inclusion of librarians and media center directors in certificated school employee contracts. Given the relatively small size of the whole group of librarians working in public libraries, it is natural enough to find some of them collected with other employee types, bargaining for comprehensive contracts.

Second, very few librarian unions have over 1,000 members. In fact, the BLS file listed none, which is at variance with information gathered previously, which disclosed that membership in the New York Public Library Guild (Local #1930, AFSCME) fluctuated between 1,500 and 1,800 workers.[1] The BLS listed the NYPL Guild as having 150 members and the NYPL Blue Collar Union as having fifty members.[2] However, setting such discrepancies aside, the file contains information of value in the understanding of library unionism.

Los Angeles County provides a good example of the extensiveness of public employee unionism. Represented by varied boards and trustees, the

BLS reported that Los Angeles County had forty-nine contracts in 1975, one of which was with the librarians who were members of the Service Employee's International Union. That contract, covering 400 employees, was for twenty-four months. The L.A. County contracts were for groups with memberships ranging from twenty-four to 19,000. Of the forty-nine contracts in file, twenty-four (including the librarians) were negotiated with the SEIU and covered 49,122 public employees. The remaining contracts were with ten other unions, covering 22,201 employees. Clearly, the SEIU was the dominant public employee union in Los Angeles in the mid-1970s. Contract duration ranged from eight to thirty-six months; twenty-three of those were for twelve months, and twenty-one were for twenty-four months.[3]

Librarians have the flexibility to affiliate in directions that they see to be to their own advantage. That flexibility is due in part to the fact that libraries have widespread acceptance as agencies promoting the development of society. Librarians can go in the direction of local strength. Contracts may be of varying length—except where statutorily restricted—as demonstrated by the fact that four of the L.A. County contracts were for more than thirty months. Contracts for librarians can be just about any of many things, reflections of strength in organizing and negotiating.

Items upon which agreement may be reached at the bargaining table must be harmonious with local statutes. To determine what kinds of items might be negotiated and later become articles or clauses in contracts, an analysis of public sector bargaining was conducted in fourteen states, and the information developed can be seen in the following three sets of items:

1. Mandatory subjects upon which there was greatest agreement among the states was:

    a. wages
    b. hours
    c. grievance procedures
    d. probationary periods of employment
    e. methods of (teacher) evaluation
    f. methods of (teacher) removal

2. Subjects about which there was most disagreement as to negotiability were:

    a. parity in wages
    b. class size
    c. retirement benefits
    d. agency shop
    e. pre-eminence of negotiated contracts over existing laws
    f. preparation time for teachers
    g. selection of textbooks
    h. in-service education of employees
    i. school calendar
    j. standards of service

3. Items which were uniformly described as management rights were:

   a. institutional mission and program
   b. level of funding
   c. hire employees
   d. supervision of employees
   e. job assignment
   f. conditions of employment for non-unit members
   g. organization
   h. size of work force
   i. standards of recruitment[4]

Although the list reflects the predominant place that teacher-board bargaining has attained within public sector labor relations, that factor does not detract from the usability of the list of items for library settings. After all, many of those item preferences arose from local organizations that included school librarians within the membership.

For librarians in colleges and universities, the list of bargained items has been discovered to be a little different. In a survey that divided concerns for bargaining into two levels, one dealing with economics and working conditions, the other with professioanl standards, the data strongly suggested that unions were the principal spokesmen on salary issues. Table 6.1 supports that finding, showing that the institutions surveyed developed contracts that gave central attention to money items. The question for academic librarians in each locality is whether they should join the departmentalized faculty in a bargaining relationship. To some extent, Table 6.2 speaks to that query, for through such data the academic librarian can begin to see the degree to which there is a shared community of interest. Additionally, librarians should candidly assess the strength of the local faculty bargaining unit and the respect the teaching faculty has for the concerns of the academic librarians. From Table 6.2, for example, the five issues

Table 6.1 **Frequency of Provision in Faculty Bargaining Agreements for Economic Issues, by Type of Provision (N=48)**

| Economic issues | *no provision* | Percentage of Agreement with | | |
		substantive provision	*process provision*	*mixed provision*
salary minima	10.4	66.7	2.1	20.8
cost of living	91.7	8.3	—	—
merit raise	62.5	8.4	22.9	—
health insurance	8.3	91.7	—	—
pension program	22.9	77.1	—	—

SOURCE: Margaret Chaplan and Charles Maxey, "The Scope of Faculty Bargaining: Implications for Academic Librarians," *The Library Quarterly* 46 (July 1976): 240.

Table 6.2 **Frequency of Provision in Faculty Bargaining Agreements for Personnel Issues, by Type of Provision (N = 48)**

Personnel issues	Percentage of Agreements with			
	no provision	*substantive provision*	*process provision*	*mixed provision*
initial appointment	29.2	8.3	56.3	6.3
promotion	16.7	4.2	70.8	8.4
tenure	18.8	—	72.9	8.4
evaluation	41.7	6.3	50.0	2.1
reduction in force	41.7	10.4	41.7	6.3

SOURCE: Margaret Chaplan and Charles Maxey, "The Scope of Faculty Bargaining," *The Library Quarterly* 46 (July 1976): 240.

surveyed within the general category of personnel were provided for in more than half of the forty-eight contracts, either procedurally or substantively. Employee evaluation, as one specific issue in which librarians might be interested, appeared in about 60 percent of the agreements.

Every worker seeks job security from every foreseeable adverse contingency. It is always high on the list of union goals. To the extent that librarians and workers in other settings are depersonalized in proportion to the bigness of the organization, job security drives will find expression in worker demands for contract treatment. In some years, job security has been the number one union goal, even superseding wages, whenever workers felt threatened about job loss. Collectively, that is a reaction by workers who, as individual consumers, have done their part in building that massive private debt which U.S. citizens have accumulated and who are aware of their need for a steady cash flow, partially to pay their personal part of that large private debt. Every American worker, from the highest paid executives to the lowest paid unskilled starter, strives for some kind of job security—or, if not security in a specific job, economic security in some form or another.

The drive for security has called for the invention of new employment relationships and new unemployment provisions. Many of those inventions have been enacted into laws. Many have been expressed as clauses in negotiated contracts. Some job protection devices have been pronounced by courts, particularly in the realm of workers who were dismissed without statements of just cause.

Public workers, along with those in private industry, want job security. Given their typical financial commitments, they need as much security in their work as can possibly be developed. To secure this need, they must be aware of protections in the contract, in state statutes, and recourse in instances of dispute. Likewise, management must be alert to new obligations, particularly procedural obligations, which put upon them new routines and techniques for contract administration and personnel supervision.

WORDS AND CONTRACT MEANING

The beauty of the English language is also one of its frailties in the sense that word meaning changes as its meaning is derived from context. Two contesting parties may, in good faith, ascribe different meanings to key words, and honest misunderstanding may erupt from wording that received too little attention at the time of contract drafting. The goal of negotiations is agreement; to have an agreement which lacks intelligible and comprehensible words in key phrases of the contract is to set the stage for disputes and occasionally for hostility and distrust. Because contracts are developed bilaterally, both librarians and library administrators must scrutinize the language of the negotiated agreement prior to its mutual adoption and make necessary changes before the agreement is set in place as the contract within which the organization must operate. Ambiguity and uncertainty need to be written out of the agreement.

Such a goal sounds worthwhile, and perhaps even easy. However, when negotiation is in progress and word clarification is being pursued, changes in wording may become part of the negotiation, especially when only one party sees the value of change.

For example, take a simple word: days. What does that mean? Are weekends included? Does it mean weekdays, only? And what is a "week" day? If the contract calls for a circumstance in which days are counted, will holidays be be included in the count? If a contract stipulated that librarians should be paid an extra stipend of $20.00 per day for hosting orientation-field day groups coming into the library, would that mean one such effort in a day, an effort to take the whole day, several such groups, all scheduled in one day? If librarians did special shift work for part days, would they receive wages on a pro rata basis? If the shift exceeded one-half day, would that count as a whole day? Or would it all be hourly?

Consider two examples of contract language. In the first occurred the phrase, "[Librarians] may be required to take a physical examination."[5] Within the experience of professional work settings, more personnel management problems arise because of mental strain and attendant failures than because of physical debilitation. A physical examination is not much of a start as a remedy for a mental problem. A superior term would call for a "medical examination," in the sense that, through extended comprehensiveness, the alleged condition could be attended within the wording of the contract. This phraseology might represent, generically, those circumstances in which unions try to restrict the power of governing boards. Closely analyzed, it becomes a kind of variable trade-off in which unions must carefully assess the consequences of managerial restrictions and extensions of protection to workers who may not be doing well. That is, bad performance by workers in public service agencies cannot redound to the advantage of either labor or management, and many unions desire language that puts the onus of personnel evaluation and management upon the agency's administrators.

In the second example, the contract included a statement of intent, a kind of preface: "The parties agree to negotiate in good faith with respect to salaries and other matters of mutual concern."[6] That statement means that everything is bargainable, that nothing can be excluded—except those things that are statutorily proscribed. It is phraseology in which a union might have an interest but one that trustees would ordinarily reject. If the library administrator wanted to indicate willingness to bargain on all matters to which there would be mutual agreement, then the contract phrasing must have been a suprise, for "mutual concern" and "mutual agreement" are terms of nearly opposite meaning. Within the bargaining context, "mutual concern" means agreement to bargain upon matters that, by contract language, become a concern to both parties when one party stipulates the concern. Such broad, glossy statements frequently occur in the opening parts of a contract, clutter it, and produce uncertain implications for both parties.

As contracts are drafted and final wordage supplied, writers need to consider the history of disputes and arguments and the altercations that might arise and to view the contract in context. Verbiage is no reasonable goal. Conscientious considerations should lead toward contracts of low dispute and satisfaction in knowing that "you got what you wrote."

CONTRACT CLAUSES

Some clauses extracted from contracts will now be discussed to show characteristics of particular types of clauses. Reflecting the comparatively low number of librarian-library contracts, none deal exclusively with librarians. However, they are suitable as patterns for libraries because they are from the public employment sector and in several instances they also could include library employees in the unit. The first three excerpts identify the parties to the contract, but in different ways.

From the State of Wisconsin and American Federation of Teachers:

This Agreement made and entered into this 28th day of September, 1976, at Madison, Wisconsin, pursuant to the provisions of Section 111.80-11.97, Wisconsin Statutes, by and between the State of Wisconsin and its Agencies (hereinafter referred to as the Employer) represented by the Department of Administration and the

Wisconsin Federation of Teachers (hereinafter referred to as the "Federation") as the representative of employees employed by the State of Wisconsin. . . .

From Miles City (Mont.) and AFSCME:

The City Council of the City of Miles City, hereinafter referred to as the Employer, and Local No. 283 of the American Federation of State, County and Municipal Employees, AFL-CIO, representing the employees covered by this Agreement, and hereinafter referred to as the Union, in order to increase general efficiency of the City Government of the City of Miles City and to eliminate as far as possible political consideration from city employments and to promote the moral well being and security affected hereby, do mutually agree. . . .

From Wayne State University (Mich.) and the American Association of University Professors:

Wayne State University recognizes the Wayne State University Chapter of the American Association of University Professors as the sole collective bargaining agent for the purpose of bargaining with the University with respect to wages, hours, and other conditions of employment for the employees in the following classifications. . . .

This set of clauses shows that employer parties to a contract may be from various political subdivisions or public service agencies with a public charge. Unions may be locals—affiliated or unaffiliated—district councils, regional associations, or any group organized under law that has received from the employer (if necessary) recognition as the sole bargaining agent. Some clauses are free flowing and sparse of words; others are cumbersome from legalese.

Two clauses, both from university settings, have been selected to show some of the detail to which the parties agreed as negotiations were completed.

From Michigan State University and the Michigan State University Employees Association:

The Bargaining Unit consists of the following: All regular clerical and technical employees of Michigan State University whether salaried or hourly paid, but excluding those clerical and technical employees who are regularly employed less than one-half ($\frac{1}{2}$) time; or temporarily employed less than one-half ($\frac{1}{2}$) or less than 90 days; or designated as assigned off-campus; also employees classified as administrative-professional; classified health professionals in recognized union or association units; student employees; supervisory and executive employees; and all other hourly paid and salaried employees.

From Rutgers, the State University of New Jersey, and the American Association of University Professors:

Excluded are all officers of administration including deans, associate deans, assistant deans, assistants to deans, academic directors who are not engaged in instruction or research for 50% or more of their time during the academic year, visiting professors, honorary professors, fellows, all members of the co-adjunct staff, all those persons who administer or help to administer a major academic unit or program of the University. . . .

Academic librarians, as different from the faculty who make up the membership of the various academic departments, need coverage of the same level of specificity shown in the inclusion-exclusion aspects of the two university examples. The need for clarity in contracts cannot be overemphasized.

THE MAKE-UP OF CONTRACTS

As the negotiators propose and counterpropose around the bargaining table, specific descriptive statements about the work setting become mutually acceptable and are written as the clauses of the agreement. Negotiators must have neat and orderly minds, for the agreement is not intended as a literary masterpiece. When stable and completed, the clauses become the articles of the contract itself. Although oversimplified, that description reveals the process through which the developed contract finally comes into place as the document stipulating how the library's work will be carried on. It should raise the level of consciousness of labor and management alike.

Each article is directed toward a separate and discrete aspect of the work setting, topically unrelated to other articles in the contract. The commonality of articles is through the fact that each article contains enough of the fundamental viewpoints of the bargaining parties to be satisfactory—which does not mean that negotiators will be wildly ecstatic in their endorsement of any particular article!

Contracts tend toward extensiveness. Only part of that is ideological. Each article has an earned place in the contract. In a survey of several library contracts developed over a ten-year span, from 1967 to 1977, it became apparent that the number of articles was increasing. Library contracts for the latter 1970s commonly consisted of more than thirty different articles. Earlier research in the public schools of four midwestern states, covering school librarians along with other certificated professionals, revealed that same tendency toward contract extensiveness and comprehensiveness.[7]

Examples of contract articles have been extracted from two library contracts

1. The Union Contract Agreement between the New York Public Library and the NYPL Staff Members Local 1930, District Council 37 AFSCME, AFL-CIO (July 1, 1973-June 30, 1976 and extended)

2. The Staff Association Contract Agreement by and between Pierce County Rural Library District and Pierce County Library Staff Association, 1976–77 [Tacoma, Wash.]

The contracts represented different regions and sizes. One was an unaffiliated union. Three articles were extracted from each contract for comparison. Each extract was labeled, at the end, with the locale from which it came.

These articles deal with recognition:

Section 1. The Library recognizes the Union as the representative of, and this Agreement shall apply to, the staff members in the titles listed below, who have submitted check-off authorizations or who make required payments of dues directly to the Union pursuant to Article III of this Agreement, with certain exceptions involving supervisory or confidential positions:

(78 job titles included; 20 positions excluded)

For purposes of this agreement, the term "staff member" shall not include a person employed on a temporary basis or compensated on the basis of per diem, per hour, honorarium or lump sum contract.

Section 2. The Library agrees that during the term of this Agreement it will not recognize any other union as the representative of the staff members (as defined in Section 1). It is agreed by the parties hereto that nothing in this Agreement shall be construed as requiring any staff member to join the union. The right of any staff member to join any union of his or her choice or to refrain from joining any union is recognized by the parties to this agreement.

The Library shall not interfere with the right of any person in its employ to become a member of the Union. . . . [New York]

1.1 The Library recognizes the Union as the exclusive bargaining unit for all permanent full-time and regularly scheduled part-time employees for whom the Union was certified by the Department of Labor and Industries, excluding the Director, Department Heads, business Manager, Bookkeeper and Confidential Secretary as set forth in Case Number 0–1518 dated May 31, 1974, and all those subsequently certified.

1.2 This Agreement is applicable to employees of the Pierce County Rural Library District as noted in the classifications of Schedule A (attached . . . in the Contract). [Tacoma, Wash.]

Differences in extensiveness and comprehensiveness of the articles within a contract are primarily local decisions. That is, the New York local apparently proposed and accomplished a more comprehensive clause than did the Tacoma local, which agreed to a recognition clause complete with legal sources but relatively brief and narrow. The Tacoma local may have accomplished some of those points of comprehensiveness elsewhere in their contract or may have experienced a low need for such comprehensiveness. Conceivably, the local wanted it but couldn't get it.

Articles in contracts have been developed from experiences in specific work settings. As such, they are union reactions to conditions from which relief is sought, and in that sense, are themselves explanations of the phenomenon of contract extensiveness.

These articles deal with nondiscrimination:

The Library and the Union do not and shall not discriminate against any staff member or applicant for employment because of race, creed, color, national origin, age, sex, marital status, or political affiliation, with respect to wages, hours, or any terms or conditions of employment, including but not limited to recruitment, employment, appointment, promotion, transfer, termination, and selection for training. [New York]

8.1 The Library and the Union agree that in their service to the public, in their mutual relations, and in all conditions of employment not limited to hiring, promotion, transfer, discharge, evaluation, wages, training, and references written or verbal, they will provide equal opportunity and treatment for all without discrimination and they shall not discriminate against anyone on account of race, color, creed, national origin, sex, sexual orientation, lifestyle, political ideology, past or present union activities, age, marital, or family status; and both parties agree to be in compliance with applicable state and federal laws. The presence or past history of any sensory, mental or physical handicap shall not be a reason for discrimination per se as long as the employee or prospective employee is capable of performing the job. The parties shall take whatever affirmative action that is necessary to accomplish these purposes. They shall ensure that the civil and constitutional rights of employees are not denied or abridged.

8.2 Wherever words denoting gender are used in this Agreement, they are intended to apply equally to either gender.[Tacoma, Wash.]

The New York contract as amended for extension from 1976 included a slight change, adding sexual preference and political beliefs to the groups protected from discrimination. The New York contract, then, protected ten groups; the Tacoma contract identified twelve groups of employees to be specifically protected from discriminatory action. Both articles go beyond the number of groups enumerated in the Civil Rights Act of 1964. All employees should watch the federal judiciary, for court pronouncements in the general realm of affirmative action are being refined as one case after another has made its way to the courts.

These articles deal with management rights and responsibilities:

The Library shall have all customary management responsibilities not otherwise limited by this Agreement, including the exclusive right to determine its services, staffing, and scheduling; the exclusive right to direct and control any and all persons employed by it, and the exclusive right, in accordance with the Library's current regulations, to hire, transfer, promote, demote, discipline, suspend, or discharge any such persons for any cause which, in the judgment of the Library, may affect the efficiency of its operations. Notwithstanding the above, questions concerning the practical impact that decisions on the above matters have on staff members, such as questions of workload or manning, may be dealt with in collective bargaining. [New York]

It is understood and agreed that the Board of Trustees possesses the responsibility to operate the Library system as indicated by state law. The Library Director has been charged by the Board with the responsibility for the orderly and efficient management and control of the Library system. Library rights and responsibilities must be exercised consistent with the provisions of this Agreement and include the following:

1. To utilize the most appropriate, effective and enlightened methods to operate the Library system;
2. To hire, promote, transfer, assign, train, direct the work of and appraise the performance of employees of the Library with due regard to fairness, objectivity, and the dignity of the individual employee;
3. To establish and communicate well-defined rules, regulations and policies which shall be uniformly applied;
4. To suspend, demote, discharge and take other appropritae remedial action;
5. To determine the size and composition of the work force, and to lay off employees in the event of documented lack of work or funds consistent with Article XXV - Layoff and Recall;
6. To determine the methods and means necessary to effectively carry out the mission and goals as determined by the Board of Trustees;
7. As delegated by the Board of Trustees, to do all other acts necessary for the orderly and efficient management and control of the Library (RCW 27.12.210). [Tacoma, Wash.]

As mentioned earlier in this chapter, the words of a contract become very important when misunderstandings or disagreements arise over contract administration. Words become weapons, so to speak. Of the two management rights clauses, swept into contracts as articles, the New York contract appeared to be more restrictive on management than the Tacoma contract, which, once again, referred to the legal basis in state statute. The New York contract kept more operational aspects open or within the possible realm of collective bargaining.

The two contract documents had exactly the same language for the first few sections of the article devoted to union security. Designed to assure exclusive recognition, maintenance of position, adequate income to the union, and so on, union security clauses obviously have much in common from place to place. Still, even such a concern, common to all unions, must be individualized to provide the authority necessary to each specific locale. Those individualized ingredients reinforce the realization that union contracts must reflect a community of interest actually held to be important by the membership. In all, the Tacoma contract had forty-two articles; the New York contract, thirty-one.

A primary area of commonality was in the shared concern for leaves of absence from work, which have come to occupy a sizeable portion of contracts. Some contracts have an article for each type of leave. For example, there may be vacation leave, sick leave, holiday leave, personal leave, terminal leave, leaves with pay, leaves without pay, and so on.

A comprehensive statement on leaves for workers from the employment setting was developed by District Council 37, AFSCME, for citywide bargaining in New York. That statement, over 10,000 words in length, stands as an excellent example from which to understand the public employment conditions that might be proposed by librarians and might have real out-of-pocket costs for any accepting library administration.

Rights to the use of leave generally are attached to longevity. More days of annual vacation leave are available for senior employees, and not only through accrual of unused days from previous years. Table 6.3 illustrates that seniority factor at work.

Presumably, the premise supporting seniority has been that older workers, through the superior performance that comes with job experience, earn more days off. In part, it is tradition, too. Not incidentally, Table 6.3 is an excellent illustration of a major understanding in bargaining. Item "c" in the table reveals the use of gradualism in bargaining. What is most desired may not always be possible of achievement at a given point in time. Agreement is reached on what is possible as a partial improvement, but with a time certain, for phasing in what was the original proposal for improving worker welfare and increasing operating cost. By inclusion for future acceptance, the union wins; by deferral into some future time, management wins. Inasmuch as negotiation is a kind of systematized compromise, the table represents the essence of bargaining.

Contracts must answer variable needs. They must address such worker concerns as salary and job security. They must address more tenuous matters, such as worker dignity. They must not hamper the administration of the library, for decreased services may well mean the alienation of users. They cannot be misleading to concerned parties. Only through negotiations carried out amicably and in good faith, and with precision writing of the document, can contracts emerge which are advantageous to labor and mangement alike.

Table 6.3 **Credit to Annual Leave Allowance**

Category	Monthly accrual rate	Annual leave allowance
a. for employees on staff prior to July 1, 1956	2½ days	27 work days
b. for employees appointed after July 1, 1956		
At the beginning of the 15th year	2½ days	27 work days
At the beginning of the 8th year	2 days + 1 more day at the end of the vacation year	25 work days
Prior to the beginning of the 8th year	1⅔ days	20 work days
c. for new employees hired on or after July 1976: after 6/30/78, (b) applies and this provision (c) shall no longer be applicable	1¼ days	15 work days

SOURCE: "Time and Leave Rules," *Public Employee Press* (New York: District Council #37, AFSCME, AFL-CIO, November 4, 1977), p. 24.

SUMMARY

Librarians who have sought the protection perceived in unions have had two opportunities for unionization: (1) with other employees over a wide spectrum of occupational areas, but all sharing a single employer, such as a county or municipality, and (2) with other librarians or library employees, as the union has been formed within the employment rubric of a single library. Research, which is sparse, does not indicate that either one of the opportunities delivers more advantages than the other. Neither conformation appears to be preferred by librarians in any one section of the nation. For example, each conformation appears on both east and west coasts.

Upon a short history of collective bargaining within the public employment sector, a consensus is beginning to emerge about what subjects are suitable for bargaining and what subjects are reserved as management rights. Among the former are wages, hours, and grievances; among the latter are institutional goal determination, funding levels, and personnel hiring and assignment. For several topics, it is still debatable as to where the prerogative for determination rests. Likewise, it is debatable as to the kind of union affiliation toward which librarians should gravitate as they consider their personal welfare in a professional setting. Conceptually, the authority that has resided in boards and administrators has become diminished, an apparently irreversible trend from within American society, which means that new forms of individualism among librarians are a natural consequence.

Contract clarity calls for careful word selection. When in formation, foresight may properly indicate a need for definition, as a minimum effort to reduce ambiguity and conflict. Public employee contracts are large in number, and some should serve as excellent patterns for later contracts in other locations. Librarians do not have to reinvent the wheel, because contracts for almost all situations can be secured and selected clauses and articles used as patterns. This relieves negotiators in newly collectivized settings of the obligation to design entirely new contracts.

To some extent, union contracts represent a decline in the legitimacy of the established social patterns; the paternalistic, "trust us for your welfare" concept of administrators and public boards is fading. Replacing that concept is the mutually accepted document, delineating the specifics of the work obligation. Little is left to trust and acceptance of traditional seats of power. Contracts are manifestations of assertiveness by individuals. That assertiveness is a new kind of authority, collectively developed within labor unions for government employees, and many librarians are viewing it as personally advantageous.

NOTES

1. Statement by David Beasely, former president of Local 1930, in a personal interview, New York City, May 25, 1978.

2. Bureau of Labor Statistics, *BLS File of State, County and Municipal Collective Bargaining Agreements, Fall 1975* (Washington, D.C.: The Bureau, 1976), p. 13.

3. Ibid., p. 45.

4. Academic Collective Bargaining Information Service, *Scope of Public Sector Bargaining in 14 Selected States* (Washington, D.C.: The Service, January 1977) ERIC ED 132 956, p. 5.

5. Fred Lifton, "Contract Language in Collective Negotiations," in Patrick M. Carlton, ed., *Ground Rules, Contract Language, Grievance and Impasse Resolution* (Reston, Va.: Proceedings of the Collective Negotiations Clinic, 1976), ERIC ED 128 940, p. 41.

6. Ibid.

7. Robert C. O'Reilly, "Living with the Negotiated Contract," paper delivered at Houston, National School Boards Association Convention, March 1977, p. 5.

CONTRACTS, DISPUTES, AND ARBITRATION   7

AGREEMENTS LEAD TO CONTRACTS

The negotiation process leads directly to the bargaining table. There, the representatives of the librarians and the spokesmen for the trustees examine and consider proposals. Counterproposals may be generated. Some proposals will result in mutual acceptance; some will doubtlessly be rejected. The librarians' union must seize the initiative for developing proposals, for they want a contract much more than do the trustees. In the bargaining procedure, a record of agreements should be kept as they occur, even though they might apply only to a part of a single proposal. Each point of agreement should be mutually acknowledged by parties for two reasons: first, it provides a record, should there later occur a lapse of memory by either party; second, it provides evidence to the parties that the bargaining talks are fruitful.

There is such a great distance between reading about performance at the bargaining table and awareness of the reality of the adverse relationships that a reader may not recognize the animosities that occasionally arise as negotiators disagree. The care suggested for details speaks directly to that tension and does much to allay it. The people who go to the negotiating table are important. Neither party should send representatives who are caustic and abrasive, who delight in playing the role of the "flamethrower."

Another concern that must be addressed early is how information will be released to the public. Although press releases issued without the knowledge of the other party may gain some short-range advantages for the negotiators making the releases, they are also destructive of trust and must work as a disadvantage over the long range. Negotiators have power and must be cautious lest they misuse it.

The goal of bargaining is to get a contract. The contract is legitimation for all that preceded it. Stalemate, embarrassment, and disruption of the services of the library cannot be goals for professionals. However, negotiations may tempt both parties toward manipulation of facts and reason, with only a short-range view—"victory" of almost any kind in the negotiating sessions. With protective protocol, the negotiating parties should work around hostilities and disagreements, moving always to points of agreement. Eventually, from all the proposals considered, a set should emerge upon which the negotiators have reached agreement. The bargaining goal may not be as difficult as it might seem at first glance, for bargaining does not start from a zero base. The parties are talking about people already in place in jobs for which there is a need and for which they have been paid. Neither is bargaining at a zero base in terms of knowing what to do and what not to do, for the history of labor relations is a ready source of information. It is reasonable to expect agreements, with a contract to follow. The protocol of bargaining is generally flexible. It may include agreements on the size of each of the negotiating teams, the frequency and length of meetings, publicity limitations, and so on. In those states that legislatively demand that all bargaining sessions be open, some of the protocol is legislatively set. Only a few items should rise to the point of bargaining protocol, and they should rise naturally, as parties for either side feel some need. The point of the protocol is to reduce unpleasant surprises, eliminate public embarrassment, and suppress hostility between the parties at the bargaining table. Protocol should make each negotiator feel more confortable with and more trusting of the negotiators on the other side of the table.

These remarks underscoring the importance of protocol in bargaining are drawn from observations of the labor relations scene over the years, with a candid admission that relationships between government as employer and professional employees is much less authoritarian than it might at first glance appear. The necessity for protocol in library labor relations is only intensified by conditions that could be seen at the end of the 1970s. Library negotiation lacks a long history and does not have a wealth of practice from which mutual trust or expectations can develop. Perhaps a more debilitating feature, adversely affecting all labor relations, has been the effect of inflation, which has led to uncertainty about the future, to uncertainty about the real value of settlements after they were reached, and to a general unease that has motivated many negotiators toward exclusively short-range advantages. Protocol is a stabilizer, and its value increases as the need for stabilization increases.

A majority of the states have statutes governing public employee bargaining, which includes librarians in public libraries and public schools. Contracts including items statutorily forbidden are not enforceable. For example, in a state whose statute mandated that tenure was possible after five years of probation, a contract provision that allowed tenure after three years of probation would be unenforceable if contested. Statutes may stipulate the terms under which contracts may be negotiated, including specific items that may be included or must be excluded, the maximum length of time to be covered, and the format of the document in which the agreements may be recorded as they form the tentative contract. Tentative, because until the agreement reached by negotiators has been submitted to the trustees and ratified by that group and until the agreement has been submitted to the union rank-and-file and ratified by that group, it is not a contract. Upon ratification, the agreement becomes the labor contract that specifies monetary and other compensation for specified services.

The time of agreement ratification is the optimum time for publicity. Negotiators generally agree that privacy is an important part of bargaining, despite advocacy from some quarters for three-party bargaining to include employees, employer, and the public. However, secrecy for public employment contracts cannot bode well for any of the three parties. Fair labor practices abhor fraud and deception, and secrecy might encourage them. Ideally, joint press releases from the library trustees and the library union minimize embarrassment and indicate to citizens generally an appropriate openness in the operation of a service receiving much of its support from taxation.

As the negotiators discuss each proposal, a list of accomplished items begins to materialize. That list constitutes the body of the draft agreement. The following rules should promote agreement development in the negotiations setting of librarians and trustees:

1. The writing of the final draft should be turned to a small, joint sub-committee of the bargaining teams.
2. Final word entries should be timely and available for criticism from both teams.
3. The contract form should clearly provide a space for sign-off by both teams.
4. After endorsement by the teams, outsiders should not be allowed to change the agreement.
5. Language should be examined for vague, ambiguous, or obscure words and the agreement presented to constituencies for adoption.[1]

In one laboratory experiment designed to simulate collective bargaining, it was hypothesized that when negotiators anticipated the entry of neutral third parties with binding powers, the negotiators had a more difficult time, encountering more bargaining difficulties than similar spokesmen facing a neutral third party of little power. Further, it was anticipated that negotiators working with a third party of known reputation would have more difficulty than those facing an unknown third party. The experiment findings have relevance for parties involved in negotiating library contracts.

The study was structured and the negotiators (spokesmen) were manipulated into certain beliefs and expectations. Observations and reports provided behavioral data for statistical analysis; a few generalizations could be made:

1. Representatives who faced a third party with binding power took more time to reach agreement.
2. Spokesmen facing third parties of unfavorable reputation were not much influenced fluenced by the extent of the power.
3. Negotiators who faced third parties of high power
   a. felt great pressure in their task
   b. had more difficulty coming to settlement.

There were consistent interplay patterns between the power and reputation of the third party, especially if the third party had high power. The data suggested that negotiators may have a tendency to let the high power neutral "take over," which freed the negotiators from the responsibility for compromise. Further, these data suggested that when negotiators faced neutrals of high power and favorable reputation, they took longer in deliberations, evidently an effort to impress the neutral who was held in high esteem.[2] As it turned out, the reputation of the neutral third party, more than his statutory power, influenced the performance of the negotiators.

CURRENT LABOR RELATIONS IN LIBRARIES

The state of the art of collective bargaining in libraries can be seen by way of an impressionistic description of pertinent conditions across the national scene of labor relations in libraries. These conditions have been developed by the craftsmen and strategists at the negotiations table. Some of that impression is revealed from the following items from contracts and court decisions.

In 1978, the Library of Congress (LC) and two locals of the AFSCME accepted a two-year contract that included two points strongly sought by employees: (1) establishment of a grievance procedure and (2) participation with management in employee hirings and library reorganization. The contract included most of the professional and nonprofessional employees of the LC. It did not require union membership of employees. Although the union was unsuccessful in its bid for a provision under which employees could grieve nonselection for promotion, a grievance procedure was established addressing such matters as interpretation or application of the contract, violations of LC regulations, and, generally, dissatisfactions of employees. In cases of disputes brought forward as grievances in which settlement attempts fail, the cases will be submitted to arbitration. Upon the union's demand, the library finally agreed that in cases of arbitration the losing party must bear the costs.

In the area of personnel management, the library agreed to new grada-
tions in personnel evaluation, with those ratings used as a basis for promotion. Library reorganization cannot occur during the term of the contract,
except upon notification to the union at least thirty days in advance of the
planned reorganization, with that period to be used for negotiation of the
impact upon personnel. In addition, new candidates for most jobs will be
rated by a screening panel consisting of two management officials and one
union employee, with actual hiring normally to occur from a list submitted
by the panel.[3]

Disputes going beyond arbitration may be resolved in courts. These cases
influence the settlement of similar disputes. The Iowa Supreme Court ruled
in *Spilman* v. *Davis County Schools* (1977), regarding the employment
status of an employee who, though certified as a school librarian, was hired
as a library clerk. After one year, Spilman was orally informed that she
would not be rehired for the approaching year. She sued for reinstatement
upon the basis that certified employees of schools may be dismissed only for
cause and by the procedures set forward in state statutes. It was found that
she was hired specifically as a library clerk, was paid less than the basic
teacher's scale, and received a contract different from that for all (other) certified personnel. The court ruled against her, stipulating that despite the fact
that she was certified as a teacher and a librarian, her employment was as a
clerk and that statutory protections were intended for functions, not for certificates.

In *Hollenbaugh and Philburn* v. *Carnegie* (Connesville, PA) *Free Library*
(1978), a federal circuit court ruled upon a question of personnel management extending beyond the confines of employment. The case involved two
public employees, both of whom were fired from the library when he, a
married man, moved in with her after she became pregnant with his child.
The library board admitted that the two were reasonably competent in their
jobs but stated that not to fire the couple would have made it appear that
the board approved of open adultery and parenthood outside of marriage.
Further, the board stated that this publicly known arrangement impaired
the effectiveness of both employees on the job. The case, appealed to the
Supreme Court, was declined even though two justices stated an interest in
it and raised some question about the circuit court decision. In any event,
within the Third Judicial Circuit (at least) came confirmation of a level of
personnel control by library trustees that can be predicted to have bearing
upon items considered for contracts in the future.

It is the intent of this book to be informative. It is not intended to be a
polemic or advocacy, and only mildly as advisory. The reader must understand that the basic intent is to portray conditions of balance between "labor
and management" in libraries, not to devise or recommend conditions under
which labor would gain ascendancy over management or vice versa. On the

other hand, it is surely true that when parties meet to contest for power and money, discernible advantages accrue to the best-informed party, for that party has the highest potential for persuasion to the acceptance of new ideas. Informed parties are the best guarantee that a contract will not be the result of a bad day's work.

FACTORS INFLUENCING THE FUNDING OF CONTRACTS

The pervasive model for Ameican labor relations was developed in the private sector of the economy. After all, unionization of large numbers of public employees had not occurred in the first half of the twentieth century. In the haste to find a workable model that would carry the burden of librarians negotiating with library trustees, the private economy model was available, visible, had a reasonable sucess record, and was adopted—and perhaps too little adapted. Be that as it may, librarians in public employment settings are involved in union activities borrowed largely from the private sector.

The preponderant factor in private employment collective bargaining has been money. Production costs, sales, and profit considerations have provided a base from which to calculate the costs of a contract. Companies negotiating contracts have been able to apply certain projections, compare with competitors, and determine their likelihood of success under any given contracts. In private enterprise, revenues must be received sufficient to pay the workers, purchase raw materials for production, replace deteriorating plant and equipment, pay dividends to stockholders, and so on. Those costs can be calculated and modeled into the future, and the company's administrators, in private planning complementing the bargaining sessions, may know the prospects for the company's continuation, be they good or bad. Such items, all parts of the money factor, lack direct application in public employment, which is not to say that they are irrelevant as general considerations.

Public schools, and to an only slightly lesser extent public libraries, are labor intensive, with labor costs typically at about 70 to 75 percent, as a minimum. They do not have many of the costs found in private settings. Likewise, private business organizations spend their money in ways they have found necessary. For example, typical U.S. corporations allocate about four times as much money to emloyee compensation as is allocated for new buildings and equipment.[4] Observing the fiscal operation of schools and libraries and the replacement rate for buildings and equipment leads to the conclusion that public agencies spend a far smaller proportion on buildings and equipment.

Library unions must recognize that a bargaining model has been borrowed and that it is something less than a precise fit. Like private employers, libraries must recruit employees from the available manpower pool. The library must offer enough compensation for the work that prospects will be attracted. The job must appear to have desirable long-range benefits. For all the similarities, it is surely apparent that the economic base undergirding private enterprise is substantially different from the area of government employment.

Other factors merit mention as they provide a unique impact on library negotiations:

1. the political nature of public employment
2. service mandates given to local agencies by the state and federal governments
3. the general economic health of the nation and the economic health of the specific locality
4. the availability or lack of local and comparative data that could be used to support or refute specific proposals at the bargaining table
5. the power dynamics of public employee unions

Another factor has been selected for more extensive treatment here because it has potential for use by both librarians and trustees, as the service of the library is considered. With more than 220 million Americans to serve, a huge potential library clientele is in existence. Service, as represented in reported circulation data, reference usage, and so on does not reveal that libraries, taken as a whole, are attracting their "fair share" of community patronage. In that swelling population is a new mix of people. Their age is changing, their locations are changing, their racial composition is changing. It may be that libraries must take yet another page from the book of private enterprise and rethink library service. How should it be changed to attract and serve a new clientele? An example of such a clientele can be seen in the initial results of some of the competency testing for high school graduation. Florida's Student Assessment Test represents the first statewide effort in testing for minimum competencies. Rejecting the extreme and simplistic contentions of racial supremacy and test bias, it is true that in two administrations black secondary students have fared badly. In 1977, the failure rate was 77 percent; in 1978, 61 percent of that group failed. As late as the 1950s, only a small proportion of eligible blacks stayed in secondary schools with graduation as a goal. By the latter 1970s, that proportion, nationwide, was nearly the same as for white students. The Florida experience is an indicator of education that "did not take," of education that did not yield cognitive intellectual development at minimal levels, for many students. Considerations of the functions of libraries surely point to some new opportunities in service to just such population segments—growing segments, at that. Librarians in public libraries and librarians in public schools may see this as an opportunity for linkage through which a specified service, an obviously valuable service, may be delivered.

Long neglected by many public service agencies, attention to unique shifts in population might so enhance the attractiveness of libraries that renewed support would materialize. Such support is needed to fund the contracts toward which library unions are striving and which, in light of the characteristically modest salaries of librarians, would move that occupational group closer to some sort of economic equity.

Compensation has always held center stage in the negotiations process, and although many conditions of work are settled through bargaining, money is central. One way to enhance understanding of equity is through interoccupational comparison of similar groups. In a study conducted by the National Education Association, Table 7.1, a comparison of mean salaries of different certificated employee groups was extended through time, allowing for historical comparisons. The table revealed that, through the years and within the four groups, compensation to public school librarians was at a higher level than that for teachers.

Table 7.1 **Mean Salaries of Public School Employees**

Year	Teachers	Librarians	Counselors	Nurses
1962–63	$ 5,747	$ 6,145	$ 7,390	$5,650
1964–65	6,222	6,721	8,058	6,215
1966–67	6,905	7,006	8,630	6,664
1968–69	7,841	8,400	10,279	7,292
1970–71	9,218	9,806	12,051	8,634
1972–73	10,254	10,566	12,817	9,571

SOURCE: "Government Employee Relations Report" (Washington: D.C.: Bureau of National Affairs, 1975), pp. 71, 1076.

Although there are a very limited number of such reports available, four annual reports of metropolitan libraries were secured for purposes of comparative analysis. They were:

Dallas. Municipal Library Advisory Board, Annual Report, 1974–75

Denver. Public Library Annual Report, 1975

Memphis-Shelby County Public Library and Information Center Financial Statements and Auditors' Report [for year ended] 6/30/75

Pittsburgh. Carnegie Library 80th Annual Report to the Board of Trustees, 1975

That analysis revealed incomparabilties due to the fact that budget line items differed in what was included or excluded from one place to another. For example, the library budgets in Denver and Pittsburgh for their 1975 fiscal years were each within a few dollars of $5,450,000. Yet, they lacked commonality in budget line titles, except for personnel payroll and books.

Some large public libraries are city-county libraries, which also distracted from efforts at comparison because some annual reports included fiscal sub-programs for specific political subdivisions without adequate documentation from which a researcher could trace the costs actually charged against the specific line items. As one example, the Carnegie Library of Pittsburgh provided some but not all services to Allegheny County. It was not possible to discern whether that budget line item devoted to book purchases included or excluded the costs of books, subscriptions, and possibly some salary costs of special programs for the county.

Nonetheless, two generalizations pertinent to bargaining can be made about the costs and operations of public libraries. First, they are labor intensive, quite comparable to public schools in that about 65 to 75 percent of the budget was expended for personnel costs—a fact alluded to earlier in a different setting. To this cost for personnel were charged such efforts as the professional reference services, inasmuch as that commodity consisted of librarians' time. Second, the inventory enhancement aspect of the budget accounted for about 12 to 18 percent when it included books, periodicals, microforms, and so on that were purchased.

CONTRACT ADMINISTRATION

Contracts are agreements entered into by competent parties to perform mutually beneficial acts. A service or thing described in some detail may be promised for money, and that in a specific amount. Traditionally, that description was applied to dealings between two citizens, but negotiated contracts represent an expansion of that concept. Contracts are for specified periods of time. Theoretically, they may be written or oral; however, in some states, oral contracts in public employment settings have no standing and written contracts are mandatory. Negotiated contracts for groups must be written. Even the form itself may be a condition of the contract. As a practical matter an unwritten contract is risky, and misunderstanding is an almost certain circumstance over extended periods of time.

Rules of work exist in all libraries. All employees must be apprised of the rules of the library, which traditionally were unilaterally developed by the trustees and found expression in policy statements and job descriptions. This was a reserved authority of management, and continuity of policy within the closed circle of board-administration was the prevailing condition under which library employees worked prior to collective bargaining.

Now, in many instances, contracts have superseded or incorporated much of what was policy earlier.

In review, when an agreement is ratified by both parties, it becomes a contract; however, this is a collectively applied contract, not a document issued to each individual employee. Collectively negotiated contracts have an inclusiveness, incorporating specifics of work by described functions or job titles and also including the policies, rules, and regulations of the board of trustees.

Contracts that apply to all the workers represented by the union have one other major difference worthy of note. In the circumstance that allowed an individual worker to accept or reject a tendered contract, there existed an option lacking in collective bargaining. Yet even that assertion merits qualification. In collective bargaining, the press for a contract originates with employees. Private employers may resist that press, if they wish, through the lockout of employees or through the even more drastic techniques of moving or closing the business. Public employers have much less leeway. In the case of the *United Steelworkers* v. *Warrior and Gulf Navigation Company* (1960) the Supreme Court noted the decreased degrees of freedom when collectively bargained contracts were at issue.

> When most parties enter into contractual relationships, they do so voluntarily, in the sense that there is not real compulsion to deal with one another, as opposed to dealing with other parties. This is not true of labor agreements. The choice is generally not between entering or refusing to enter into a relationship, for that in all probability pre-exists the negotiation. Rather, it is between having that relationship governed by an agreed-upon rule of law or leaving each and every matter subject to a temporary resolution dependent solely upon the relative strength, at any given moment of the contending forces.

Although most public employers are vocal in their opposition, the characteristic of article accrual in contracts seems to be universal. Employees are quite unwilling to return to an utterly fresh starting point when new contract talks are initiated. In the sense that continuity of service is a valuable part of the total function of a library and with the experience background that new contracts are sometimes late in coming, accrual and continuity may be factors that go together and sometimes work to the benefit of "management," the library administrators and trustees. If, for example, a library union contract came to its termination time and a new contract had not been developed, how could services be determined, salaries paid, and service continued, except by the past practice of accrual? In a way, the accrual factor provides a little more flexibility to the negotiating process. Learning occurs through preparation, implementation, and analysis and acts as a barrier against unfair advantage by either employers or employees. Accrual, when it represents what has been learned through experience in labor relations, must be a positive factor in maintaining quality of work.

The government employers are typically in a wait-and-see posture when new contracts become the topic. In most states, if employees do not seize the initiative and petition for bargaining, the board is free to ignore any employee group and operate in a more traditional authoritarian manner, telling employees what their jobs and compenation will be. Lulled into that frame of mind, boards too frequently ignore their opportunities to seize the intiative when considering how the library should operate. The development of operational goals, both short-term and long-term, should allow any board to also be an assertive, originating party in negotiations. To the extent that negotiated contracts are seen to be in contradiction to the goals of a board of trustees, the approach of a new "negotiations season" should be seen as an opportunity for remedy and advancement. This certainly does not mean that every goal that might be developed for a library should be negotiated. Many goals will be incorporated into policy as a unilateral act by the administration. The placement into contract or into policy should not be accidental, should be done after thoughtful consideration by trustees and administration, and should not produce unpleasant surprises. Wherever goals or other items should be articulated, planning and preparation are essential, lest the board of trustees be subverted in negotiations. The balance of competing interests represented by the trustees and the library employees will be articulated in the contract.

The services of some public employees are of urgent need, and that need is unequal to other similar employees. Some of those needs are so fundamental that they nearly escape notice. A city needs streets and street maintenance crews; a city needs buildings and the police and firefighters who protect them. A city needs librarians—but how badly? How strong a case can be made for library services? Librarianship is not a vital service in the sense that a firefighter performs a critical incident service. Despite such differences in the urgency of job performance, statutes frequently address the conditions of a like class of workers, the employees of political subdivisions. For the states that, by law, have made final and binding arbitration applicable to all public employees, such laws are as much a part of each contract as if an actual article in the contract.

In the same way that every contract incorporates the policies, rules, and regulations of the governing board, each public employment contract also incorporates and accepts the statutes of the state. When omitted as specific parts of the contract, it only means that they do not have to be incorporated; however, they apply.

Contracts have historically been made to get the most for the least. As both parties enter negotiations with that mind-set, neither is likely to be well satisfied by the contract. The same viewpoint prevails in private dealings of all sorts, when sellers and buyers would each like to get more for less. This unharmonious condition cannot be altered, given the nature of things. It applies to contracts developed by and for libraries, and it must mean that disputes over the meanings of a contract will arise, despite the best efforts of the negotiators to address all foreseeable conditions. Candid recognition that disputes will come should not decrease the enthusiasm at the negotiation table to anticipate and allay, in advance; nor should the disputes that arise lead an observer to conclude that the contract itself did not support good labor relations. Anyway, because negotiations recur periodically, there is a built-in, self-correcting aspect.

DISPUTES AND GRIEVANCES

Who has seen the library where working conditions were so perfect that no one grumbled? Who has seen the library where the workers were so productive that the administrator never criticized? Who has seen the library where the director's decisions were always accepted by the librarians as fair and unbiased? No such places exist. Disputes arise. Some are real and some are not, but any of them, if not resolved, may come to be labeled as grievances. As general guidelines in dispute resolutions, libraries should stipulate through policy or contract the following structures as arrangements to encourage the settlement of grievances within the library.

1. Informal procedures: usually no more than a provision that the grievant and the supervisor attempt to resolve the problem before an appeal to a formal mechanism;
2. Written complaint: a provision that, when informal procedures have failed to resolve a conflict, the grievant will indicate in writing to an appropriate person or committee the nature of the complaint, the evidence on which it is based, and the redress sought;
3. Grievance Committee: this term . . . refers to an individual, a committee, or a combination of the two, whose functions are to consider the written complaint and to resolve it or refer it to where it can be resolved;
4. Hearing Committee: this term refers to a committee especially established to consider a particular case in which it is mandatory or desirable to provide for a quasi-judicial process, and where major policy issues or severe sanctions (e.g., dismissal) are involved.[6]

It can be seen that the structure is arranged from the simpler to the more complex. When grievances are not resolved within the organization, the services of neutral parties can be secured from such agencies as the American Arbitration Association or a state mediation board. There is cost attached to grievance resolution within an organization, for at minimum it must involve time lost from assigned jobs. If outsiders are brought in to assist, out-of-pocket costs develop. Characteristically, for libraries those costs would be assessed to both the administration and the employees, and about equally.

Grievances have to do with perceived inequities. Generally, they involve individuals, although, given the costs of grievance resolution, all the members of an organization might hope that resolution would have wide application.

In contemplation of disputes at work, employees must take care that they do not place themselves in a position of insubordination. For example, if a supervisor faces a manpower shortage in some area of the library and directs another librarian into that area, it may be that the directive originated in the supervisor's interpretation of the management rights article of the contract. On the other hand, the directive may be viewed by the librarian as usurpation by the supervisor and disregard for the employee classification in the contract. To reject the directive would place the employee in a position of insubordination, which might be grounds for reprimand, demotion, or dismissal. The employee must accept the directive, do the assigned work, and lodge a grievance through established procedure to dispute the suitability of the order. The four-part structure just given could then be brought into play.

Contracts can never be so specific as to attend all disputes that in hindsight are identifiable but were not addressed by the negotiators. Although the inadequacy of oral contracts has been discussed, every contract, as it becomes the operational guide for the work setting, must have an element of trust. Unfortunately, one of the pervading characteristics of all kinds of hired labor has been distrust. Workers distrust the employer, and the employer distrusts the workers. Pangs of insecurity, inadequacy, and distrust are not strangers to negotiations or to employers working under contracts—or to library directors administering a contract.

Yellow-dog contracts were made illegal by federal legislation of the 1930s. As a condition of employment, workers were given no choice but to sign a pledge that if they were ever involved in union organizing activities, dismissal would be automatic. Based upon intimidation, those contracts denied workers the Constitutional freedom of association. Fear and distrust were obviously strong parts of such work settings. Although now past, those contracts have had a historical carryover, even into public employment, that mitigates against openness and candor, both of which must somehow be recaptured, for both are essential for dispute settlement.

Even though there are several large libraries in the nation, the prevalent library is a small organization. Hundreds of libraries have fewer than fifty employees in the whole organization. The distance from the director of the library to the most junior professional is not great. Small size coupled to the recency with which libraries have entered the unionizing arena provides only a partial explanation of the hostile attitude administrators have toward grievances. The remainder of the explanation must come from three other sources: (1) employees who file grievances just to make trouble for the administration, (2) administrators expecting more workplace stability from a contract than it can deliver, and (3) inept administration.

As all these explanations may hold, it is unreasonable to focus upon bad contract management by the administrator as the source of grievances. Yet trustees hold the administrator responsible for the management of the library; even though it is a much too severe view to jump to the conclusion that grievances equal mismanagement, it happens. That is one indication of the inadequacies of a personnel evaluation system. Such attitudes diminish receptivity to the fact of grievances by many library administrators, although the grievance procedure must have openness if it is to function as an attitude adjustment safety valve.

Disputes may be of many kinds. To air them, employees must see that they run no professional risk in raising such issues. Only through a conscious effort can such an environment be developed. Employees can contribute to the development of that environment, which will redound to their benefit, by strict adherence to three simple rules.

1. Employees should not contrive problems or constantly hunt for situations only because they want to raise grievances.
2. Employees should not hesitate to grieve any problem in the work setting that diminishes, personally or professionally, any employee.
3. Employees should strive for grievance settlement at an informal level, quickly, quietly, and with the least disturbance possible.

If a bad intent has been the motivation for the grievance, if rancor and malice support the grievance, it will be destructive of good faith between the librarians and the administration. Disputes must be raised with the intent of settlement and with no subterfuge.

Observations of employment settings have revealed that some issues arise as grievances more often than others. Major sources of issues have been ". . . the recruitment and selection of all employees, their assignment, working conditions, promotions, salaries, layoffs, terminations, retirement and fringe benefits."[7] Four general issues have emerged as most grievable in public schools as faculty, including librarians and media center directors have filed for formal hearings: (1) nonrenewal of contracts for probationary teachers, (2) termination of tenured teachers, (3) contract termination prior to its term, and (4) misunderstandings of entitlements about the several kinds of personnel leave programs. The issues are uneven, from state to state. In some states, probationary personnel may be released for no stipulated cause, depending upon the wording of the contract, statutes of the state, and rulings of the public employment relations board of the state. Similarly, some political subdivisions have seized the initiative in reducing misunderstandings of personnel leave by collapsing several different kinds into a single category of personal leave. Not incidentally, bearing upon the issue of generalized personnel leaves was the passage in 1978 of P.L. 95–555, which denied to any employer the right to discriminate against pregnant females, effective April 29, 1979.

As especially complex and troublesome grievances may eventually be referred to an outside, neutral party for arbitration, a reasonable target would be an earlier and cheaper settlement. Some contracts contain rather comprehensive statements on disputes and grievance procedures. One such statement can be found in the contract for the Lincoln (NE) Public Schools. In an introductory statement that spoke of good morale contributing to job performance and designed to clarify the intent of the contract clauses dealing with grievances, a grievance was defined as follows:

> Grievance shall mean a claim by one or more employees of a violation, a misapplication or misinterpretation of the state statutes, board policies, administrative directives or regulations under which such employees work, specifying that which is claimed to be violated and the specifics of such violation. The term "grievance" shall not apply to any matter for which (1) the method of review is prescribed by law, or (2) the Board of Education is without authority to act.
>
> Should a teacher have a claim based upon an event or condition which affects the teacher's welfare or morale, but may not be processed under the above definition, the teacher shall have the right to use normal administrative channels to solve the problem. This process shall commence with a conference with the teacher's immediate supervisor.[8]

A contract whose terms are well defined and in which grievance procedures are mutually understood will have done much to set a tone where grievances become that safety valve needed to smooth over the rough spots of contract administration. Such arise even where good labor relations prevail. The terms of the Lincoln Public Schools contract could be used in public library settings as well. As mentioned earlier, a librarian may not refuse a directive from an administrator just because, for example, it may be perceived as some sort of misapplication, lest the librarian be identified as insubordinate. Despite the unpleasantness, refusal would show short-sightedness. However, in a dispute setting, the aggrieved librarian has the opportunity later to seek redress through a grievance procedure. The mere existence of the procedure tends to halt repetitions of maladministration.

CASES AT ARBITRATION

From among the many grievances that rise to arbitration annually from within libraries, six have been selected from the files of the American Arbitration Association. They portray the kind of disputes in which librarians and library union officials become involved. Timeliness in pursing a grievance cannot be disregarded; abuse of latitude in the work setting may be reason for dismissal. Several other areas of personnel management are involved in this first set of six cases, devoted to public libraries.

Local 1321 AFSCME and Queens Borough Public Library LAIG 658 (1972)

A librarian received a call to jury duty. He gave that notice to his supervisor. During the week of jury duty, he had been scheduled to work M-T-W-Sat-Sun, with Thursday and Friday off. He served on the jury from Monday through Friday and turned in his jury pay, including that for Thursday and Friday. He was paid in regular fashion by the library, but it was insisted that he work Saturday and Sunday, as in the original schedule; he worked seven consecutive days.

He contended that his schedule should have been changed to coincide with the jury duty, which would have made Saturday and Sunday overtime work. The library's policy covered leave with pay for jury duty. Testimony about previous situations and in comparable settings revealed conflicts in operating procedure about rescheduling. There was a paucity of similar circumstances and such procedural irregularity that the arbitrator decided no discernible past practice could be used as a reference point.

Supervisory discretion dictated the need to assess the manpower situation, library usage patterns, and the effect of the jury service absence on other employees. Rescheduling would have compelled another employee to work Saturday and Sunday to accommodate the relatively higher use rate of those days, the arbiter observed.

The grievance was denied.

City of Boston Library Department and AFSCME Local 1526 LAIG 2195 (1978)

An employee who was a member of the Association Executive Board had been told, specifically, that grievances had to be processed during his break periods. Yet, he took time off to process a fellow employee's grievance, leaving his work area in the face of a direct order not to do so. The contract stipulated that although the library was liable to provide reasonable time for processing grievances, no employee could absent himself from his work station and thereby hamper the "operating needs" of the library.

The arbitrator noted the contract; he also noted the employee's violation of the established labor relations practice of obey now and grieve later, and then upheld the library administration as it disciplined the worker by docking his pay in the amount of time he took off from work. That is, inasmuch as the employee chose to be insubordinate, the library's action was held to be reasonable, and the grievance was denied.

Local 1930 AFSCME and New York Public Library LAIG 620 (1972)

As a consequence of a service review of a librarian (also serving as president of the library's union) in which the work quality level was questioned, this grievance was initiated. It asked that the questioned personnel evaluation be expunged from the record.

The grievant noted that the review was extraordinary, not conducted according to the policy of the library and timed to occur when he was deeply involved in negotiating a new contract. He produced a memo from the director of the library to his division chief, directing the division chief to grant requests to the union president for time off to work on union business. Even after that, the grievant, as union president, after submitting a leave request saw it torn up in anger by the person who, shortly after, did the negative service review.

The arbitrator recognized three questions:

1. Was the timing of the service review motivated by anti-union bias and an attempt to intimidate the grievant in carrying out his functions as Union president?
2. Was there a violation of the library's own procedure in rendering the service review? If so (was this) an attempt to intimidate the grievant?
3. Was the contested service review inconsistent with other reviews and unsupportable by the record?

In conclusion, the arbitrator decided that the review was unduly influenced by the grievant's functioning in union matters and ordered the review expunged from the personnel record.

District Council 37 and Local 1930, AFSCME and NYPL LAIG 195 (1971)

In the latter 1960s the St. George Branch Library suffered extensive vandalism and harassment of staff and public alike. The perpetrators were mainly teenagers who were dropouts or truants from nearby high schools. During cold weather, they came to the library; between December 1969 and April 1970 the police were called fifty times. The public and staff were abused, threatened, and intimidated. There were no male librarians on the St. George staff.

The staff got informal support through the library administration, which assigned a private investigator to assist. The assistant librarian successfully brought criminal and juvenile charges against a number of individuals and spent time appearing in court against them. She was threatened by some, but the rate and intensity of vandalism dropped markedly.

The union asked for protection and safety in the workplace. The library management replied that it wasn't in the contract or in the budget. The arbitrator ruled that it was an implicit management obligation that did not need to be part of the contract. He also observed, however, that the rate of vandalism had dropped so substantially that it appeared that the branch was, once again, a reasonably safe workplace. Therefore, he concluded that the library had failed, in 1969/70, to provide a safe workplace but provided no other relief for the grievant.

District Council 37 AFSCME and Queens Borough Library LAIG 35

Over a period of five years, the grievant had worked in several branches of the Queens Library and had received favorable personnel evaluations. The library policy stipulated that in personnel evaluation, "Comments will cite specific examples to support positive and negative aspects of ratings."

In March 1969, the grievant was rated "average or good." He was shown the rating and asked to write any comments upon it he desired, and he did so in a "constructive and sophisticated manner." A regional librarian changed that rating to "weak average." A department head changed that rating to "marginal average" and called for another rating. The terms lacked standard definitions. That grievant was not shown those later ratings, and no specific examples were cited.

In July 1969, the second rating was conducted, and the grievant was placed on special probation, to be reevaluated in September and November. He was told that if either of the reevaluations were "below average" he would be immediately terminated.

The arbitrator concluded that the library violated its own rules and procedures and thereby developed the ratings through which the grievant was placed on probation. It was ordered that the service rating reports of March and July and the letter of probation should be removed from the personnel files.

District Council 37 AFSCME and NYPL LAIG 24 (1970)

This controversy involved some members of the cataloging staff at a time when the temperature humidity indicator (THI) exceeded the upper limit stipulated in the union contract (THI = 80). The union contended that, with the THI at 80.6, the library was required to operate on a skeleton staff, releasing all others on compensated leave. The library contended that since the particular catalog staffers worked neither in a branch nor in the Central Building but were in still another facility, they were excluded from that aspect of the contract. In that facility, the airconditioning failed to function and the THI was 80.6 in May of 1970.

The agreement included allusions to facilities of the library that were air-conditioned. However, the arbitrator would not accept the argument that any facility having airconditioning, even though not functioning, was exempt from the THI clause.

On the day in question, after discussions of the high THI by a steward with a supervisor, the employees stayed until 10:00 A.M., waiting to see if the airconditioner would be fixed. As they departed, they were told they would be considered on annual leave. Were they on annual leave, or were they on leave under the contract's THI clause, for which they deserved compensation?

The arbitrator ruled that the leave was as per the contract and compensable and that the library owed money for five and one-half hours to each of the cataloging staff. The library was ordered to re-credit the annual leave time.

The set of six cases from library disputes is not a large group. Examination of the American Arbitration Association records revealed that a very small number of cases had been filed with the AAA publications division. Comments from within AAA confirmed that finding and also revealed that, primarily, this small number of arbitrated cases on file was a consequence of a strong, explicit preference by the library unions in the New York area.[9] In a way, this was a contradiction to the general condition of public sector arbitration as an increasingly popular method for the resolution of disputes. In 1970, public sector arbitration represented about 5 percent of the total effort of the American Arbitration Association. In 1977, it was about 50 percent.[10]

The following cases comprise another set. This set originated in school settings and are school library related. The preceding set of cases were abstracted in the AAA publication, *Labor Arbitration in Government*. The following set came from cases abstracted in a companion publication, *Arbitration in Schools* (AIS). In the second set are ten cases, with citations and a title for each. Only two of the cases have been presented at length.

Common School #16 (Sussex, WI) and Hamilton Education Association 65-AIS-5, "The Library As a Study Hall"

On short notice, two industrial arts teachers were absent. Those students were assigned to a study hall in the library to be supervised by the librarian. The principal offered to close the library to all but the industrial arts students, who at no time numbered more than thirty-four. The librarian declined, wanting the library open to all students. The library was never filled to capacity. The librarian did not consent to the student assignment and filed a grievance alleging violation of local policy on load.

The arbitrator ruled that the policy language was ambiguous and that librarians were teachers, in the broad sense. An overload for one day was deemed insignificant.

Longmeadow (MA) School Committee and Longmeadow Education Association 60-AIS-19, "A Dependency Allowance for a Librarian"

The grievant, a librarian, was denied a dependency allowance. The contract allowed a dependency allowance, $250 for each major and $150 for each minor dependent. Dependency was defined as IRS registration of declared dependents and head of household. The grievant had three children and an employed husband. The arbitrator ruled in favor of the grievant and directed payment of the dependency allowance.

Brown University (RI) and SEIU Local 134 59-AIS-8, "Status of a Student Library Assistant"

A dispute arose in Brown University, a private institution. The hearing was in accord with the negotiated agreement. As a student employee working full time in the summer and part time in the school year, the grievant was not a member of the bargaining unit. He dropped out of school and became a full-time library assistant. Then, he once again registered to be a full-time student and sought to have his hours reduced to 15 hours per week. He did not resign. Contractual revision and development included definitions of the category of student employee. As a full-time employee, he gained seniority, within contract definitions. He was awarded damages by the arbitrator.

School and Weedsport (NY) Teachers Association 92-AIS-14, "Appropriate Duties for Library Aides"

The question revolved about use by the district of library aides to perform library teaching duties. Literally, this was a contest between the association's drive to protect positions against the district's desire to maintain manpower flexibility and low operational costs. Resolution turned upon the application of regulations established by the State Department of Education—in this case, treating of tasks to which noncertificated personnel may be assigned. Those included (1) managing records, materials, and equipment; (2) attending to the physical needs of children; and (3) supervising children as directed to by teachers and when teachers are present. The ruling was that "aides may not conduct any kind of planned program for children in the library, as this would enter into the realms of teaching." The award was to the association.

Hillsborough (NJ) Board of Education and Education Association 90-AIS-23, "Abolishing and Creating Positions"

A negotiated agreement was the reference point to determine if the board was in violation when it abolished a library aide position, a position given limited coverage in the contract. This library aide had worked for eighteen years in the system and managed a middle school library independent of a certificated librarian. When a librarian was hired, the aide position was abolished and a new position, assistant, created. (The pay difference was downward, from $6,800 to $4,800.) The association contended that there was no real change in jobs, but only a title change. The arbitrator ruled that real change occurred and that the board was within its rights in the treatment of nontenured employees.

Sparta (MI) Schools and Sparta Education Association 90-AIS-20, "Personnel Types Included in Contracts"

Should ten-month librarians be expected to work on days when ten-month teachers are not required to work? The contract was examined for precise definitions of teaching faculty and nonteaching faculty, and librarians were listed in the second category. The contract also spoke at length on the professional obligation, locating it on the calendar, and including a stipulation that all employees have to recognize their obligation in their work area. The grievance was sustained, upon the limiting clauses of the contract.

San Francisco Unified Schools and S F Federation of Teachers 71-AIS-11, "Librarians and On-the-Job Preparation Times"

The question: Shall counsellors and/or librarians be allowed a preparation period, and may they be required to work a total of 34 hours per week? Board policy, memoranda, and court decisions were reviewed as part of the pertinent evidence. A tenured librarian received a directive that her work week would be 35 hours, at least six hours per day, "plus lunch periods with no preparation periods." The contract clause stated, "We agree in principle that a curriculum preparation period will be available to every teacher K-12. The Superintendent agrees that the necessary funds will be included in the preliminary budget for consideration at that time." The teacher's representative testified that teacher, as used herein, referred to any certificated employee who was not an administrator or supervisor. Decision: (1) Counsellors and librarians were entitled to a daily preparation period, and (2) they could be required (as per board policy) to work 35 hours per week.

Cumberland (RI) Schools and Cumberland Teachers Association 95-AIS-8, "Librarians as Student Supervisors"

Did the school violate the agreement when they increased noninstructional duties for a librarian in 1977? In ten years with the district, this librarian had never been assigned to hallway or recess supervisory duties. A change in the number of pupil lunch periods called for adjustment of the schedule of certificated personnel in the building, including the librarian. After examining the pertinent articles of the contract and past practice, the arbitrator concluded that the reassignment was in violation and prohibited the school from any other such assignments for the duration of the contract, except by mutual agreement.

Middletown (OH) City Schools and Middletown Teachers Association 99-AIS-19, "Librarians and Planning Time"

The negotiated agreement provided that classroom teachers should have one planning period for each day of school. Should certificated librarians, a category also included in the agreement, also have one planning period per day? Even though they do not teach classes, grade papers, or meet with parents, the arbitrator decided that they were entitled to the same rights and obligations as classroom teachers because they were included in the negotiated contract. Moreover, it was stipulated that the librarians' settlement could not be satisfied by designating the teacher work days, before and during the pupil attendance year, as preparation time (which would have been an equivalent of 176 planning periods). Although librarians had, in a contractual supplement, provision for additional work times, this supplement in no way detracted from their general rights and entitlement found in the main body of the agreement.

However, in this particular instance, a librarian had demanded the planning period upon one day's notice. The board was upheld in denying such a short-notice request because it would have denied access to the library to some teachers and students. There was no suitable local public library that could have been used as an alternative by either teachers or students. To resolve the dilemma, the arbitrator directed that planning periods should be scheduled one semester in advance. Necessary exceptions to that schedule should be made with one week's notice, protecting the rights of students and teachers in their anticipated use of the library.

Sergeant Bluff-Luton (IA) Education Association and SB-L Schools, unpublished AAA decison, 1978, "Should A-V Directors Get Extra Pay?"

Several events occurred at about the same time. The school hired a new librarian, moved into a new school building, and signed a first-time master contract. Although this case involved the question of timely filing of a grievance, the central question was, "Did the employer violate the master agreement, supplemental pay provisions?"

In the supplemental pay provisions of the master agreement, Appendix B, it was stated,

Following are the extracurricular and extra duty assignments. The salary percentages are multiplied by the beginning B A base salary to determine the dollar compensation:

. . . .

Audio Visual Director   1.5%

The agreement covered the period July 1, 1976-June 30, 1977.

In 1975 a teacher performed the duties of A-V Director and was paid a supplement of 1.5%. In 1976, the duties were performed by an administrator and no supplement was paid. In 1977, the grievant was hired as librarian for the school and was assigned responsibility for all audiovisual materials. All those duties were assigned and performed within the regular work day of 8:00 A.M. to 4:00 P.M. Her individually executed contract specified extracurricular pay for services as senior sponsor but not as A-V Director.

The arbitrator interpreted the term "extra duty" to mean work over and above the normal work day. The grievant performed the work during the regular eight-hour day. The grievance was denied.

THE RIGHTS OF INDIVIDUALS AT WORK

It should be pointed out that there are, technically, two kinds of grievances. Disputes called interest grievances arise at the time of negotiations. Such grievances are natural events, occurring as negotiators try to dominate the other team. Ideas are presented in ways to be persuasive and powerfully favorable to a particular position. From the discussions at the table that precede the contracts, the negotiating parties sometimes arrive at an impasse in which disagreement is obvious and neither party can or will move to resolve it. Most states provide a structure within which some outside third party, a neutral person, may work with the negotiators to see if some settlement can be created. The focus of this chapter has been upon disputes involving the interpretation of contracts, as individual concerns and conflicts arise after the contract. Yet a brief recognition of interest disputes seems necessary.

Every occupational setting has an aspect of tension. Part of that is fear; part is the drive for independence. In the mind of each employee, the question must sometimes arise, "Do I really have to do that?" Likewise, every administrator must have a complementary question arise, "Why must I explain yet again how to do that job?" Such professional work settings as libraries feature less of the telling simply because there is a dependence upon and confidence in the performance level of the workers. Professional workers tend to see what needs to be done, and to do it.

The cases presented reveal that grievances do arise, however, as librarians want something more in their jobs or seek relief from what is seen as unjust. From among those cases, only a few (five) centered upon a dispute involving more than one librarian. Typically, grievances are filed by one employee who feels wronged; yet class actions are possible. Occasionally, groups of workers in a common setting, finding that they are all suffering from a particular aspect of contract management may join in a class action, except that in the nature of disputes, the record clearly indicates a preponderance toward individual work problems.

Contracts themselves are private, in essence. Although a librarian might work under a collectively negotiated contract, and although all other librarians of identical job title might be assigned to identical tasks even for identical pay, the contract should still be understood as a private agreement. It is an agreement between one worker to deliver services under certain work conditions for specified pay. Other workers may also have an agreement with the same employer, but for each worker it is a private, individualized agreement, another reason that grievances tend to be private causes.

Out of the 1960s and 1970s came a flurry of law-making bearing upon public employment. Court decisions, state and federal statutes, and rulings from attorneys general have comprised the bulk of that rapidly developing law. Pensions were influenced, as were modes of pay (such as equal pay), safety in the workplace, and so on. Unresolved work disputes, rising to calls for outside arbitration, have themselves become the basis for part of this law, as decisions of arbitrators in one dispute have influenced decisions of arbitrators in similar later disputes. The situation in which courts are increasingly receptive to hearing appeals from rulings or awards of arbitrators is becoming still another source of law bearing upon grievance resolution.

This latter phenomenon has drawn the attention of the American Arbitration Association and the National Academy of Arbitrators. The effect of appealing arbitration awards has opened for judicial review the performance of the arbitrator. Some judges have been displeased with what they found, and in their decisions reversing awards from arbitrators they have been intemperate in their criticism of arbitrators and arbitration.

Given the number of disputes arbitrated in the nation, it could hardly be expected that every dispute, in its hearing and in the consideration and the decision of the arbitrator, would be exemplary.

A judicial tolerance focused upon balance should be a positive contribution to all of labor relations. The judiciary has become more socially active over the past three or four decades. Its influence is impinging more and more into the realm of labor relations. Its increasing willingness to review arbitral awards carries two costs which should be understood by both labor and management, by both librarians and administrators: (1) additional dollars of cost and (2) extended time prior to settlement. The point of the contract is to ensure stability at the work setting. The point of the grievance in labor relations is to provide relief for injured parties, cheaply and promptly. Judicial review of arbitration awards may not, in the long run, serve workers well. Judicial restraint would seem to guarantee that ". . . then (we will) obtain the requisite measure of predictability as to the firmness of results coming out of the arbitral sphere, . . . if effective collective bargaining is still to be considered a cherished national goal."[11]

NOTES

1. "Government Employee Relations Reports" (Washington, D.C.: Bureau of National Affairs, 1970), p. 61, 1006.

2. Richard J. Klimoski and others, "Third Party Characteristics and Intergroup Conflict Resolution," ERIC ED 116 081, 1975.

3. W. Dale Nelson, "LC Pays Its (Union) Dues," *Wilson Library Bulletin* (September 1978), p. 22.

4. Michal W. Granof, *How to Cost Your Labor Contract* (Washington, D.C.: Bureau of National Affairs, 1970), pp. 1-2.

5. Robert C. O'Reilly, "Living With the Negotiated Contract," paper delivered at Houston, National School Boards Association Convention, March 1977, p. 3.

6. W. Todd Furniss, *Grievance Procedure: A Working Paper* (Washington, D.C.: American Council on Education, 1975), p. 2.

7. Ibid., p. 5.

8. Lincoln Education Association and Board of Education, *Negotiated Settlement* (Lincoln, Neb.: Lincoln Public Schools, May 1974).

9. Statement by Earl Baderschneider, AAA publications associate editor, in a personal interview, New York, October 13, 1977.

10. Ibid.

11. Rolf Valtin. "The Presidential Address: Judicial Review Revisited—the Search for Accommodation Must Continue," in Barbara D. Dennis and Gerald G. Sommers, eds., *Arbitration—1976: Proceedings of the Twenty-Ninth Annual Meeting of the NAA* (Washington, D.C.: BNA Books, 1976), p. 11.

UNIONIZED LIBRARY
SUPPORT PERSONNEL 8

INTRODUCTION

Libraries are employers. Each has a work staff. People are hired, and they fit more or less well within some sort of occupational hierarchy. Even though only a few occupational titles might be found within a single small institution, a simple task analysis would only confirm the existence of an occupational hierarchy. Librarians themselves would be found at the top of the hierarchy, for they are the employees possessing the basic professional competencies through which the several aspects of information science are handled, not only to communicate among themselves, technically, but to increase the effectiveness of the total library service. They may do this as they perform their work in selection, reference, cataloging, circulation, interlibrary loan, or some other specialty.

Professionals discharge their jobs with a sense of urgency and efficiency that comports with the generally held understanding that part of professionalism is prompt and efficient performance. Every library cannot be located on Melvil Dewey Avenue, so to speak, and ALA research indicated that staff training was a real problem for some libraries. Yet, that same research indicated the value of librarians as trainers for nonprofessional staff in the observation that ". . . the level of professionalism at the top has improved library service in many systems all down the line," and the level of service was declared to have risen considerably over the past few years; i.e., the latter 1960s.[1]

Other employees, essential to the operation of the library but lacking designation as professionals, cannot be disregarded or underestimated in the whole picture. Without a direct need to understand many of the professional aspects of library service, nonprofessional employees do have a need to perfom well whatever tasks to which they have been hired. Their primary responsibility is to support the professional endeavors of the library through tasks that may be small but are not unimportant. Like librarians, in the search to improve their personal welfare and working conditions they too may organize and bargain with the library administration and board, and that large group comprises the group called the library support personnel.

SOME MANAGEMENT ATTITUDES

Within the twentieth century, there have risen—and fallen—several theories of personnel management. A brief examination of only a few such theories should provide insights into reasons that nonprofessionals might be more interested in unionization at some times, and while at work under some theories, than at other times.

Running through many of these theories has been the viewpoint that as the difficulty of task performance decreases, so also must increase the specificity of personnel managment. Implicitly, this viewpoint assumes that the simpler the task, the less intelligent the worker and the greater the need for direct supervision. That assumption of linked circumstances had much larger acceptance early in this century than now, but it has not disappeared from the concepts of management either. This basic viewpoint, which was part of several theories of management, assumed that workers needed authority imposed; that workers' own best interests were served when management plainly and directly stipulated acceptable behavior at the work site.

Current theories of personnel administration have, in part, evolved from just such basic viewpoints. Among many persons who now are prominent on the management theory scene are Maslow, McGregor, and Griffiths. Their viewpoints must influence the articles of a contract addressed to the conditions of work, and their viewpoints can be seen as representative of some kinds of administrative attitudes within which library support personnel must work. Of course, contract articles are also greatly influenced by the statutes under which public employment bargaining is carried on in the various states; however, in some instances, even those statutes have been influenced by the management theoreticians, whose ideas deserve the attention of librarians and library support employees alike, for they influenced the thinking of workers who were considering unionization. Even if workers are unaware of management theory, they are aware of its practical manifestations.

Maslow believed that man is not motivated solely by economic incentives or mainly by social needs, but that the "whole individual is motivated, rather than just a part of him."[2] He developed and articulated a series of five basic needs in man, organized in a hierarchy of importance, and he stipulated that one need must be at least partially satisfied before another need can emerge. For example, physiological needs are food, water, and oxygen. These are among the needs at the first level of Maslow's motivational theory, for they are those basic things through which life is sustained.[3]

When the physiological needs are reasonably satisfied, safety needs begin to dominate man's thinking and behavior. These needs include protection against danger, threats, extremes in climate, and tyranny and violence. For example, a person's preference for a job with tenure as opposed to short-term or indefinite employment would fall under the second category of needs, safety. The needs for belonging and love constitute the third level. Maslow felt that if man's need for group contact were thwarted, his behavior would incorporate such characteristics as to defeat organizational goals. The esteem needs occupy the fourth level on the hierarchical ladder. The esteem, egoistic needs are of two kinds: self-esteem and reputation or status.[4]

The highest need in the hierarchy is self-actualization—to be what one can be. When a person achieves self-actualization, he becomes a self-starter; he becomes responsible for himself and is able to express himself creatively.[5] Practically, not all work settings can readily accommodate the advanced needs categories; to insist upon their inclusion would be to put the goals of the organization at too low a level. Yet, a good manager must do all that is possible to allow each worker to come as near as possible to self-fulfillment on the job, whether a nonprofessional or professional. In that kind of managerial setting, library support personnel must be ready to accept responsibility and assume initiative when opportunity is presented.

McGregor systematically articulated divergent theories, allowing for comparative evaluation. Theory "X" is a traditional view of human behavior in industry: the control of workers through the exercise of authority. Theory "Y" is based on an integration of goals and upon conditions created in such a fashion that the organization can achieve its goals best by directing workers' efforts toward the success of the enterprise. Theory "Y" relies on self-control of human behavior. In a simplified explanation, if a manager follows Theory "X," employees would be treated much as children. If following Theory "Y," the worker would be treated as an adult.

Some of the supportive themes in Theory "Y" are

1. the failure of unilateral decision making to utilize human resources
2. the threat that the organization may suffer unless the integration of goals is achieved
3. the integration of personal objectives with the objectives of the organization to accomplish new occupational objectives[6]

In some part, then, the role accepted by a library director indicates what roles would be encouraged or allowed or accepted for such workers as the clerks, secretaries, analyists, and custodians. Expectations of managerial roles are established from a local history of interpersonal relations between the director and the supervised employees. Consistent management style on the part of the director, in harmony with worker expectations, allows workers to respond toward goal accomplishment and diminishes work tensions and conflicts.

From a lifelong history of study and institutional analysis, Daniel Griffiths has come forward, asserting that new theories in the administration of many kinds of educational institutions will have to be developed because people do not want to be governed. "The new Machiavelli can't make people do what he wants them to do."[7] Griffiths also feels that each individual in an organization chooses his own group. This has special meaning in the context of unions. Administrators in all kinds of educational agencies, including libraries, must be aware of the fact that as unions become a strong force in the organization, "each individual assumes at least four postures: formal and informal in the library, and formal and informal in the union."[8]

Every management theory must have justification within the organization where the work is to occur, as well as in the larger society. There is not categorically any correct style, but the message from the larger society clearly states that presently the do-it-when-I-tell-you authoritarian style, holding workers in little regard, would encounter large operational difficulties. Every leader must respond through the work force to the tasks of his agency but must move toward task accomplishment with some discernible concern for the individual workers, and those workers must perceive that concern. In too many instances, unions have been organized as a reaction to callous management, to styles that flourished many years ago and were continued long after they had lapsed out of phase with American culture, generally. On balance, it must be observed that unions occasionally have forced administrators into corners from which the only response could be hostility and antagonism. In regard to libraries, neither posture bodes well, either for the personnel or for the quality of service clients have a right to expect—and which they will support.

CONTRACTS FOR SUPPORT PERSONNEL

There are two possibilities for library support personnel, in terms of contractual status. They may be included along with the librarians in a comprehensive contract, or they may be excluded from the professional group and treated in some kind of separate contract. There are some minor modifications of those two contractual situations, but for purposes of analyzing contract conditions they will serve.

In the New York Public Library, Local 1930, AFSCME District Council #37, the contract for 1973-76 (and extended) stipulated that all staff members were included. That contract was inclusive, with some few specific positions being identified for exclusion from the bargaining unit. Also excluded were some employees, few in number, who belonged to unions prior to the time that Local #1930 was organized, such as the stationary engineers.

Excluding all occupational categories having the word librarian as any part of the job title, the contract for Local #1930 included sixty other job titles. Included were such jobs as clerk, community liaison, computer operator, illustrator, programmer, proofreader, typist, and telephone operator. Many titles were specialized into some specific work settings of the library and specialized as well by grade.

The contract itself consisted of thirty-nine articles. The articles were more uniform than unique. That is, although some articles were specific to occupational titles, they were very few. Article IV, "Salaries," wsa devoted exclusively to the professional categories. It was a record of the NYPL's obligation to "follow the terms of the applicable Labor Relations Order implementing applicable agreements. . . ."

Much more characteristic of the contract was Article XI, "Leave Regulations." Subsections were addressed to procedures and qualification. Section 1, "Annual Leave," stated that all employees could pursue "A combined vacation, personal business, and religious holiday leave with full pay, known as 'annual leave.' " All staff members had equal entitlement governed only by years in position and hours of work per week, as shown in Table 8.1. Regularly employed part-time workers are included. That table reveals that a large library may develop an inclusive union and write a comprehensive contract for all employees in that varied work force, including support personnel, with benefits accrued for all on the basis of seniority and extent of the work week.

Table 8.1 **Annual Leave in the New York Public Library**

Normal Work Week Schedule (in hours)	Less than 8 years		8-15 years		15 or more years	
	Hours of		Hours of		Hours of	
	Annual Credit	Monthly Credit	Annual Credit	Monthly Credit	Annual Credit	Monthly Credit
40 or more	160	13:20	200	16:40	216	18:00
35–39	140	11:40	175	14:35	189	15:45
30–34	120	10:00	150	12:30	162	13:30
25–29	100	8:20	125	10:25	135	11:15
20–24	80	6:40	100	8:20	108	9:00
17–19	70	5:50	88	7:20	95	7:55
15–16	60	5:00	88	7:20	95	7:55
10–14	40	3:30	50	4:10	54	4:30
9 or fewer	none		none		none	

Table 8.2 **Support Personnel in the Omaha Public Library**

Occupational Category	Number of Employees	
clerks	41	union workers
paraprofessionals	21	
professional librarians	39	non-union workers
executive secretaries	1	
building managers	1	

SOURCE: Statement by Frank Gibson, Director of the Omaha, Neb., Public Library, in a personal interview, Omaha, February 16, 1978.

To provide a geographical contrast, the Omaha Public Library was selected. The personnel roster for 1978 included 103 persons in addition to the director. As shown in Table 8.2, most workers were not in any union. The library administration was not a party to negotiating the contract for those who were union members. The agreement was between the City of Omaha and the Omaha City Employees Local #251, AFSCME, AFL-CIO. That agreement included several fiscal and operational departments of the municipality. The library was one of those. The union included persons working in any of the included occupational categories, without regard to the place to which they were assigned and where they actually performed their task. Such a contract could not have a strong community of interest developed from the place of employment

This type of contract represents a leveling of the represented work force. Only a small part, and that a narrow part of the work force, was under a union contract. A portion of the contract was devoted to identification, providing a title for each classification of employee. In fact, many classifications not covered were nonetheless listed. Such extensiveness might be seen as a union provision for future hires. Professional employees were defined but were not included in the contract. Clerks, the single worker group covered from the library work force, could possibly develop a community of interest with other clerks employed by the municipality.

That contract was compared to others between the City of Omaha and (1) the police and (2) the firefighters. The contracts for the police and the group including the library clerks were in identical formats. Pay for a Police I (beginner) and a Clerk III (most advanced) on the fourth column of the salary schedule was identified. For the beginning policeman or policewoman, the city provided compensation of $1,273 per month. For the experienced clerk III, the city provided compensation of $942 per month, calculated as a month of four forty-hour weeks ($5.89 per hour $\times$ 40 $\times$ 4 =

$942.40). Acknowledging that police protection is a more critical service than would be rendered to a citizen by a library clerk, a very substantial pay difference exists too. It is true that interoccupational pay comparisons are not very helpful as action bases for unions, even when the employer is the same and the level of job preparation can be compared favorably. Interoccupational information is helpful in making occupational choices. The fact is that American capitalism has never pretended that there is equity in pay for work performed, in terms of its frequency, strenuousness, beauty, value to society, or many other factors. A given public employer develops particular rationales under which pay is delivered to the specific jobs done by employees, and that is maintained by comparisons with pay for similar job titles in other geographic settings.

The Omaha library organizational pattern divides the work force into union and non-union employees. The excluded group consisted of people within the professional work titles:

1. library assistants
2. library specialists
3. librarians, I, II, III
4. assistant library director

All support personnel, the nonprofessionals, were union members for whom bargaining was carried on with the fiscal agency for the library, the municipality. The local of AFSCME was their bargainer.[9]

From the west coast, the contract between the Pierce County (Tacoma, WA) Library Staff Association for 1976/77 was selected as another geographic representative. An unaffiliated union with comprehensive membership, the contract included nineteen nonprofessional job titles and six professional job titles. Largely devoted to such broad matters as compensation, conditions of work, and personnel administration, only a few articles of the contract differentiated between professionals and nonprofessionals. One such was Article XXXII, "Resignation."

In the case of resignations, professional librarians and others of designated equal status are expected to give the Library one (1) month's notice; clerical employees, two (2) weeks' notice. More notice is desirable if possible.

The nonprofessional staff was ranked, each position being indexed to a salary range, but only at a specified level. That is, library pages, the lowest ranked position, could earn only within the range from $2.28 per hour to $2.65 per hour. The highest ranking was shared by two job titles, senior library associate and graphics specialist. The pay rate for those job titles ranged from a low of $4.94 to $5.72 hourly. For purposes of pay increments related to seniority, even title was extended across six proficiency columns on the salary schedule.

In discussing the values of unionism for nonprofessionals employed in library settings, it is necessary to explicitly point out that library clerks employed in public school libraries and media centers form a subgroup of their own, so to speak. Table 8.3 contains comparative average salary information for that subgroup by size of school district. Typically, the public school nonprofessional, employed as a clerk in a school library, would also be non-union. That is, they would be excluded from membership in either the NEA or the AFT, while the school librarian would probably be a member of one or the other "teacher union." Using the salary of the experienced Clerk III in the Omaha Public Library for comparison, those unionized municipal library clerks would be paid at an annual salary of $11,304 ($942 per month × 12 months). That puts the relative financial positions of the two categories of library clerks, both working in public employment settings, in sharp perspective. The comparison also points up information that would surely influence decisions about occupational choices and places of work, and that unions would use as cause-and-effect arguments.

COMMUNITY OF INTEREST

It appears that each locality has exercised its own unique thinking when approaching the problem of union membership and the degree of inclusiveness that should be denoted by that membership. Without trying to identify the factors bearing upon decisions of exclusivity in membership or of comprehensiveness, the central question is the identification of an employee group that will have a shared community of interest and still be an influential organization. When considering starting and maintaining a

Table 8.3 **Means of Wages or Salary Rates for Library Clerks in Schools, by Level and Size (1975-76)**

Groups by arithmetic mean	School System Size		
	25,000 students or more	*10,000-24,999 students*	*300-9,999 students*
Lowest mean	$5,123	$5,063	$4,696
Highest mean	6,887	6,737	6,070
Mean of means	5,867	5,879	5,333

SOURCE: "Wages and Salaries Paid Support Personnel in Public Schools, 1975–76" (Arlington, Va.: Educational Research Service, Inc., 1976), pp. 15–17.

viable union, harmony and solidarity must be accommodated. It is a question of two parts:

1. How many members must a union have to be viable, to be influential, to accomplish goals of personal welfare for members?
2. How broad, how inclusive of the range of occupational titles can a union be and still embrace shared causes?

Libraries have long been users of part time and volunteer labor. The former group, the part-timers, is a growing group. Several studies on the performance of part-timers in government jobs indicate that the employing agency benefits despite increased costs in personnel management, social security, and unemployment insurance. This is true because, among part-timers, productivity is higher, absenteeism and turn-over are lower.

Across the United Staes there is a thrust at all levels of government to increase the number of permanent part-time employees. This comes in response to large numbers of people seeking such work, and to evidence that those employees work just as hard, if not harder than their full-time colleagues.

A half dozen states (Calif., Mass., Colo., Oregon, and Wisconsin) now have specific programs or policy directives to increase the number of part-time employees in state government. Washington state is considering legislation along these lines.[10]

Many of these employees will be nonprofessionals. Are these employees, working as support personnel in libraries, going to be in or outside the unions? What is their part in the community of interest?

The problems of community of interest are not new. In 1968, the ALA surveyed library administrators and library union spokesmen. Responses to two key questions pinpoint the dilemma:

1. Should a bargaining unit include all library employees, or should a bargaining unit consist only of employees in certain grades or departments of the library?

Administrators:
     An argument can be made for the establishment of a bargaining unit for non-librarians, since, in some cases, the interests of these two groups do not necessarily coincide. On the other hand, a single bargaining unit, which includes all categories of employees, will probably be a stronger and more effective organization.
     From the management point of view, a single bargaining unit is desirable because the necessity of bargaining with a multitude of units and the inherent complications under such circumstances are obviated.

Union Spokesmen:
     All library employees; to maintain a sense of fairness, and develop an atmosphere of loyalty and responsibility.

2. Should library employees be part of the bargaining unit or units including other municipal employees?

Administrators:
Such would be dependent on the relationship of the library to city government: Is the library a department of city government or a school district library or a separate autonomous commission? Are the employees under civil service? These are factors which would have bearing on the separateness or inclusiveness of bargainig units involving library employees.
Would prefer to see a library group if large enough to have real power.

Union Spokesmen:
Yes. So that library problems will be considered with those of other municipal departments and that other department representatives will understand the problems and working conditions peculiar to the library staff.
No, Particularly not professional librarians who have no counterparts in other city departments.[11]

It appears that for the nonprofessional employees in library settings who may be considering unionization—or who may be members of unions—the questions of comprehensiveness of membership can best be addressed as a local question. Each worker trying for the improvement of personal welfare must seek the best advantage that can be offered locally. For some, it might be better to be a tiny minority within a much larger union that would cut across several municipal departments. For others, the primary advantages might accrue as members of the nonprofessional division within a single employment setting. For library support personnel, the goal is surely the same as for other workers, to seek that pattern of organization through which a high quality of representation of worker interest seems likely, in terms of salary advancement and the development and maintenance of desirable working conditions.

SUMMARY

The viewpoints under which the management of institutions has carried out its obligations have varied, by time and place. In libraries, it has been presumed that the intellectual distance between professional librarians and librarian-administrators is not great. That minimal intellectual distance is, partially, a reflection of the fact that the next librarian-administrator may come from the professional librarian group, within that library or from another similar place.
For most of the typical library support staffs, the intellectual distance from worker to director is substantial. Viewpoints from which to administer a library have been evolving, along with changes in theories and

concepts of administration generally. Distance between workers and managers creates its own set of problems. More than many other kinds of institutions devoted to the broad development of the citizenry, libraries employ proportionately larger numbers of nonprofessionals. For example, compared to an elementary or secondary school, the much larger proportion of nonprofessionals in a library is quite noticeable.

That disproportion, unique to libraries, creates equally unique problems in personnel administration. In some libraries, the support personnel may belong to a union of similarly qualified persons who work in many other but occupationally comparable settings in a municipality. They may have little if any loyalty to the library, relating to some central personnel office instead. On the other hand, they may be a part of the library union, in which they see themselves as always on the "bottom rung" of the pay ladder for that library. Comparing themselves and their functions to other municipal workers, they may perceive a condition of less pay for more work. These are less natural groupings of workers than ordinarily collectivize into local unions. Such variable personnel conditions, the intellectual distance involved, and membership in an assertive union call for new appreciations and sensitivities in administering a library on the part of both the director and the trustees. Lack of it will contribute to resentment, decrease job satisfaction and performance, and diminish the institution or the workers—or both.

NOTES

1. Nelson Associates, *Public Library Systems in the United States* (Chicago: American Library Association, 1969), p. 244.

2. Abraham H. Maslow, *Motivation and Personality* (New York: Harper and Row, 1979), p. 19.

3. Ibid., p. 38.

4. Ibid., pp. 44–46.

5. Ibid., pp. 160–70.

6. Douglas McGregor, *The Human Side of Enterprise* (New York: McGraw-Hill Book Company, 1960), pp. 49–60.

7. Daniel E. Griffiths, "The Individual in the Organization: A Theoretical Perspective," *Educational Administration Quarterly* 13 (Spring 1977): 3.

8. Ibid., p. 13–15.

9. Statement by Frank Gibson, Director of the Omaha (NE) Public Library in a personal interview, Omaha, NE, February 16, 1978.

10. *Administrator's Digest* 13 (April 1978): 27.

11. American Library Association, "Collective Bargaining: Questions and Answers," *ALA Bulletin* 62 (December 1968): 1387–88.

EQUAL EMPLOYMENT OPPORTUNITIES, LIBRARIES, AND UNIONS
9

JOBS AND EQUALITY

Societies are continually engaged in questions bearing upon employment preference. Factors that influence societies to confer work preference and therefore economic preference are changeable. For example, with the consecutive influences of World War II, the Korean War, and then the Viet Nam War, American veterans who served during the time of conscripted armies received preferential treatment in the nation's manpower pool upon their return to civilian life. Not all of the qualifications that lead to preference have been directly related to job readiness; the veteran's preference is just one such category.

Preferences developed to confer employment and economic advantage by sex that are a little less explicit than veteran's preference can be seen by glancing back only a few years. American social structure has featured a strong dependence upon the family. Family formation has been encouraged, for example, by tax laws providing exemptions through a numbering of dependents. Family formation was seen as the best way for procreation, a necessity for any society. Because the family was held in such high esteem as a social unit, preferential treatment came to heads of households. When coupled with the fact that the number of conventional American households that are split by separation and divorce is at the highest rate in the nation's history, that uniquely modern characteristic bears upon the question, too, as reformers and lawmakers strive for equity. The imbalance of employment in libraries, with females predominating, makes this larger question a legitimate concern for librarians.

Courts have been instrumental in recent American social reform. The decision of the Supreme Court in *Brown* v. *Topeka* (1954) identified racial discrimination as a social pattern to be eliminated in certain public institutions, initially public schools. In its emphasis upon equality, the court ushered in a new social atmosphere and established a criterion against which a citizen might measure his own condition in society. The court called for change, and the nation started to move toward equality. Now, the rate, direction, and inclusiveness of that change are in dispute. For citizens who see advantage in rapid change, it is never fast enough. For citizens who see disadvantage in change, any rate may be too fast. In many communities, those two groups live side by side, sharing the ups and downs of the community. In many settings, they work side by side. What is seen as a reasonable expectation by one group is seen by another as threatening. Can the American political system deliver economic equity within such a mixed citizenry? Can unions of workers, as part of the whole political system, be a positive force in such a mix of motives and desires? Inasmuch as money is the common denominator of employment and the primary concern of unions, the answer appears to be not only that they can be helpful but also that under legislative mandate, they must be.

Equality is a word of many facets; equity is more specific, implying an assurance that the librarian will get, for service delivered to the library, fair and suitable compensation. Its emphasis is economic. There is more to equality than just equity, for it is broad in application. It is the more desired circumstance. It is political in nature and power is part of equality, just as equity is part. American governments have a central tenet that power is derived through the consent of all citizens, and that the power must be used fairly for all citizens. This means that all citizens should have an equal voice in the process of governance:

> But the idea of citizenship which embodies this conception has in the past 100 years been expanded to include equality not only in the public sphere, but in all other dimensions of social life as well—equality before the law, equality of civil rights, equality of opportunity, even equality of results—so that a person is able to participate fully, as a citizen, in the society.[1]

The difficulty of establishing equality as a pervasive and dominating factor in social and economic life can be domonstrated by contriving a situation based upon facts. In a recent longitudinal study of 2,352 prominent women, the subjects were separated into fifteen categories of work, one of which was "archivists, librarians, museum directors and curators." In that group were 161 women. The mortality rate for the entire group of women who excelled in their work was 29 percent below that for their contemporaries in the general population. The community service group, which included archivists and librarians, had the lowest mortality rate of the fifteen groups—less than half that recorded by their contemporaries in the general population.[2] Now, putting this fact together with only two pieces of federal legislation from the 1960s and 1970s—the Age Discrimination Act and the Equal Pay Act—and it becomes apparent that equality is extremely difficult to establish, even when reduced to a single occupational category. That is not to say that equality is an undesirable national goal; it is only to say that many factors operate in a free society against its accomplishment. In many ways equality seems more compatible to a politically rigid system.

Equality can be approached from another vantage point, which is now being explored in America. When looking backward, an observer can see injustices perpetrated against groups of citizens. One reasonable response is to identify those victimized groups and name them groups worthy of special governmental protection. That has happened. Political coalitions have formed to secure the expansion of those groups. As the groups have changed, the trend toward greater inclusiveness can be discerned. Special protection is now offered to people who have in the past been discriminated against on the basis of sex, race, politics, religion, handicaps, and national origin. Much of that protection has taken form within the principle of compensation, payment now for injustices of the past.

Western societies do not entertain that principle of compensation at the level of individual arguments. Statutes of limitations stipulate that citizens cannot be held accountable for alleged injustices beyond a certain number of years. For an injustice done at some point far back in time, the offspring of the perpetrator may not be held accountable. People committing acts later on declared unlawful cannot be held accountable for what was done earlier. Several basic fair play ideas stand—at the individual level—in opposition to the principle that compensation is a suitable device through which to address inequalities of the past.

The national political arena is another thing. Guilt for the crime of human slavery can be declared; guilt for taking unfair advantage of Native Americans can be declared. Such declarations do not involve trials or individuals. Declarations as admissions of guilt raise the question of what can be done to compensate for the injustice. Compensation may be seen as one form of preference. Through compensation there is no need to fumble with the questions of who did what to whom. Rather, the victimized group is identified for special consideration, and all individuals who appear to qualify as members of that group come under the protection of those special legislative considerations. Compensation can be operated at a group level, even though it has been rejected at an individual level.

The principle of compensation has been an increasingly pervasive force on the American political scene since the end of World War II. It rests upon the position that some citizens, earlier, took things of value from other citizens that should not have been taken so cheaply, if taken at all. It says that as forebears were cheated, now it is time for restitution to their descendants. Elected officials have found in this circumstance a condition they could easily support, addressing social problems while helping the downtrodden of society. Applied, the principle of compensation directs that through the assistance of the fortunate in society, those who are disadvantaged and unfortunate should be helped toward equality. The essence of that application, helping the disadvantaged, is a visible and viable part of the American culture. The application has been expressed in civil rights legislation, affirmative action obligations, and court interpretations of statutes and regulations from the Civil Rights Acts (of 1866 to 1964) to the U.S. Office of Education Regulation 504 (of 1978).

Although the principle of compensation has proven its political popularity, it carries within itself the seeds of other problems that will not go away. Reasonable questions are being asked, such as

1. How is membership in a protected group determined?
2. Who in the government should name and define the protected groups?
3. How can the contradictions between affirmative action and equality be ameliorated?
4. Who determines how far back in time we should go to discover citizens deserving of compensation?
5. Should all citizens bear, equally, the burdens of compensation?

A much longer list of questions could be made. But, regardless, there is now a commitment to certain groups that a new equality will be achieved. That commitment affects employment in many ways. In employment settings where one sex (female) predominates and where sex is a protected group, there are several explicit consequences, even if they differ by the locale in which some specific plan for compensation is instituted.

Unions have a leveling effect upon any workplace, libraries included. They effectively dilute the budget of public agencies and spread out the money. Services tend toward what is uniform for any particular employee classification, if only through peer pressure. Contracts provide uniform compensation by grade, by year, and so on. Yet some librarians become recognized by their high professional accomplishment, as seen in the study of prominent women cited earlier. This is only one more piece of evidence pointing out why equality is so elusive. Americans are free to follow their ambitions, to compete, and to perform in ways that are clearly outstanding. No governmental restraint is put upon citizens who are energetic, inventive, and aggressive. Such performance in a job setting means that some employees will be seen as better performers than others. Effort and accomplishment is prized. Differentiated rewards may follow. It appears that, really, equality is a political position that is widely advocated but may mean more of a guaranteed minimum as it cannot literally mean equality in the current American technological society. It is a tangled and complex group of principles and practices that bear upon collective bargaining.

Current economic data speak to the point. Economists Welch and Smith investigated the relative positions of Americans by sex and by race in 1955, 1965, 1975. That report revealed that within the groups, black females had made astounding progress in two decades until, in 1975, they earned 98.6 percent of what was earned by white females. For males, the story was less impressive, but in the same period, the black males had risen from earning 64 percent as much in 1955 to 77 percent as much in 1975. These positive findings were in contradiction to the predictions that had been made by Welch in 1966. The differentials and progress by sex were unreported.[3]

SEXISM AND LIBRARIANS

Within the concept of employment equality for librarians, there is an ambiguous aspect, the disproportionate representation of females within the occupational category. Table 9.1 reveals this phenomenon clearly. Although restricted to a recent graduating class from the ALA-approved schools of library science, the data are generally descriptive of the phenomenon of disproportionality as it has existed through many decades and in other types of preparing institutions as well. That is, the colleges of education have been the preparing institutions for the bulk of persons seeking certification as school librarian-media specialist and finding employment as librarians in elementary and secondary schools. Stated as a ratio, females predominate in the occupation about four to one. Conservatively stated as a percentage of the total, females occupy about 75 percent of the jobs.

Table 9.1 **Class of 1975 Graduates from Fifty-One Schools of Library Science**

	Male	Female	Total
Graduates	1,285	4,573	6,010
Known Placement	781	2,641	3,467

SOURCE: Carol L. Learment and Richard L. Darling, "Placements and Salaries in 1975: A Difficult Year," in Nada Beth Glick and Sarah L. Prakken, eds., *The Bowker Annual of Library and Book Trade Information*, 22nd ed. (New York: R.R. Bowker Company, 1977), p. 346.

There is another difficulty in addressing the topic of equality of employment opportunity in this occupational category, which is so strongly dominated by one sex. Table 9.2 is based upon the same data as were used in the preceding table; however, in a new arrangement by type of employment setting, the data reveal a striking dissimilarity between the sexes as they accepted jobs in school libraries and in college and university libraries.

Table 9.2 **Placement of 1975 Graduates by Sex and Type of Library**

Sex	Total Placements	Public Libraries	School Libraries	Colleges and Universities	Other
Women	2,595	30%	28%	21%	1%
Men	773	29%	11%	39%	21%
Total	3,668*	30%	24%	25%	21%

SOURCE: Carol L. Learment and Richard L. Darling, "Placements and Salaries in 1975: A Difficult Year," in Nada Beth Glick and Sarah L. Prakken, eds., *The Bowker Annual of Library and Book Trade Information* 22nd ed. (New York: RR. Bowker Company, 1977), pp. 348–51.
* Does not include 91 placements lacking differentiation by type of library.

A substantially smaller number of men were placed in elementary-secondary school libraries; however, a substantially larger number of men than women were placed in college and university libraries. Admittedly, this difference may reflect a difference in the accomplishment of academic degrees. That piece of information cannot be separated from these data, if it is known. To some extent, however, librarians are statisticians. Any statistics that relate discrimination or hardship, however, can hardly be accepted happily, and these statistics appear to reveal either discrimination or hardship.

However, two other factors surely bear upon this phenomenon to some degree or another, and both contain the potential for unequal treatment by sex. First, and whether it has real justification or not is immaterial, there is a presumption abroad that a college or university work setting would be a more desirable place to work than an elementary or secondary school. Those more desirable work settings are claimed by many more males than females. Second, to some extent, the elementary-secondary school employment setting has evolved from, and still includes, the "schoolmarm" heritage of lesser esteem. That heritage seems to say that females should dominate the jobs in schools, and in fact they do. Neither factor can withstand severe scrutiny when exposed to inquiries based upon examination for sexism in job settings.

In a field numerically dominated by the sex supposed to be the "protected group" in the current concepts of equal opportunity, the question of equality is especially troublesome. In the interpretation of sexism as discrimination against females in a field where females predominate, the number of questions about balance of placement that should be raised may be small—just as a matter of politics. One thing that is reasonable, however, is to assure equality in treatment toward promotion and to make that a specific assurance through a contract clause.

THE FEDERAL GOVERNMENT AND EQUALITY

Through the 1940s the United States Supreme Court heard cases from Texas, Oklahoma, and Missouri raising questions about the constitutionality of separate but allegedly equal university educational opportunities for blacks. Uniformly, the Court ruled against the states. *Brown*, in 1954, was a reasonable follow up in elementary and secondary education. As a landmark case it came as something of a social shock that, by the Court's decision, the nation was obligated to see questions of discrimination and inequality in a new light—and to provide new answers to those questions, from questions of race discrimination, to discrimination on the basis of sex, age, religion, and so on. Currently, topics under the heading of discrimination at the workplace include questions of hiring, promotion, dismissal, and salary and fringe benefits.

Indicators of the political attractiveness of equality and of the principle of compensation can be seen in a sampler of Congress.

1. The Civil Rights Acts of 1957 and 1960 were forerunners of later legislation and were devoted to voting rights and the desegregation of schools.
2. The Equal Pay Act of 1963 was aimed at eliminating pay differentials based upon sex.
3. The Civil Rights Act of 1964 was an extended statute of many parts, aimed at problems of citizen inequality.
4. The Civil Rights Act of 1969 was developed to control citizen riots, halt racial discrimination in housing (both rental and purchased), and extend constitutional rights to American Indians.
5. Other statutes of the 1960s and 1970s included the Voting Rights Acts, the Model Cities Act, the Equal Employment Opportunities Act, and the Pregnancy Discrimination Act of 1978.

The federal judiciary opened this era of social reform—and has kept it in motion with thousands of decisions addressed to questions of inequality—but Congress has been active, too. Many congressional acts have influenced, and will continue to influence, the public employment setting.

One problem in the area of equality for the sexes in employment should serve as an example of its complexity. Within university settings, librarians are members of and contributors to the Teachers Insurance and Annuity Association (TIAA). Males and females make deposits of equal amounts into their retirement annuities; that is, the base contribution is the same percentage of salary for all employees of a given institution. Contributions are equal among the sexes. Those annuities have calculated values to be paid out to qualified retirees upon an actuarial differential by sex. In that actuarial differential, retiring females live longer than do retiring males. In practice, the allowed claim by females against the annuity has been for fewer dollars per month. Now, courts are hearing cases from the entire employment-retirement spectrum proposing that the Equal Pay Act should be applied to the monthly annuity payments of retirees and that males and females should not receive different amounts, monthly, if they contributed equal amounts. Several courts have found for the female claimants, noting that actuarial tables or mortality have little application to individual cases. That is, some females have died very soon after entering retirement. It is a practical problem, for it raises the question of who should pay the additional premiums to fund the greater aggregated pay-out to female annuitants. The money must come from some source. It raises subsequent questions: (1) Should male workers, on the average, receive less money for their retirement because they die younger than do females and by death are denied an opportunity to claim an equal amount? (2) Should universities pay a larger retirement fringe benefit for females than for males and thereby provide the additional money needed to fund the longer life expectancy of the female retirees? Equality is, indeed, a complex question at the point of employment for when its achievement involves cost, someone must pay that cost. It is easier to claim as an ideal than to implement as an actuality.

With new legislation, new regulations, and new court interpretations, it is not entirely possible to predict the direction of equality in employment by sex. Yet, some movement toward governmental uniformity of interpretation is discernible and is surely desirable. The Departments of Labor and Justice, the Equal Employment Opportunities Commission, and the U.S. Civil Service Commission issued uniform guidelines in 1978, providing a single source of information to employers concerning nondiscrimination and suitable modes of employee selection. Such joint efforts speak to criticisms of governmental proliferation and contradiction. Although these specific guidelines were aimed at racial discrimination, it seems likely that they will impinge upon discrimination by sex, age, and other categories, eventually.[4] In libraries, with their unique imbalance of employment by sex, such guidelines are bound to have application, even if only in the sense of vocabulary adaptation to questions of sex inequality.

THE CIVIL RIGHTS ACT OF 1964 (PL 88-252, July 2, 1964)

This was a comprehensive statute to prevent discrimination, assure voting rights, and confer extended powers of supervision to the federal judiciary. The act consisted of eleven major divisions, or titles, and those titles reveal the extensive coverage of the act.

Title I   Voting Rights
Title II   Injunctive Relief Against Discrimination in Places of Public Accommo-
             dation

Equal Employment Opportunity (Title VII) was, by far, the longest portion of the act and started with a very specific definition of such key words as person, employer, and employee. A few excerpts reveal much of the intent of Title VII, especially as applicable to libraries and library unions and provide some understanding of the Equal Employment Opportunities Commission.

It shall be unlawful employment practice for an employer—
(1) to fail or refuse to hire or to discharge any individual, or otherwise to discriminate against any individual with respect to his compensation, terms, conditions, or privileges of employment, because of such individual's race, color, religion, sex, or national origin; or
(2) to limit, segregate, or classify his employees in any way which would deprive or tend to deprive any individual of his employment opportunities or otherwise adversely affect his status as an employee, because of such individual's race, color, religion, sex, or national origin.
It shall be an unlawful employment practice for an employment agency to fail or refuse to refer for employment, or otherwise to discriminate against, any individual because of his race, color, religion, sex, or national origin, or to classify or refer for employment any individual on the basis of his race, color, religion, sex, or national origin. [Sec. 703 a and b]

It shall be an unlawful employment practice for an employer, labor organization, or employment agency to print or publish or cause to be printed or published any notice or advertisement relating to employment by such an employer or membership in . . . such a labor organization or relating to any classification or referral for employment by such an employment agency, indicating any preference, limitation, specification, or discrimination, based on race, color, religion, sex, or national origin, except that such a notice or advertisement may indicate a preference, limitation, specification, or discrimination based on religion, sex, or national origin when religion, sex, or national origin is a bona fide occupational qualification for employment. [Sec. 704 b]

The statute was rigid, with exceptionality provided on a narrow basis, as might be needed for the hiring of personnel who would work in a library sponsored by a religious organization. The five-member Equal Employment Opportunities Commission was described. It was empowerd to

. . . furnish to persons subject to this title such technical assistance as they may request to further their compliance with this title or an order issued thereunder;

upon the request of (1) any employer, whose employees or some of them, refuse or threaten to refuse to cooperate in effectuating the provisions of this title, to assist in such effectuation by conciliation or such other remedial action as is provided by this title:

to make such technical studies as are appropriate to effectuate the purposes and policies of this title and to make the results of such studies available to the public. [Sec. 705 a-j][5]

The extensiveness of coverage, the elimination of all but a very few exceptions, and the establishment of a commission to oversee the intent of the statute made the 1964 act a potent piece of legislation, affecting employers and unions alike.

THE EQUAL EMPLOYMENT OPPORTUNITIES ACT OF 1972 (PL 92-261, March 24, 1972)

This act was a consequence of precedent orders and legislation and the experience of the EEOC in implementing the Civil Rights Act. It was enacted after the concept of equal employment had been in place for several years. It included all of Title VII of the Civil Rights Act of 1964 and established new methods by which to assure enforcement and compliance. An employer was defined as a person or agency with fifteen or more employees. The act exempted all elected officials from the employer class. Broad powers of investigation were granted to the EEOC and new personnel record keeping obligations were demanded of employers. A person(s) suffering from discriminatory, unlawful employment practices could file charges against the employer, employment agency, or labor union. So could an EEOC member file, on behalf of a citizen.

In the case of any charge filed by a member the Commission alleging an unlawful employment practice occurring in a State or political subdivision of a State which has a State or local law prohibiting the practice alleged and establishing or authorizing a State or local authority to grant or seek relief from such practice or to institute criminal proceedings with respect thereto upon receiving notice thereof, the Commission shall, before taking any action with respect to such charges, notify the appropriate State or local officials and, upon request, afford them a reasonable time, but not less than sixty days . . . unless a shorter period is requested, to act under such State or local law to remedy the practice alleged. [Sec. 706 d][6]

Initially, when Title VII was enacted, the EEOC was given hardly any powers of enforcement. It was a commission limited to persuasion. The EEOA changed that and settled great power upon the Commission, taking that jurisdiction away from the Justice Department. That 1972 act forbade discrimination by sex, age, race, and so on but also acknowledged that imbalances could exist, for many reasons, and were not of themselves conditions which required redress by programs of affirmative action.[7]

In fairness, it should be pointed out that much of the thrust for equalizing opportunities came from the executive branch of government. Actions by the judiciary and legislative branches have been presented. Through the use of executive orders, presidents of the 1960s exerted pressure for new opportunities. Executive orders have been serially numbered since 1907. In Executive Order 10988 President Kennedy created a condition for the organization of (federal) public employees that was quickly accepted as a pattern by many states as they passed laws enabling collective bargaining for their own public employees. Several executive orders have been influential in public employment and did frankly draw the political applause for which they were also designed.

E.O. 10095. MARCH 6, 1961. ESTABLISHING THE PRESIDENT'S COMMITTEE ON EQUAL EMPLOYMENT OPPORTUNITIES

In this order, the president reviewed the conditions for employment and stipulated that job opportunities should exist without regard to "race, creed, color, or national origin." Declaring that the federal government employment practices should set an example for all employers, the president established the committee. With the charge that the committee should keep surveillance, analyze data, and generally strengthen efforts to achieve full equality of employment opportunity, the committee membership was identified. Chaired by the vice-president, membership consisted of several cabinet secretaries plus the heads of those major divisions of the federal government that budgeted for large capital expenditures and such other members as the president might appoint. The committee was directed to report at least once each year to the president.

The President's Committee on Equal Employment Opportunity established by this order is directed immediately to scrutinize and study employment practices of the Government of the United States, and to consider and recommend additional affirmative steps which should be taken by executive departments and agencies to realize more fully the national policy of nondiscrimination within the executive branch of government.

Continuing, the order expanded the concept of EEO into many other government areas, including a contract clause demanding that the contractor to any government agency stipulate to nondiscrimination among their own employees. Finally, the committee was given broad powers from which it could discover compliance or lack of it.[8]

E.O. 10988. JANUARY 17, 1962. EMPLOYEE-MANAGEMENT CO-OPERATION IN THE FEDERAL SERVICE

The basis for this order rested upon research indicating that in work settings, generally, employee productivity and morale correlated positively with opportunities to influence management decisions. The order allowed for the collectivization, organization, and unionization of employees in the federal service. First, disclaimers were entered, such as a denial of the right to strike, a denial that managers could join employee unions, and a denial of membership in organizations discriminating on the basis of race, color, creed, or national origin. (Other "territorial" exclusions came later in the order.)

Then, the order stipulated that exclusive rights of representation could be granted by a federal agency, and that

An agency shall accord an employee organization formal recognition as the representative of its members in a unit as defined by the agency when (1) no other employee organization is qualified for exclusive recognition as represenative of employees in the unit, (2) it is determined by the agency that the employee organization has a substantial and stable membership of no less than 10 per centum of the employees in the unit, and (3) the employee organization has submitted to the agency a roster of its officers and representatives, a copy of its constitution and by-laws, and a statement of its objectives. When, in the opinion of the head of an agency, an employee organization has a sufficient number of local organizations or a sufficient total membership within such agency, such organization may be accorded formal recognition at the national level, but such recognition shall not preclude the agency from dealing at the national level with any other employee organization on matters affecting its members. [Sec. 5a]

The order directed that after recognzing the newly formed local, officials should consult with the organization on matters affecting personnel policies and practices and matters affecting working conditions. Likewise, it became appropriate for the organization to raise certain matters for discussion.[9]

E.O. 11264. SEPTEMBER 24, 1965. REASSIGNMENT OF CIVIL RIGHTS FUNCTIONS

It was the goal of this order to secure from all contractors to the federal government a more vigorous affirmative action, to ensure that

The contractor will not discriminate against any employee or applicant for employment because of race, creed, color, or national origin. The contractor will take affirmative action to ensure that applicants are employed, and that employees are treated during employment, without regard to their race, creed, color, or national origin. Such action shall include, but not be limited to the following: employment, upgrading, demotion, or transfer; recruitment or recruitment advertising; layoff or termination; rates of pay or other forms of compensation; and selection for training, including apprenticeship. The contractor agrees to post in conspicuous places, available to employees and applicants for employment, notices to be provided by the contracting officer, setting forth the provisions of this nondiscrimination clause. [Sec. 202–1]

The order also stipulated certain sanctions and penalties, as the Secretary of Labor implemented the order, publishing the names of companies and unions found to be in compliance as well as those failing to comply and allowing the Secretary to cancel, terminate, and halt contracting, when violations were discovered.[10]

E.O. 11375. OCTOBER 13, 1967. EQUAL OPPORTUNITY FOR WOMEN IN FEDERAL EMPLOYMENT AND EMPLOYMENT BY FEDERAL CONTRACTORS

In this order, attention was called to Title VII of the Civil Rights Act of 1964, which had been aimed at the private employment sector, and then clarified the position of the federal government as a public employer. It amended E.O. 11246 to "expressly embrace discrimination on account of sex."

It is the policy of the Government of the United States to provide equal opportunity in Federal employment for all qualified persons, to prohibit discrimination in employment because of race, color, religion, sex or national origin, and to promote the full realization of equal employment opportunity through a positive, continuing program in each executive department and agency. The policy of equal opportunity applies to every aspect of federal employment policy and practice. [Sec. 101][11]

The tendency toward extension of governmental protection to more and larger groups of citizens can be seen as a certain and steady aspect of the interest of all branches of the federal government.

AFFIRMATIVE ACTION

Affirmative action goes beyond organizational openness and receptiveness. It involves a commitment to a conscious and sustained effort toward the elimination of barriers to equal employment opportunities. It incorporates much of the social and economic philosophy explained earlier when the principle of compensation was discussed. Legislatively based in the statutes treating equal opportunity, affirmative action goes one step further. Spurred by the federal government's Equal Employment Opportunity Commission and the Equal Employment Opportunity Coordinating Council, states have enacted their own statutes aimed at reducing the power of vested interests and assisting the equalization of opportunities. In 1977, the California legislature considered S.B. 179, which attended all of the discrimination categories mentioned in the Civil Rights Acts of 1964, along with some additions:

. . . discrimination in employment on the basis of race, sex, color, religion, age, physical handicap, ancestry or national origin (must be eliminated) in every aspect of personnel policy and practice in employment, development, advancement and treatment of persons employed in the public school system, and (public schools) must promote the total realizaiton of equal employment opportunity through a continuing affirmative action employment program.

The impression that women, as compared to men, have suffered substantial job discrimination is held widely. There is abundant evidence of a great variety to support the impression. Assistance to local government employers as they face the obligations of affirmative action has come from federal agencies, talking about recruitment, skill utilization, career ladders, upward mobility, and so on. Together, the Office of Federal Contract Compliance, the U.S. Civil Service Commission, the Department of Justice, and the Equal Employment Opportunity Commission developed guidelines designed for adaptation and adoption in local and state governments. In turn, those guidelines were based upon five principles designed to eliminate discrimination in employment. They would be suitable for any public library and in some form are now actually in place, not as part of a negotiated contract but as antecedent to any contract and a part of every contract. The four agencies agreed that the following principles should be followed:

1. Whenever it is appropriate to establish goals, the goals and timetables should take into account anticipated vacancies and the availability of skills in the market place from which employees should be drawn. In addition, where unlawful discrimination by the employer has been established, the corrective action program . . . should also take into account the need to correct the present effects of the employer's past discriminatory practices.
2. The goals should be reached through such recruiting and advertising efforts as are necessary and appropriate, and the selection of persons only from amongst those who are qualified. A goal, unlike a quota, does not require the hiring of persons when there are no vacancies, nor does it require the hiring of a person who is less likely to do well on the job ("less qualified") over a person more likely to do well on the job ("better qualified"), under valid selection procedures. . . . valid selection procedures should be developed as soon as feasible. . . .
3. In no event does a goal require that an employer must in all circumstances hire a specified number of persons, because such a goal would in fact be a quota. It is,

however, appropriate to ask a court to impose goals and timetables, including hiring goals, on an employer who has engaged in . . . unconstitutional or unlawful employment practices.

4. Relief should be provided to those persons who have been adversely affected as a consequence of the employer's unlawfully discriminatory practices. . . . all agencies will seek to have those persons who have been excluded from consideration or employment because of such discriminatory practices allowed to compete for future vacancies on the basis of qualifications and standards no more severe than those utilized by the employer in selecting from advantaged groups, unless the increased standards are required by business necessity. Such relief will be sought to prevent the erection of unnecessary barriers to equal employment opportunities . . . .

5. When an employer has utilized a selection device which is itself unlawfully discriminatory, relief should be sought to prohibit the use of that and similar selection devices (i.e., devices which measure the same kinds of things) together with the development of an appropriate affirmative action plan which may include goals and timetables. . . .[12]

The evidence that allows determination of discrimination can be discovered in at least two ways: (1) general or national information, usually in comparative data form, and (2) individualized or specific information, frequently a grievance involving a person who alleges discrimination on an unlawful basis in an organization. Tables 9.1 and 9.2, presented earlier in this chapter, reveal some general aspects of inequality, as it might be discovered by inference. Table 9.3 reveals information specific to one employing organization and the existence of some comparatively small groups in protected citizen categories that, if their condition is to change, need the advantages of affirmative action.

Table 9.3 contains the kind of information that an employer needs and from which action could result. It is used here as a procedural example that could be used by librarians in employment settings other than in a university. First, the employer must conduct a self-examination and record information by job titles, sex, age, race, or whatever factors appear to need scrutiny. That information is compared to the manpower pool available for each job title. If any disparity is evident, that is the cue for the employer to initiate affirmative action, perhaps including the establishment of short-range, mid-range, and long-range goals to modify the personnel condition. In Table 9.3 all employees were assigned into a major occupational activity of the university as the employing organization, then cross-tabulated by race and sex. The table serves as a good example of the sensibility necessary for the discovery of sex bias.

Does affirmative action include preferential treatment? Yes, it appears that one cannot exist without the other. Doesn't this contradict the principle of equality? No, not if the consideration includes the principle of compensa-

Table 9.3 University of Nebraska at Omaha Equal Opportunity Compliance Survey

M.O.A.	Male					Female				
	White	Black	Spanish	Indian	Oriental	White	Black	Spanish	Indian	Oriental
Admin./Managerial	43	2	0	0	0	5	2	0	0	0
Instructional	329	6	4	0	1	89	7	2	0	0
Professional	67	2	2	0	0	29	6	0	0	0
Unclassified	0	0	0	0	0	0	0	0	0	0
Technical	16	1	0	0	0	3	0	0	0	0
Clerical/Secretary	16	2	0	0	1	173	15	1	0	0
Crafts/Trades	20	0	0	0	0	13	4	0	0	0
Service Workers	81	4	0	1	0	12	9	0	0	1
Total	983					Non-Citizens				14

SOURCE: University of Nebraska, "Policy Statement and Affirmative Action Program," (Lincoln, Neb.: The University, 1974), p. 11.

tion. The Commission on Civil Rights stated that Affirmative Action should attend

[Those] steps taken to remedy the grossly disparate staffing and recruitment patterns that are the present consequence of past discrimination and to prevent the occurrence of employment discrimination in the future.[13]

With the many federal courts called upon to decide questions of equality, and its absence, there is a lack of harmony in the judiciary. All judges do not see the circumstances alike. In *Gramercy* v. *Virginia Commonwealth University* (1976) a federal court ruled that the Equal Pay Act does not apply to local governments as long as males and females receive equal pay for equal work. As late as 1979, the circuit courts of the nation were split as to whether the Justice Department could sue a local government agency for alleged sex or race discrimination in employment.

The discord that surrounds affirmative action appears to be an unavoidable part of it. It is "built in" with the ambiguities and contradictions that must accompany different definitions of equality. When bargaining, employers must be careful not to bargain away any policy statements developed to keep the agency in compliance with affirmative action obligations. In libraries, for example, those obligations would influence recruitment, hiring, assignment, and promotion.

BUILDING EMPLOYMENT EQUALITY INTO CONTRACTS

Many decades ago, jobs in public employment were part of the "spoils system." Political candidates who were elected rewarded their supporters by getting job appointments for them. This meant that all those people already holding jobs who had supported the other candidate would be fired to make room. If that employment condition seems a chancey one, it is largely because nowadays job security is much greater.

The spoils system had severe shortcomings as a routine through which jobs were filled. With its short-term, career-interruption characteristics, it fostered low morale and discouraged professional development. Civil service was an employment routine developed to replace the spoils system by assuring job continuity upon good performance. It disallowed the use of political preference as a basis for hiring and incorporated several of the basic principles of equal employment opportunity. One goal of a complete contract is to restrict supervisors and department heads in the exercise of personnel management authority. The union's safeguard proposals may only fill a vacuum, but in matters of affirmative action, administrators often view them as undesirable and unnecessary encroachments upon personnel choices that were once local administrative prerogatives.

Within political subdivisions, librarians may find employment in public school districts, municipal and county libraries, and state universities and colleges. If unionized, those librarians will find many of their assurances of equal treatment incorporated into the contract. Such contract clauses are specific to local job settings because they may reflect the composition of the community and the composition of the manpower pool by sex. Excerpts from three different contracts stand to reveal the attention given to equal employment opportunities by the unions of professional employees, and the public agency employing them.

From the contract between the Detroit Board of Education and the Detroit Federation of Teachers (librarians included) for July 1, 1975 to July 30, 1977, came the following clause:

II. FAIR PRACTICES
    A. In accord with Board policy, no person or persons, departments or divisions responsible to the Board shall discriminate against any employee on the basis of race, creed, color, national origin, sex, marital status, or membership in, or association with the activities of, the Union.
    B. In accord with its Constitution, the Union will admit persons to membership without discrimination on the basis of race, creed, color, national origin, sex or marital status.
    C. The Union and the Board agree to continue to work affirmatively in implementing their mutual objective of effective integration of faculties and student bodies in all Detroit schools.

In New York City, the agreement covered 60,000 teachers, including several hundred public school librarians, and was negotiated between the Board of Education and the UFT #2, AFT, AFL-CIO. The contract covered three years, September 9, 1972, to September 9, 1975. It contained the following clauses aimed at nondiscriminatory employment.

ARTICLE II
Fair Practices

The Union agrees to maintain its eligibility to represent all teachers by continuing to admit persons to membership without discrimination on the basis of race, creed, color, national origin, sex or marital status and to represent equally all employees without regard to membership or participation in, or association with the activities of, any employee organization.

The Board agrees to continue its policy of not discriminating against any employee on the basis of race, creed, color, national origin, sex, marital status or membership or participation in, or association with the activities of, any employee organization.

The Board agrees that it will not require any teacher to complete an oath or affirmation of loyalty unless such requirement is established by law.

The contract between the New York Public Library Staff Members, Local 1930, AFSCME, and the New York Public Library, 1973-76 and extended, spoke to a nondiscrimination policy:

ARTICLE II—*Non-Discriminatory Policy*

The Library and the Union do not and shall not discriminate against any staff member or applicant for employment because of race, creed, color, national origin, age, sex, marital status (see Letter of Agreement, dated January 16, 1975, printed at end of this agreement), or political affiliation, with respect to wages, hours, or any terms or conditions of employemtn, including but not limited to recruitment, employment, appointment, promotion, transfer, termination, and selection for training.

The controversy surrounding equality of opportunity is not entirely nor exclusively idealistic. The American ethic of fair play, when consciously and thoughtfully articulated, proves acceptance of the notion of equal opportunity—without regard to sex, age, race, political creed, or religion. It is at the point of implementation that problems arise because, after all, affirmative action does not call for and may expressly disallow strict equality of treatment. It calls for some structured preferential treatment as a means to address past years of imposed inequality.

With librarians as a female-dominated group, what evidence of past inequality can be cited? Some miscellaneous data, by sex, describe conditions of employment having negative themes. Of women employed by the federal government, about 15 percent earn more than $10,000 per year; in private employment, about 7 percent do. One of every four black heads of household is a woman; in the general population, the number is one in nine. From that one in nine group, 40 percent fall below the government-defined poverty level. Two-thirds of all women who are gainfully employed earn less than $7,000 per year or are married to men earning less than $7,000. Only 4 percent of the federal government employees earning more than $19,700 per year are females.[14] The data are not supplied to indicate some necessity for preferential treatment upon the principle of compensation, but only to demonstrate with lucidity that from some perspectives it is an entirely rational view.

Remedy for disparities in pay came many years ago to professionals in public education. In a preponderantly female occupational category, pay for females had been less, a pattern borrowed from the private sector and sanctioned in the view that heads of households, assumed to be married men with families, needed more money. The issue was reduced to a sharp focus: how to eliminate the pay differentials based upon sex. The solution was the single salary schedule. The printed schedule reveals publicly what salary is being paid for a given function, with two variables: (1) years of experience as a professional and (2) extensiveness of academic preparation. As those two variables are equally attainable by any employee, the schedule speaks to most of the specific concerns of equality of opportunity.

Not all public employees want the kind of single salary that dominates the pay delivery systems of public schools. Librarians tend toward the single salary schedule with an added refinement, personnel classifications related to the difficulty and complexity of the work done. For public school librarians, the single salary schedule is a nationally accepted device. It allowed public school boards to show an early posture of philosophical compliance with the specifics of the Civil Rights Act of 1964 and subsequent related legislation. Because it delivers pay to a function and not to a personality, it cannot be influenced by sex, age, race, and so on.

The U.S. Civil Service has a salary delivery system that is comparable in many ways. It allows for no input by sex, race, politics, and so on. Like the single salary schedule, it delivers salary to a function at some demonstrable level of efficiency. Although both salary systems have much to commend them, neither addresses such substantial problems of sex imbalance in libraries as promotion and assignment, which must be remedied if economic equity is a goal.

Domestic violence and destruction have been part of the social discord that accompanied directives, generally from the federal government, moving citizens toward prescribed equality. Every society, if it is to remain viable and stable, has some rate at which major social changes can occur. If exceeded, social and political disintegration follow. The American polity has not come near such a chasm; this is a comment upon facts revealed in history and human nature about the ability to assimilate change.

Enforcement and compliance agencies are criticized from both sides. On the one hand, they hear they are too lax and too slow. On the other hand, they hear that they are unreasonable and that they lack faith in American citizens and those local government agencies that control public schools and public libraries. New terminology with special definitions has come into use. Preference has been identified as the heart of affirmative action. Sometimes, affirmative action has been called reverse discrimination. One observer of American society, describing that whole political action concept designed to accomplish equality of opportunity, has called it affirmative discrimination.[15] With the professional intelligence incorporated into collective bargaining, librarians in every job setting will surely wish to address this overshadowing question, using the opportunities of the American political system to shape an understanding of equality of employment opportunities. In the sense that librarians are in the business of constructing the intelligence of their clientele, they could easily turn some of that developmental energy toward their unique problems of inequality.

SUMMARY

American society, in flux on the general matter of equality, presents several opportunities for sex identification to females. Yet, evidence of discrimination against females can be seen in many settings. Among librarians, females prevail. Many of those women recognize unpleasant or demeaning conditions in their work settings, held over from sex stereotypes of another day. As union members, such librarians will bargain hard and long to rid themselves of such burdens—whether they be policy or contractual conditions—and to move toward what they perceive to be equal employment opportunities. Unions thrive on volunteerism. When union members invest themselves in their own union and accept internal constraints, the union should flourish.

Among professional librarians, females outnumber males by about three to one. This characteristic itself reveals bias when seen in some of its particulars. Among jobs generally esteemed as most desirable, the disproportion by sex shrinks; among jobs generally seen as least desirable, the disproportion by sex increases. That is, not only do women predominate in the occupational group, but among the least desirable library jobs, women predominate in much greater numbers. Activity, originally political in nature, has now filtered down to local settings as equality of employment opportunity and affirmative action in recruitment have become parts of local library unions—contract or policy, or both.

That political activity, much of it at the federal level, has included executive orders, statutes from the Congress, and decisions from the judiciary. The Civil Rights Acts of the 1960s and other legislation aimed at equalizing employment opportunities have had a salutary effect upon employment conditions in libraries. It is now unlawful to ". . . discriminate against any individual with respect to compensation, . . . (or) conditions . . . of employment, because of . . . race, color, religion, sex, or national origin."

Viewed chronologically, affirmative action, as applied to the public employment of professionals, received initial impetus from the executive orders issued by the presidents in the 1960s. Some of those orders were ahead of legislation; some followed and reinforced the new laws. For example, the E.O. 11375, "Equal Employment for Women in Federal Employment and Employment by Federal Contractors," reinforced and made emphatic Title VII of the Civil Rights Act of 1964. It also made explicit the desire that EEO programs should allow for no discrimination on account of sex.

Ironically, it seems certain that some conflicts in affirmative action must occur, as preferential provisions extended to females will clash with preferential provisions extended to black employees, older employees, handicapped employees, and so on.

Since 1964, an increasingly larger number of contracts for employment has included statements of fair practices in employment. Unions and employers have pledged to act to eliminate discrimination on the basis of sex, race, creed, national origin, and so on. The statements are explicit and clear. Salary delivery sytems are, more and more, reflecting the statements of intent and are less and less sensitive to bias by such characteristics as sex, race, age, and religion. Other conditions of work important in libraries, such as job security and autonomy in performance, are receiving attention. The prospect for EEO in libraries appears good.

NOTES

1. Daniel Bell, *The Cultural Contradictions of Capitalism* (New York: Basic Books, 1976), p. 11.

2. "Longevity in Prominent Women," *Statistical Bulletin* 60 (January-March, 1979): 2–9.

3. *Time* 3 (May 22, 1978): 76.

4. *Education Daily* 11 (August 4, 1978), p. 4.

5. *United States Statutes at Large* 78 (Washington: Superintendent of Documents, 1964): 241-68.

6. *United States Statutes at Large* 86 (Washington: Superintendent of Documents, 1972): 103.

7. Bureau of National Affairs. *The Equal Employment Opportunity Act of 1972* (Washington: The Bureau, 1973), pp. 3–7.

8. *Code of Federal Regulations, Title 3—The President* (1959-1963) (Washington: Superintendent of Documents, 1963), pp. 448–54.

9. Ibid., pp. 521–38.

10. *Weekly Compilation of Presidential Documents* 1 (Washington: Superintendent of Documents, 1964) (September 27, 1964): 305-7.

11. *Weekly Compilation of Presidential Documents* 3 (Washington: Superintendent of Documents, October 16, 1967): 1437–38.

12. Permissable Goals and Timetables in State and Local Government Employment Practices," in *Affirmative Action Planning for State and Local Governments* (Washington: Superintendent of Documents, 1973), pp. 1–8.

13. United States Commission on Civil Rights, *Last Hired, First Fired—Layoffs and Civil Rights* (Washington: The Commission, 1977), p. 14.

14. Dorothy Jongeward and Dru Scott, *Affirmative Action for Women: A Practical Guide* (Reading, Mass.: Addison-Wesley, 1973), pp. 9–13 and 75–81.

15. Nathan Glazer, *Affirmative Discrimination* (New York: Basic Books, 1975).

MONEY, SPENDING, AND CONTROLS   10

The vast majority of all the librarian-media specialists are employed in public settings—public libraries, public schools, and public universities. If all those persons plying their trade as librarians in private schools and universities and in special private libraries were counted, the total would hardly exceed 10 percent of the entire occupational category. By way of a sweeping observation of those employment settings, it seems safe to suggest that the library support personnel—another occupational category—working in private settings would be a percentage of about equal size. The point is that the great preponderance of library associated workers are in public settings, drawing a salary from public funds. Unionized librarians, with very few exceptions, work under contracts based upon tax funds.

An uneasiness settled upon the American citizenry in the latter 1970s, a mood related to questions about the effects that energy deficiencies will have upon a technological society. It is related to inflation and to the sagging imbalance in the nation's balance of payments as goods are imported and exported. It is related to the shift within the population through which the proportion of older persons has increased and the proportion of younger persons has decreased. Narrowly, it is related to the question of how to provide social and economic stability in the face of world shortages and fierce competition. There are many other factors, but these are adequately suggestive of the unease that has given rise to notions of restriction, limitation, and reduction, especially in the realms of government services. This might be called the new dynamic in American politics; in some circles it was being described as a tax revolt. Initiative and referenda designed to diminish tax collections came before the voters in sixteen states in the general election of 1978. Tax or spending limits were endorsed by voters in eleven of those sixteen states.[1] Such an obvious mood cannot lead public employees toward a feeling of confidence or security in their jobs.

This situation has become a problem, partially because much of the support to libraries comes from property taxes. The evidence is clear that property taxes occur unequally; i.e., as levied on citizens, that tax payment varies substantially from one place to another.

A 1977 study of the economics of taxes highlighted this locational variation. Rather standard assumptions were made about family characteristics as family income and taxes were compared. For example, a fairly typical family consisting of four persons living in their own house in New York City and earning $50,000 annually would pay about $7,875 in state and local taxes (including property taxes), over 15 percent of their gross annual income. That same kind of family, living in Jacksonville, Florida, would face a total state and local tax bill of about $1,236, about 3 percent of their gross annual income. Admittedly, this comparison disallows indication of narrower differences found among the sixty-two cities studied through the identification of different income levels. Nonetheless, the difference in tax burdens were substantial in many of the comparisons, and increasingly people have named the property tax as the least fair of the several taxes.[2]

Public libraries, dependent upon the property tax for the bulk of their operating funds, face a critical problem. Extraordinary competence is one basis from which to approach problems of financial welfare during times of fiscal stress. Many citizens have lost sight of the fact that libraries have demonstrated extraordinary ethics in handling funds through which services are provided. Corruption, common enough in the business world and the world of big federal government, has been exceedingly uncommon in the relatively small local libraries from which people may borrow books at no cost, for self-improvement and entertainment. The service itself is a magnificent concept, and has been delivered at a conspicuously high quality level. That tale merits retelling, though it is obvious. It has been too well hidden.

Without discussing whether taxes are regressive or progressive, without attempting to determine the taxes that would be equitable when collected against the market value of real estate property being taxed, it is only realistic to acknowledge that owners of houses are seeking tax relief. State legislatures are responding, studying the problem of equitable tax assessment or initiating legislative changes to provide some relief.

Intense political conflict is part of the current American scene. Many factors indicate some uncertainty for the gains in welfare made by librarians as employees within the American public enterprise. Generally, no librarian can any longer expect uninterrupted welfare gains through the leverage of collective bargaining in the 1980s, speaking realistically.

LIBRARY POLITICS AND REVENUE

Traditionally, personal prosperity has been accepted as a reasonable goal for all American workers. That includes librarians of all kinds who provide a valuable service for some compensation, which is, by any comparative measure, quite modest. In the sense that libraries are social services, their value to society can be observed as holding less importance than some other agencies involved in services generally agreed to as more basic to the social condition, such as transportation or agriculture. As demands for tax relief mount, the threat of reduced library services and of reduced employment must be squarely faced. For librarians to act otherwise would be evasion and pretense. Sentiment for tax relief may tip the balance of bargaining power more toward management and less toward employees. It is, after all, a balance; it has changed from time to time, affected by different variables, and sometimes by outside variables. That condition would very likely produce its own effect in library labor relations:

1. It would cause a moderation of demands by union leaders as long-range effects receive increased attention in the development of strategies aimed at enhancing worker welfare.
2. It could cause an increased solidarity and a new awareness of the community of interest in each local library, as employee groups retrench to gain strength and find their best strength within their own group.

If operational funds drop, and the trustee-director response is to cut the number of library employees or to reduce the compensation to those remaining, the unions will surely languish or even disappear. Historically, unions have flourished when they have appeared to protect workers and enhance worker welfare. Members have not tolerated organizations proven inadequate to the task of job protection. There is little reason to think that library unions would be different. Obviously, library unions have a big task just before them.

The gains in American longevity are continuing. One citizen group most vociferous in seeking tax relief because theirs is so often a stable income is the older Americans group. The average life span for the resident population of the United States reached seventy-three years in 1977. For males the expectation was sixty-nine years, and for females it was nearly seventy-seven years.[3] Just as a matter of sensible response it might be well for librarians to examine their services and their clientele and make modifications through which older Americans will be pleased to support libraries.

The National Commission on Libraries and Information Science has recently authored two studies published as government documents: *Public Libraries: Who Should Pay the Bills?* and *Our Nation's Libraries: An Inventory of Resources and Needs.*

The NCLIS states that 82 percent of the cost of public libraries is derived from property taxes. They found the balance to be paid by state taxes, about 11–13 percent; and, from federal funds, about 5–6 percent. NCLIS recommended that states should pay 50 percent of the cost of public libraries. The commission found that the 8,307 public libraries and the 74,725 public school libraries and media centers were alike underfunded. Both agencies stipulated substantial staff deficiencies. Public libraries indicated a need for 9,000 more professionals; public school centers indicated a need for 101,000 new professional postitions.[4] The commission's findings highlighted the different perceptions of library service as seen by providers of the professional services against the backdrop of tax conservatism.

PROBLEMS AND OPPORTUNITIES

The problems do not all center upon financial restrictions, although that is the major problem. For example, as the University of Massachusetts moved through the steps of unionization, contracts were finally developed for 1,900 professional faculty and staff in the latter 1970s. Through long bargaining sessions, agreement was reached on thirty articles. Ironically, the status of over sixty librarians was in doubt, as management stipulated that they should be excluded from the substantive articles of the contract. The administration of the university sought faculty agreement to the contractual exclusion "of librarians' workloads, personnel procedures, job security, and other issues" to be considered by another bargaining committee that would commence sessions after contract ratification.[5]

Comments about librarians in any setting of private employment have been restricted in this text only because of the size of that group. A ruling by the Second Circuit Court of Appeals in the *National Labor Relations Board* v. *Yeshiva University* (1980) and also filed as *Yeshiva University Faculty Assn.* v. *Yeshiva University*, however, provided a valuable insight for that smaller group and revealed a new uncertainty for professionals employed in certain kinds of private institutions. The National Labor Relations Board had, since about 1970, assumed jurisdiction over private educational institutions. The Yeshiva faculty formed a bargaining unit in 1976. When the university's administration refused to bargain, the dispute went through administrative hearings and into a circuit court. Yeshiva argued that the professionals were, themselves, managerial through their collegiate units and committees, and the court agreed. The effect of that ruling removed Yeshiva from under the jurisdiction of the NLRB, and all such other similar institutions likewise. As every private institution is excluded from the public employment bargaining laws of the several states, the position of librarians in private universities or private libraries, as related to collective bargaining, is uncertain.

That basic question has been extended into certain elementary and secondary schools. In the fall of 1978 the Supreme Court heard arguments in the case of the *NLRB* v. *Catholic Bishop of Chicago* as to whether the NLRB could compel parochial school officials to bargain with the elected lay faculty representatives. In this case, elementary-secondary librarian-media specialists working in sectarian schools found their status in labor relations determined by the high court. In 1979 the Court stated that the NLRB had no jurisdiction over professional employees in church operated schools, and that such schools could not be compelled to bargain with an association formed to represent teachers, librarians, counsellors and so on.

Although the "tax revolt" and service reductions have become a national phenomenon, the tax reduction sentiment gained its primary impetus from Proposition 13, passed in California. What was its impact there? Some news comments from various localities just a few months after its passage are instructive.

The Long Beach Public Library is losing 37.5 FTE staff positions, including 17.8 professionals from a complement of 175 FTE.

San Luis Obispo City-County Library is anticipating a 25 percent cut in budget, losing approximately $279,000.

Beaumont District Library, suffering a 60 percent cut in funds, will reduce its hours by 34 per week and eliminate all materials purchases, allowing periodicals' subscriptions to expire.

The Tulan County Library will be cut 50 percent. Of a staff of 79, 37 are being laid off.

The Bruggenmeyer Library in Monterey Park is absorbing its 25 percent cut in part by reducing staff hours. The assistant librarian was reduced to 20 hours, as were two senior librarians. Three junior librarians were reduced to 27 hours, seven clerks to 32 hours and three other staff members were laid off.[6]

That grim picture of service reduction has an equally unhappy aspect for library directors, who must identify and inform professional colleagues who will be adversely affected. Doubtless much enmity and resentment will be aimed toward them personally, for all that they are not basically responsible. Imposed job curtailment is an angry time for all.

In such a problem based setting, what are some opportunities? Some have been addressed earlier in this text under the general rubric of improved services. Other possibilities include an extended political action base. For the librarians who are members of the NEA or AFT, or to some extent the AAUP, those organizations carry on a political action program. Especially, the NEA and AFT speak to all federal questions of appropriations for educational agencies and libraries and to many state legislative actions also. The NEA has been restricted in the manner in which it may raise funds for political action but will doubtless develop new ways to secure financial support. In addition, continued political action by inter-union affiliations and coalitions seem assured, for many unions of public employees have common goals and can, through their combined membership, deliver substantial political clout.

New kinds of contracts may be drawn in which both employees and

management recognize, in advance, that there is but little likelihood of total
fiscal fulfillment. In a time of increasing COL, employees dislike a reduced
or steady state rate of pay, for both are actually reductions in buying
power. When an employer lacks the actual dollars stipulated in the contract, and cannot meet the payroll, initiative passes to the employees. They
can decide to

1. work as volunteers
2. reduce the magnitude of the service
3. close the institution and take a holiday—without pay

That type of contract has several attractions for employees, perhaps
foremost of which is the accumulation of base dollars in successive contracts, with hope of eventual recovery of the entire stipulated salary
amount. National experience is not conclusive presently to indicate whether
the hope is reasonable or not.

Employee grievances may rise in number. Disputes over equitable and
accurate fulfillment of contractual obligations seem increasingly likely as
financial stress will lead directors and trustees to exploratory positions in
curtailing operational costs. Particularly, such topics as residence, layoff,
and reinstatement seem likely candidates for dispute arbitration. In light of
the number of challenges that have been carried to the courts, consequent of
dissatisfaction with arbitration awards, and of the receptivity of state courts
to hear such litigation since 1975, disputants should be ready for extended
hearings before a final settlement.[7]

Some libraries are turning to differentiated funding. More than one local
library has a Friends of the Library group composed of several hundred people
and now approaching the task of fund raising in a modest way. A few
libraries have private foundation support and substantial endowments.
Candidly, however, neither scheme seems promising for causing relatively
substantial sums of money to flow into large numbers of libraries.

Free libraries may cease to exist. As a matter of fact, most libraries other
than the very smallest already charge fees for some of their services;
however, few developed fees with the intention that such receipts would be
a major factor in library financing. Now that idea is gaining consideration.
The ALA president has remarked that libraries in California and elsewhere,
which had never thought of charging fees, are proposing five-dollar
subscription or membership fees, a fee for each visit through the entry turn-
stile, or book rental charges. Other observers have noted that the future
holds high likelihood of combining fee and free services.[8]

Despite so many grim factors, which can be seen by anyone looking upon
libraries and librarians, and despite the fact that the cost of operating
libraries at constant service levels increased about 10 percent from 1976 to
1977,[9] there are some happenings around the nation in which high support

for libraries has been shown. Higher state appropriations for public libraries have been reported from South Carolina, Florida, and Maryland. In Oklahoma, citizens in Tulsa and Oklahoma City voted for higher tax levies earmarked for library service.[10] Other states which increased appropriations were New York with a $3 million, 10 percent boost; Alabama, with a $750,000 augmentation, an increase in state funding for libraries of 38 percent; and Oklahoma, where passage of an additional $150,000 appropriation expanded the per capita aid from five cents to eleven.[11] The end of the 1970s may finally emerge as a transitional period, from which the great social service available to citizens will emerge as a strong, viable institution nationwide.

The prospect for librarians as an occupational category is unclear. The factors of support for typical current library operations are mixed. The prospect for substantial growth in library services seems as bright in some regions of the nation as it seems dim in others. Librarianship is still a very desirable occupation; but, to speak without equivocation, it must be acknowledged that fund restrictions, so evident in some states, have a way of taking a toll on any organization, libraries included. In such times, professional inventiveness, imagination, and the community of interest in each local library may prove to be the most stabilizing factors in librarian employment that librarians can cultivate to continue to make of the job a personally and socially satisfying one.

NOTES

1. "Cut Taxes Loud Message," *Omaha World-Herald* (November 8, 1978), p. 34.

2. "State and Local Tax Bills: A Report from Sixty-Two Cities," *Changing Times* 32 (November 1978): 25–29.

3. "Gains in Longevity Continue," *Metropolitan Statistical Bulletin* 59 (July-September 1978): 7.

4. "Libraries Need State Support, Report Says," *Education Daily* 11 (November 3, 1978): 6.

5. "A Mass Faculty Struggle for First Master Contract," *NEA Advocate* (October 1978), pp. 1 and 5.

6. "Impact of Proposition 13," *Administrator's Digest* (September 1978): 63.

7. Judith H. Toole, "Judicial Activism in Public Sector Grievance Arbitration: A Study of Recent Developments," *Arbitration Journal* 33 (September 1978): 7–15.

8. "Free Libraries: On Way Out?" *Administrator's Digest* (September 1978): 57.

9. "Public Library Costs Up Again in 1977," *Library Journal* 103 (October 1, 1978): 1896.

10. *Library Journal* 103 (October 1, 1978): 1901–03.

11. *Library Journal* 103 (November 1, 1978): 2160.

GLOSSARY OF COLLECTIVE BARGAINING TERMS*

Agency shop: A condition specified in an agreement that requires all employees in the negotiating unit who do not join the exclusive representative to pay a fixed amount as a negotiation service fee. The payments may not be allocated to the organization's political action fund. An agency shop may operate in conjunction with a modified union shop. (See union shop.)

Agreement: A written agreement developed through negotiations between an employer and an employee organization. Usually for a definite term of one year or more, the agreement defines conditions of employment, rights of employees and the employee organization, and procedures to be followed in settling disputes or handling issues that arise during the life of the agreement.

American Arbitration Association (AAA): A private nonprofit organization with regional offices in major cities established to aid professional arbitrators in their work through legal and technical services and to promote arbitration as a method of settling commercial and labor disputes. The AAA provides lists of qualified arbitrators to employee organizations and employers upon request.

American Federation of Labor-Congress of Industrial Organizations (AFL-CIO): A federation of autonomous national-international unions created by the merger of the American Federation of Labor (AFL) and the Congress of Industrial Organizations (CIO) in December 1955. The initials AFL-CIO after the name of a union indicate that the union is an affiliate.

American Federation of State, County and Municipal Employees (AFSCME): The federation, in 1978 the largest AFL-CIO affiliate, accepts memberships from workers in professional, craft, and unskilled set-

*Adapted for specificity to library employment settings from the U.S. Civil Service Commission and augmented.

tings—the entire labor spectrum. It is the most common national affiliate for unionized library employees of all kinds.

American Federation of Teachers: A union that represents the welfare of all certificated school employees, except administrators. Membership includes school librarians and media specialists who may wish to join. Smaller than the NEA, the AFT is affiliated with the AFL-CIO and headquartered in New York City. (See National Education Association.)

Arbitration: A method of settling employment disputes through recourse to an impartial third party, whose decision may be final and binding. Arbitration is voluntary when both parties agree to submit disputed issues to arbitration and compulsory if required by law. Arbitration may be mandated by contract, statute, or court order.

Arbitrator: An impartial third person to whom disputing parties may submit their differences in anticipation of a settlement, which is called an award. An ad hoc arbitrator is one selected to act in a specific case or a limited group of cases, either of which might be typical of disputes arising from library employment.

Authorization card: A statement signed by an employee authorizing an organization to act as his representative in dealings with the employer, which may be a part of the union organizing activity.

Bargaining rights: Legally recognized rights to represent employees in negotiations with employers.

Bargaining unit: The group of employees recognized by the employer as appropriate for representation by an organization for purposes of collective bargaining.

Certification: Formal designation by some outside agency, such as the AAA, of the organization selected by the majority of the employees in a supervised election to act as an exclusive representative for all employees in the bargaining unit.

Check-off (payroll deduction of dues): A practice in which the employer, by agreement with the employee organization (or, after written authorization, by individual employees where required by law), regularly withholds organizational dues from each employees' salary and transfers those funds to the union treasury. The check-off is a common practice and may also provide for deductions of initiation fees and assessments.

Collective bargaining: A process in which employees act as a group and vis-à-vis their employers make offers and counteroffers in good faith on the conditions of employment for the purpose of reaching a mutually acceptable agreement and determining the written document incorporating any agreement that becomes the contract for work. Also, a process whereby representatives of the employees and their employer jointly determine the conditions of employment.

Cooling-off period: A period of time that must elapse before a strike or lockout can begin or be resumed by agreement or by the law. Common in private sector bargaining, the term derives from the hope that the tensions of unsuccessful negotiations will subside in time so that a work stoppage can be averted. As a technique to avert work stoppages, the tool has proven its value in private employment labor relations.

Credited service: Years of employment counted for retirement, severance pay, or seniority.

Crisis bargaining: Collective bargaining taking place under the shadow of high tension and threats, such as strikes, as distinguished from extended negotiations in which both parties enjoy ample time to present and discuss their positions.

Decertification: Withdrawal by an authorized agency of an organization's official recognition as exclusive negotiating representative.

Dispute: Any disagreement between employers and the employee organization that requires resolution, such as inability to agree on contract terms or unsettled grievances from the work setting.

Downgrading (demotion): Reassignment of workers to tasks or jobs requiring lower skills and with lower rates of pay.

Escalator clause: Provision in an agreement stipulating that salaries or compensation are to be automatically increased or reduced periodically, according to a schedule related to changes in the cost of living, typically, as measured by the Consumer Price Index.

Exclusive bargaining rights: The right and obligation of an employee organization designated as majority representative to negotiate collectively for all employees, including any nonmembers in the unit of employment.

Fact-finding board: A group of individuals appointed to investigate, assemble, and report the facts in an employment dispute, sometimes with authority to make recommendations for settlement. Structure and function of fact-finding vary from state to state, reflecting state statutes on public employment, but the technique is widely used in public employment.

Federal Mediation and Conciliation Service (FMCS): An independent federal agency that provides trained mediators to assist the parties involved in negotiations or a labor dispute in reaching a settlement, provides lists of suitable arbitrators on request, and engages in various types of "preventive mediation."

Fringe benefits: Supplements to wages or salaries received by employees at some cost to employers. The term encompasses a host of practices (paid vacations, pensions, health and insurance plans, and the like). No common agreement prevails as the list of practices that should be called fringe benefits. Other terms for fringe benefits include "wage extras," "hidden payroll," and "nonwage labor costs."

Grievance: Any complaint or expressed dissatisfaction by an employee in connection with his job, pay, or other aspects of his employment. Whether such complaint or expressed dissatisfaction is formally recognized and handled as a "grievance" depends on the scope of the grievance procedure in the specific employment setting.

Grievance procedure: Typically a formal plan, specified in a contract or state statute, which provides for the adjustment of grievances through discussion at progressively higher levels of authority in management and the employee organization, usually culminating in arbitration if necessary. Formal plans may also be found in public agencies having no organization to represent employees, but mandated by statute, regulation, or order.

Injunction: A court order restraining one or more persons, corporations, or unions from performing some act the court believes would result in substantial injury to another's rights or property. In public employment, a common use of the injunction is in the form of a court order demanding the return to work of employees engaging in (illegal) strikes.

Job posting: A public listing of available jobs, usually on a bulletin board or through publication, so that employees may apply for promotion or transfer, with no partiality shown.

Labor grades: Rate steps in the salary structure of an organization. Labor grades are typically the outcome of some form of job evaluation or of wage-rate negotiations, by which different occupational categories are grouped so that approximately equal value jobs fall into the same grade and rate. Grades provide an appropriate pay differentiation for both professional and support workers in libraries.

Labor-Management Relations Act of 1947 (Taft-Hartley Act): Federal law that amended the National Labor Relations Act (Wagner Act) of 1935 and, among other things, defined and made illegal a number of unfair labor practices by unions. It preserved the guarantee of the right of workers to organize and bargain collectively with their employers or to refrain from such activities.

Labor-Management Reporting and Disclosure Act of 1959 (Landrum-Griffin Act): Federal legislation aimed at the prevention or elimination of "improper practices on the part of labor organization, employers," and so on. The statute includes protection of members in their relations with unions and standards for elections.

Management prerogatives (management rights): Rights reserved to management that are usually specifically defined as such in a contract. Management prerogatives usually include the right to schedule work, to maintain order and efficiency, to hire, promote, transfer, and generally, to administer personnel in the organization.

Master agreement: A single or uniform collective agreement covering a number of installations of a single employer or the members of an employer's association. In libraries, the master agreement may occur in the first condition in which all librarians of like grade are compensated alike, without regard to the location in which they work.

Mediation: An attempt by an unbiased third party to help in negotiations or in the settlement of an employment dispute through suggestion, advice, or other ways of stimulating agreement, short of dictating its provisions (a characteristic of some kinds of arbitration). Mediation is akin to persuasion. A mediator is a person who undertakes mediation of a dispute. Mediation is synonymous with conciliation.

Merit increase: A technique in employee compensation in which increases are given on the basis of outstanding individual efficiency and performance.

National Education Association: The NEA is the largest organization that represents the welfare of all certificated school employees, generally excepting administrators. Practically, it is a union and includes school librarians and media specialists who may elect to join. It is headquartered in Washington, D.C. (See American Federation of Teachers.)

National Labor Relations Act of 1935 (Wagner Act): The basic federal statute guaranteeing to employees the right to organize and bargain collectively through representatives of their own choosing was passed in 1935. The act also defined "unfair labor practices" as regards employers. It was amended by the Labor Management Relations Act of 1947 and the Labor Management Reporting and Disclosure Act of 1959. Its application to public sector employment is more conceptual than substantial.

National Labor Relations Board (NLRB): The agency created by the NLRA (1935) and continued through subsequent legislation. The extensive and specific functions of the NLRB are confined to the private employment sector.

National Right to Work Committee: A loosely knit national group that advocates right to work legislation and opposes the concept of the agency or closed shop.

Open end agreement: A contract with no definite termination date, usually subject to reopening for additional negotiations or to terminate at any time upon proper notice by either party to the other. (See zipper clause.)

Open shop: A policy of not recognizing or dealing with a labor union; or a place of employment where union membership is not a condition of employment. With but very few exceptions, public employment occurs in open shop meetings.

Package settlement: The total money value, which may be quoted in cents per hour, of a change in wages or salaries and supplementary benefits negotiated by the employee organization in a contract renewal or reopening.

Past Practice clause: Existing practices that have gained acceptance through use and are not specifically included in the contract, except perhaps by reference to their continuance.

Pattern bargaining: The practice whereby employers and employee organizations develop and accept collective agreements quite similar to those reached by other employers and employee organizations in that field. It includes comparison with the prevalent, a common technique in public employment settings.

Payroll deductions: Amounts withheld from employees' earnings by the employer for social security, federal income taxes, and other levies by some government unit; it may also include organization dues, group insurance premiums, and other assignments authorized by the employee.

Picketing: Patrol duty, usually near the place of employment, by members of the employee organization to publicize the existence of a dispute and to persuade employees and the viewing public to support the unions' position.

Probationary period: Usually a stipulated period of time during which a newly hired employee is on trial prior to establishing seniority or otherwise becoming a regular employee. Professionals generally pass through a probationary period before they are granted tenure. Such time periods may range from a few weeks to several years, the longer time spans generally being the obligation of professional employees such as librarians. The duration of the period of trial is presumably related to the complexity of the task; the more complex the work, the longer the probationary period.

Real wages: Purchasing power of money paid as wages or the amount of goods and services that can be acquired with the money wages. An index of real wages takes into account changes over time in earnings levels and in price levels as measured by an appropriate index such as the Bureau of Labor Statistics' Consumer Price Index (CPI).

Recognition: Employer acceptance of an organization as authorized to negotiate, usually for all members of a negotiating unit, occurring after election by the members or certification of the unit.

Reopening clause: A clause in a contract stating the time or the circumstances under which negotiations can be requested, prior to expiration of that contract. Reopenings are usually restricted to salaries and other specified economic issues, not to the agreement as a whole.

Representation election: Elections are conducted to determine whether the employees in a discrete employment unit, such as a library or school district, desire an organization to act as their exclusive representative.

Right-to-work: Legislation that forbids the inclusion in any contractual agreement the requirement that an employee join the organization in order to get or to keep a job. Fewer than half of the states have such laws.

Seniority: A term used to designate an employee's status relative to other employees, as in determining order of promotion, layoff, vacation, and so on. It may be of several types:

straight seniority—seniority acquired solely through length of service
qualified seniority—other factors, such as technical ability, considered along with
        the length of service
department of unit seniority—seniority applicable to a particular department or
        agency, rather than the entire employment unit

Seniority list: Individual workers ranked in order of seniority.

Shop steward (union steward or building representative): A local union's representative in a location or department, elected by union members or appointed by the union. Stewards carry out union duties, adjust grievances, collect dues, and solicit new members. Shop stewards are usually fellow employees and perform duties similar to those of building representatives in public school districts or public libraries with branches.

Standard agreement: The collective bargaining agreement prepared by a national or international union for use by or guidance of its local unions, designed to produce standardization of practices within the many locals of the union's bargaining relationships.

Strike: A temporary work stoppage by a group of employees to express a grievance, enforce a demand for changes in the conditions of employment, obtain recognition, or resolve a dispute with management. A slowdown is a deliberate reduction of output without an actual strike in order to force concessions from an employer. A sympathy strike is a stoppage among employees who are not directly involved in a dispute but wish to demonstrate support and solidarity or to bring additional pressure upon employers. A walkout is the same as a strike.

Sweetheart agreement: A collective agreement exceptionally favorable to the employer, in comparison with other similar contracts, implying less favorable conditions of employment than should have been obtained through negotiations.

Unfair labor practice: Action by either an employer or employee organization that violates certain provisions of national or state employment relations acts, such as a refusal to bargain in good faith.

Union security: Protection of a union's status by a provision in the collective agreement establishing a closed shop, union shop, agency shop, or maintenance-of-membership agreement. In the absence of such provisions, employees in the bargaining unit are free to join or support the union at will and thus, in the eyes of the union, are susceptible to pressures to refrain from supporting the union or to the inducement of a "free ride."

Union shop: A provision in a contract that requires all employees to become members of the union within a specified time after being hired (typically, about one month), or after a new provision is negotiated, and to remain dues-paying members of the union as a condition of continued employment. A relatively rare practice in public employment because of limitations about what public boards may bargain, this practice is common in the private employment sector.

Whipsawing: The tactic of negotiating with one employer at a time, using each negotiated gain as leverage against the next employer. Teacher unions, including librarian members, are major users of this technique, making comparisons within states or regions of what has been agreed to at another place.

Zipper clause: A provision within an agreement that specifically bars any attempt to reopen negotiations during the term of the agreement. The opposite of reopening clause.

SELECTED BIBLIOGRAPHY

The items listed in this selected bibliography pertinent to libraries and labor relations are in addition to those cited in the notes. These citations are supplied to allow readers to pursue the topic further. Annotations have been made for authored books; exemplary essays have been selected from edited books and arranged topically. Finally, a miscellany of current articles has been provided.

PERSONNEL MANAGEMENT

Conroy, Barbara. *Library Staff Development and Continuing Education*. Littleton, Colo.: Libraries Unlimited, 1978.
> This comprehensive approach to the development of personnel systematically treats many aspects including careful delineation of administrative responsibilities. Suggesting that descriptive data and well-formulated objectives will provide clear guidelines for personnel development plans, none of the exemplary models include union participation—but they could.

Maloney, R. Kay, ed. *Personnel Development in Libraries*. New Brunswick, N.J.: Rutgers Bureau of Library and Information Science Research, 1977.
> Jeffrey J. Gardner. "Performance Evaluation in Libraries," pp. 1–16. Myrl Ricking. "Task Analysis in Libraries," pp. 17–26. Paul S. Strauss. "Is Job Enrichment Really the Answer?" pp. 27–44.

McCoy, Ralph E. *Personnel Administration for Libraries: A Bibliographic Essay*. Chicago: American Library Association, 1953.
> With a wealth of citations, this monograph addresses the working conditions found in various kinds of libraries—public, university, school, and special. Hiring, classifications, and interstaff relationships receive attention.

Myers, Margaret, and Scarborough, Mayra, eds. *Women in Librarianship*. New Brunswick, N.J.: Rutgers Bureau of Library and Information Science Research, 1975.
> Harold Wooster, "How the Library Changed its Spots—An Ain't So Story,"

pp. 2-10. Anita R. Schiller, "Sex and Library Careers," pp. 11-22. Carolyn
W. Sherif, "Dreams and Dilemmas of Being a Woman Today," pp. 27-48.
Herman Greenberg, "Sex Discrimination Against Women in Libraries," pp.
49-62.

Schlipf, Frederick A. *Collective Bargaining in Libraries*. Urbana-Champaign, Ill.:
University of Illinois, 1975.
> Don Wasserman, "The Unionization of Library Personnel: Where We Stand
> Today," pp. 23-29. Martin Schneid, "Recognition and Bargaining Units," pp.
> 43-53. Milton Byam, "Implications for Public Libraries," pp. 117-21. R.
> Theodore Clark, Jr., "The Duty to Bargain," pp. 54-75.

Special Libraries Association. *Special Libraries: A Guide for Management*. New
York: The Association, 1975.
> Primarily, this book is oriented toward space, inventory, and service. Yet, at
> least one-third of the book is devoted to organization, staffing, and
> budgeting, including some current data on proportions for salaries.

Vignone, Joseph A. *Collective Bargaining Procedures for Public Library Employees*.
Metuchen, N.J.: Scarecrow Press, 1971.
> This research investigates attitudes toward collective bargaining of librarians,
> directors, and trustees. Different views prevail, even though (in Penn-
> sylvania) the librarians have a legal right to collectivize and even though all
> three categories from a single library might hold memberships in a common
> professional organization, the American Library Association.

Wertheimer, Barbara Mayer. *We Were There: The Story of Working Women in
America*. New York: Pantheon Books, 1977.
> This extensive history of women at work in the United States portrays mainly
> the industrial unions in which women played integral parts. The essence of
> the problems of women as unorganized workers, such as sex discrimination,
> is attended; the roles of government and families are considered.

TRUSTEES AND PUBLICS

Batchelder, Mildred L. *Public Library Trustees in the Nineteen-Sixties*. Chicago:
American Library Association, 1969.
> This scholarly treatment includes history and the basic question of whether
> library boards should exist. The relationships of trustees to communities,
> politics, and personnel are discussed.

Sinclair, Dorothy. *Administration of a Small Public Library*. Chicago: American
Library Association, 1965.
> Much of this book is given over to a generalized treatment of small libraries.
> Yet much of it focuses upon the board of trustees and the relationships fanning
> out from that board into the community as well as relationships between the
> administrator and the board. The likelihood of a union in such a small library
> is remote, but the transference of the labor relations concept of employees
> voicing needs to trustees, however informally, is very real—and this applies
> to such real prospects.

Young, Virginia G., ed. *The Library Trustee: A Practical Guidebook*. New York:
R. R. Bowker, 1969.
>Virginia G. Young, "Qualifications of Trustees," pp. 14–18. Virginia G. Young,
>"The Trustees as Policy Makers," pp. 24–36. C'Ceal Coombs and Germaine
>Krettek, "The Trustee and the Political Process," pp. 80–89. Virginia H.
>Mathews and Dan Lacy, "The Trustee and Public Relations," pp. 134–39.
>"Statement of the Brooklyn Public Library Trustees," pp. 207–12.

PUBLIC EMPLOYEES

Bryan, Alice I. *The Public Librarian*. New York: Columbia University Press, 1952.
>The value of this book lies in its historical treatment of librarians working in
>public employment. Historical narration is skillfully supportive and inter-
>pretative of data from many aspects including work, education status,
>employee characteristics (by sex), morale, and personnel practices.

Chickering, A. Lawrence. *Public Employee Unions*. Lexington, Mass: D.C. Heath,
1976.
>Robert A. Nisbet, "Public Unions and the Decline of Social Trust," pp. 13–34.
>Harry H. Wellington and Ralph K. Winter, Jr., "The Limits of Collective
>Bargaining in Public Employment," pp. 51–76. Daniel Orr, "Public Employer
>Compensation Levels," pp. 131–44. George Meany and Jerry Wurf, "Union
>Leaders and the Public Sector Union," pp. 165–82.

Labor Management Relations Service. *Second National Survey of Employer Benefits
for Full-Time Personnel of U.S. Municipalities*. Washington, D.C.: The Service,
1974.
>A data source, revealing the kinds of fringe benefits for categories of
>employees. Fringe benefits are itemized and priced, revealing the costs to sus-
>tain them, by size of city and geographic area. Interoccupational comparisons
>can be made.

Zagoria, Sam, ed. *Public Workers and Public Unions*. Englewood Cliffs, N.J.:
Prentice-Hall, 1972.
>Arvid Anderson, "The Structure of Public Sector Bargaining," pp. 37–52.
>Henry Maier, "Collective Bargaining and the Municipal Employer," pp.
>53–62. Victor Gotbaum, "Collective Bargaining and the Union Leader," pp.
>77–88. Sam Zagoria, "The Future of Collective Bargaining in Government,"
>pp. 160–77.

UNIVERSITY LIBRARIANS

American Library Association. *Personnel Organization and Procedure*. Chicago:
The Association, 1968.
>This is a manual on the administration of personnel in university
>libraries. It is a "how to" book. Although it antedates much union activity, its
>practicality and generous use of illustrative material provides strong basis
>from which both library employees and officers can think about working
>conditions for contracts.

Marchant, Maurice P. *Participative Management in Academic Libraries*. Westport, Conn.: Greenwood Press, 1976.

> Upon a strong data base, the author suggests the need for management participation, if academic librarians are to achieve high job satisfaction and high performance. Although library unions are not treated, the implication is clear that the part of the labor relations model which demands labor-management communications would fit the advocate for joint participation.

Massman, Virgil F. *Faculty Status for Librarians*. Metuchen, N.J.: Scarecrow, 1972.

> This book attends a basic question for university librarians: How can academic rank be accomplished? It is a research effort, partially designed to discover similarities and differences between librarians and the academic professoriate. With extensive data and copious citations, the researcher concludes that for financial reasons, librarians need faculty rank but that they frequently lack the academic credentials upon which that rank generally rests.

Rogers, Rutherford D., and Weber, David C., *University Library Administration*. New York: The H.W. Wilson Company, 1971.

> This book provides a comprehensive view of university libraries. Nonetheless, about half of the book is devoted to labor relations topics of university librarianship. Some such topics include library planning, personnel selection, budgets, job classification and salaries, and associations and unions.

Weatherford, John W. *Collective Bargaining and the Academic Librarian*. Metuchen, N.J.: Scarecrow, 1976.

> This is a basic book about unionization in universities by a librarian with service on a bargaining committee. Concise and practical, the book covers such topics as compensation, working conditions, and contract administration. A comprehensive description of university bargaining in the nation, and of librarian participation, is included.

CURRENT ARTICLES

Alperin, Susan. "Sexism in Story-telling Hour Spurs Consciousness-Raising Group [in Portland, Oregon]." *Interracial Books for Children* 9 (1978): 10–13.

Asheim, Lester. "Librarians as Professionals." *Library Trends* (Winter 1979): 225–57.

"Attorney's Union Calls Librarians Nonprofessional." *American Libraries* 9 (October 1978): 523.

Beatty, LaMond F. "Impact of Public Law 94–142 on the Preparation of School Media Coordinators." *Educational Technology* 18 (November 1978): 44–46.

Brandwein, Larry. "From Confrontation to Coexistence." *Library Journal* 104 (March 15, 1979): 681–83.

Burrows, D. "Up the Profession—Down the Library." *P.L.A. News* 16 (Winter 1977): 14–15.

Casey, Genevieve M. "Cooperation, Networking, and the Larger Unit in the Public Library. *The Library Quarterly* 48 (October 1978): 447–63.

"A Comparative Study of Job Satisfaction: Catalogers and Reference Librarians in University Libraries." *Journal of Academic Librarianship* 4 (July 1978): 139–43.

"Current Issues in Librarianship." *Catholic Library World* 49 (May 1978): 412–40.

Dickinson, D. W. "Some Reflections on Participative Management in Libraries." *College and Research Libraries News* 39 (July 1978): 253–62.

"Embattled Unions Strike Back at Management." *Business Week* December 4, 1978, pp. 54–58.

"The Employment of Professionals in Support Positions: A Symposium," *Journal of Academic Librarianship* 3 (January 1978): 320–27.

Essex, W. W. "Trustees: You Too, Can Be Sued." *Wisconsin Library Bulletin* 74 (1978): 15.

"Fighting Back," *Women Library Workers*, no. 17 (October-December 1978): 8–10.

Gerhardt, L. N. "Teeth for the Professionally Nameless." *School Library Journal* 24 (December 1977): 7.

Hall, M. A. "Funny Thing Happened on the Way to a Performance Appraisal Forum." *Public Libraries* 17 (Spring-Summer 1978): 8–19.

Heim, Kathleen M., and Kacena, Carolyn, "Sex Salaries and Library Support." *Library Journal* 104 (March 3, 1979): 675–80.

Johnson, Shirley B. "The Impact of the Economy on Libraries and the Impact of Libraries on the Economy of New York State." ERIC, April 1978, 20 pages, ED 157 523.

"The Library Committee—Its Role in Library and University Governance." *Catholic Library World* 49 (September 1977): 54–56.

MacDonald, A. H. "Constraints of Restraint—Doing More with Less." *Atlantic Provinces Library Association Bulletin* 41 (3): 55–58 and (4): 87–89.

Molz, R. Kathleen. "Issues of Governance and their Implications for Libraries." *Library Trends* (Winter 1979), pp. 299–313.

Morgan, D. R., and Kearney, R. C., "Collective Bargaining and Faculty Compensation: A Comparative Analysis." *Sociology of Education* 50 (January 1977): 28–39.

Nye, P. "Bargaining for the City: A New Breed of Specialists is Working for Municipal Management." *Nation's Cities* 16 (June 1978): pp. 4–8.

Pemberton, M. A., and Smith, E. P., "Comparison of Role Perceptions of the School Media Specialist Among Administrators, Classroom Teacher and Modern Library Specialists." *Southeastern Librarian* 28 (Summer 1978): 92–95.

Pisano, Vivian H., and Skidmore, Margaret. "Community Survey—Why Not Take an Eclectic Approach?" *Wilson Library Bulletin* 53 (November 1978): 250–54.

Preston, M. B. "Minority Employment and Collective Bargaining in the Public Sector." *Public Administration Review* 37 (September 1977): 511–15. Reply with rejoinder by J. Adler, 38 (May 1978): 294–95.

"School Librarians Can Cope." *Catholic Library World* 49 (September 1977): 58–63.

"Sex Discrimination in Employment: Highlights of Relevant Laws and Executive Orders." *Education Libraries* 4 (Fall 1978): 10–11.

Sexton, Michael J., and others. "The Scope of Teacher Collective Bargaining." *Collective Negotiations Public Sector*, no. 2 (1978): 145–66.

Shirk, J. T. "Research in Action—An Introduction to Strategy for Change: the Librarian as Change Agent." *Public Librarian* 17 (Spring 1978): 1–10.

Smith, John. "The Problem of the Cuts or the Way to Examine Your Feet is to Remove Your Tight Shoes." *Service Point* (September 1978), pp. 6–11.

Snyder, Carolyn. "Personnel Evaluation in Libraries." *Illinois Association of College and Research Libraries Newsletter* 5 (Winter 1978): 1–6.

Tennessee Library Association. "Grievance Procedure of the Tennessee Library Association, Adopted November 12, 1977." *Tennessee Librarian* 30 (Spring 1978): 10–14.

"U.K. Library Association Protests Job Downgrading." *Library Journal* 103 (December (December 1, 1978): 2371.

Watkins, Alice. "Implications of Hiring a Nonprofessional to Do a Professional Job." *COLT Newsletter* 11 (November 1978): 1–4.

Wedgeworth, Robert. "Prospects for and Effecting Change in the Public Library." *The Library Quarterly* 48 (October 1978): 531–42.

INDEX

About the Authors

ROBERT C. O'REILLY is Professor of Educational Administration at the University of Nebraska at Omaha. He is the author of *Understanding Collective Bargaining in Public Education* and *Understanding Nebraska School Boards* (with Marjorie I. O'Reilly).

MARJORIE I. O'REILLY is a media specialist in the Wegner School, Father Flanagan's Boys' Home, Boys Town, Nebraska. She co-authored *Understanding Nebraska School Boards* with Robert C. O'Reilly.